D1488717

SARA TEASDALE
A Biography

By Margaret Haley Carpenter

Co-Editor with William Stanley Braithwaite:
ANTHOLOGY OF MAGAZINE VERSE FOR 1958

SARA TEASDALE: *A Biography*

Williamina Parrish

Sara Teasdale
1908

SARA TEASDALE

A Biography

BY

MARGARET HALEY CARPENTER

THE SCHULTE PUBLISHING COMPANY
NEW YORK CITY
1960

•

PRINTED IN THE UNITED STATES OF AMERICA
BY WHITTET & SHEPPERSON, RICHMOND, VIRGINIA

To the Memory
of
DAVID MORTON

Preface

SARA TEASDALE once said, in reference to her projected biography of Christina Rossetti, that writing about this English poet was like writing about "polished granite" because of her reticence and the uneventfulness of her outer life. One may almost apply this in a modified sense to writing about Sara Teasdale herself, for her life, too, was one of inner richness rather than outer excitement and activity. One cannot make her into a colorful, dramatic literary personality, for such a thing was alien to her spirit. The most her biographer can hope to do is to present the facts of her life in an orderly, accurate fashion and attempt to give the reader some insight into her nature and the impulses that lay behind her creative gift.

This book was completed before the recently issued biography of Vachel Lindsay, *The West-Going Heart*, by Eleanor Ruggles was published; and I have had access to the letters that Vachel Lindsay wrote to Sara Teasdale, which have previously been unread and unpublished, and which were not available to Miss Ruggles to use. This was because of an agreement made with the Yale University Library that these letters, which I used before they became the property of Yale, would be sealed until my book was published. I am exceedingly grateful to Miss Ruggles, Mr. Nicholas Cave Lindsay, and Mr. Donald Gallup, Curator of the American Literature Collection of Yale University Library, for scrupulously abiding by the terms of this agreement.

Sara Teasdale did not want her letters published, and this, in addition to the fact that the majority of them have been destroyed as she requested, accounts for their absence in these pages. Those to Vachel Lindsay, John Hall Wheelock, Margaret Conklin, and most of those to Williamina Parrish are no longer in existence. Dr.

Stafford Hatfield's were lost in England in the last World War. Also, with the exception of copies of a very few of them, the letters of Ernst Filsinger to Sara Teasdale have been destroyed.

In quoting from Vachel Lindsay's letters and from other letters and documents, I have used three asterisks (* * *) to denote omission of one or more paragraphs. The usual three dots (. . .) denote omission of a few words or sentences within the same paragraph.

It was apparent to me, after careful study of Vachel Lindsay's letters and after a serious comparison of his poems in manuscript with those in printed form, that the dashes that he used for punctuation could be interpreted as commas, periods, or dashes, as the occasion demanded. Also, it was apparent that he frequently used capital and small letters interchangeably. I have earnestly endeavored to preserve the intent of his message in each case, without changing his actual words whatsoever, by interpreting as best I could the meaning of the many dashes and of the small and capital letters, as well as the arrangement of his paragraphs. Where it was obvious that he had made an unconscious error in spelling or in the omission of punctuation (needed for clarity's sake), a silent correction has been made.

Since I have had access to material that will never be available again, I have purposely devoted much space to the Potters, that group of girls who were close early friends of Sara Teasdale's, and who exerted an immensely important influence on the young poet. It would be difficult to give the essence of this group in a few words, paragraphs, or even a few pages. The Potters created their own universe, and one must savor their thoughts, activities, and records to absorb the climate of their days. It is this world, this climate, that I have tried to recreate, for this was the world of Sara Teasdale's girlhood, and to know her fully, one must also know fully this part of her life, about which little in detail has ever been published.

Never has it been more truly said that without the help of others, this book could not have been written. For behind its completion lie the generosity and continuing interest of the many individuals to whom I turned for aid, who gave unselfishly of their time and of their memories to me, a total stranger. I only wish that I could repay them in some more adequate way than by merely listing their names here.

I am especially indebted to Sara Teasdale's close friend and literary executor, Miss Margaret Conklin, who has given me invaluable assistance and critical guidance. Miss Conklin made it possible for me to have the opportunity to consult priceless source materials, and I am exceedingly grateful to her for this and for her permission to quote from various documents.

To Sara Teasdale's nephew, Mr. John Warren Teasdale, III, I am also deeply indebted for his kind and faithful coöperation in answering my many questions, lending me genealogical data, sharing his memories, and granting permission to quote from certain material. To his brother, Mr. Kenneth Teasdale, I also owe my sincerest thanks for his assistance.

Mr. Nicholas Cave Lindsay has been of inestimable aid in helping me locate and allowing me to quote from his parents' papers.

Mrs. Irma Filsinger Wetteroth, Mrs. Edna Wahlert McCourt, and Mrs. Vine Colby McCasland have been unfailing sources of help over a long period of time, writing numerous letters in answer to my many questions, lending me valuable materials, and granting me their kind permission to quote from materials under their jurisdiction.

I am also deeply grateful to Mrs. Betty Parrish McCormick Morency, who made certain materials available to me, granted me permission to quote from letters and documents, and gave me much needed information.

Mr. William Stanley Braithwaite has been a continuing source of encouragement in the completion of this biography and has given generously of his reminiscenses.

Of those who helped me greatly, but died before this book could be completed, I am especially obligated to Sara Teasdale's sister, Mrs. Mamie Teasdale Wheless, Miss Grace Parrish, Mr. Bruce M. Stanley, and Mr. Poultney Bigelow.

Mr. John Hall Wheelock graciously shared his materials and memories with me, as did Mr. Witter Bynner and Mrs. Jean Starr Untermeyer.

Dr. Henry Slonimsky very kindly placed at my disposal many papers concerning Marion Cummings and gave his permission to quote from these as I needed.

Mr. Harold Strong Latham, the editor of Sara Teasdale and Vachel Lindsay at the Macmillan Company, has generously contributed much of his time, patience, and wisdom to this book.

I am also indebted to Dr. H. Stafford Hatfield of England, and to Mrs. Aline Risque Chalker, Miss Alice Ernst, Mrs. Nancy Coonsman Hahn, Miss Celia Harris, Mrs. Susan Creighton Williams Porter, and Miss Caroline Singleton for lending me precious materials or drawing on their recollections of the past for me.

Mrs. Louada Burr Voellner and Mrs. Janet Amitin have been of the greatest aid, over a long period of time, in checking certain bits of information pertaining to St. Louis, supplying needed names and addresses, and helping me in other ways literally too numerous to mention.

Mrs. Charis Johns Buckminster, Mrs. Norma Millay Ellis, Mr. Cloyd Head, Mr. F. Winston Johns, Mr. Virgil Markham, Mrs. Edgar Lee Masters, Mr. Carl Sandburg, Mrs. Rittenhouse Simms, and Mr. Henry Staunton Monroe have all graciously given me permission to quote from the material that they control.

Dr. Oscar Darter went to much trouble to locate for my use several rare books concerning members of the Teasdale family.

Others to whom I owe a debt of thanks for sharing their memories, giving me information, or aiding me in some other way, include: Mrs. Johanna D. Bemis, Mr. Ogden Bigelow, Dr. Walter Russell Bowie, Miss Grace Burnham, Mrs. Linda C. Campbell, Mrs. Elsie Williams Chandler, Professor Charles Cory, Mrs. Julia Barclay D'Arcy, Miss Helen DeFrance, Mrs. Fran Dolliver, Mr. Hugh Ferriss, Miss Pearl Gehner, Mrs. Corinne S. Hall, Mrs.

Olive Harris, Mrs. Josephine B. Hubbard, Dr. Robert Majer, Mrs. Edna P. Morrison, Miss Abbie Paige, Mrs. Helen Pratt, Miss Marguerite Lois Rickert, Mrs. Jennie Rosecrans, Mrs. Ninita M. Savage, and Mrs. Minnie Clay Wuerpel.

Director Charles Nagel of the City Art Museum of St. Louis, Mrs. Otie Linn Durbin of the St. Louis Artists' Guild, Alice Dahm of Mary Institute, Dean Kenneth Hudson of the Washington University School of Fine Arts, and Director O. W. Wagner of Washington University have all been most cooperative in providing the information that I requested.

I am also deeply indebted to a number of individuals in various libraries who have been wonderfully kind in helping with my research: Mrs. Judith Bond, Curator of the Harriet Monroe Modern Poetry Collection, University of Chicago Library, and Director Herman Howe Fussler of that Library; Librarian Stanley Pargellis and Mrs. Gertrude L. Woodward, Custodian of the Rare Book Room, of the Newberry Library; Miss Viola C. White, formerly of the Abernethy Library, Middlebury College; Mrs. Frances Biese and Mrs. Barbara Kell Strudell, formerly of the Missouri Historical Society, and Mrs. Frances H. Stadler, currently with this Society; Miss Anna Russell of the University of Buffalo Library's Poetry Collection; Miss Hannah D. French of the Wellesley College Library; Mr. Rutherford D. Rogers, formerly Chief of the Reference Department of the New York Public Library; and Mr. Donald Gallup, Curator of the American Literature Collection of the Yale University Library.

Other cooperating libraries that I have called upon include the Norfolk Public Library, the Henry E. Huntington Library, the St. Louis Public Library, and the libraries of Brown University, Columbia University, Harvard University, Rollins College, the University of California at Berkeley, and Wagner College.

MARGARET HALEY CARPENTER

Norfolk, Virginia
January 23, 1960

Acknowledgments

The following are in addition to the acknowledgments given in various footnotes throughout this book.

•

Copies of the letters to Sara Teasdale from Ernst Filsinger, quoted in this book, are in the collection of the Missouri Historical Society, St. Louis, Missouri, of which Mr. Charles van Ravenswaay is the Director.

•

The letters to Harriet Monroe from Vachel Lindsay and Elizabeth Conner Lindsay, certain passages of which are quoted in this book, are in the Harriet Monroe Modern Poetry Collection of the University of Chicago Library, of which Mrs. Judith Bond is Curator. Excerpts from these letters are used with the kind permission of Director Herman H. Fussler of that Library.

•

The Diary of Sara Teasdale, kept on her first trip abroad in 1905, and the letters of Vachel Lindsay to Sara Teasdale are now in the American Literature Collection of the Yale University Library, of which Mr. Donald Gallup is Curator.

•

The letter written by Ernst Filsinger to Jessie Rittenhouse, part of which is quoted in this book, is in the Rollins College Library.

•

Other letters that were consulted but not quoted are in the University of Chicago Library; in the Newberry Library's Rare Book Room under the care of Mrs. Gertrude Woodward, Custodian, and

Librarian Stanley Pargellis; in the University of Buffalo Library's Poetry Collection under the care of Miss Anna Russell; in the Abernethy Library, Middlebury College; in the Henry E. Huntington Library, and in the Libraries of Harvard University, Columbia University, and Wagner College.

•

The fragments of the poems from volumes by Vachel Lindsay, which appear in this book, are used through the courtesy of the Macmillan Company, which controls the world rights to them.

•

The various poems from books written by Sara Teasdale, which are quoted in these pages, also appear with the permission of the Macmillan Company, which controls the world rights to Sara Teasdale's books.

BOOKS BY SARA TEASDALE

Sonnets to Duse and Other Poems	(1907)
Helen of Troy	(1911)
Rivers to the Sea	(1915)
Love Songs	(1917)
Flame and Shadow	(1920)
Dark of the Moon	(1926)
Stars To-night	(1930)
Strange Victory	(1933)
Collected Poems	(1937)

ANTHOLOGIES EDITED BY SARA TEASDALE

The Answering Voice:
  Love Lyrics by Women   (1917, 1928)

Rainbow Gold:
  Poems Old and New, Selected for Boys and Girls (1922)

Contents

·

Illustrations

I cannot die, who drank delight
  From the cup of the crescent moon,
And hungrily as men eat bread,
  Loved the scented nights of June.

The rest may die—but is there not
  Some shining strange escape for me
Who sought in Beauty the bright wine
  Of immortality?

—SARA TEASDALE

SARA TEASDALE

A Biography

Chapter 1

ANCESTRY AND THE EARLY YEARS

·

SARA TEASDALE was born on August 8, 1884, in St. Louis, Missouri, the youngest child of Mary Elizabeth Willard and John Warren Teasdale. At the time of her birth, the older of her two brothers, George Willard, was almost twenty, and the younger, John Warren, Jr., was fourteen. Sara's only sister, Mary Willard, fondly called "Mamie," who was seventeen, adored the baby and gave her a loving, protective care from the very first.

The poet was born in the family residence, 3668 Lindell Boulevard, a picturesque old mansion, which has long since been torn down to make way for the more modern buildings of St. Louis University. She was named Sarah Trevor Teasdale for her maternal grandmother, but she later dropped the final "h" in Sarah. For years, she was affectionately known by her family and friends as "Sadie."

Thoroughly American on both sides, Sara's family was old, established, and respected. One of Mrs. Teasdale's most illustrious ancestors, Major Simon Willard, came to America at the age of twenty-nine from Horsmonden, Kent, England, in 1634. He joined the Puritans in New England, living for a time in Cambridge, Massachusetts, and in 1635 he helped found the town of Concord on land that he and others purchased from the Indians. Here he lived for twenty-three years, serving the settlers in many invaluable ways; in 1885, residents, honoring his memory, marked the site of his farm, and fifty years later a granite monument was dedicated on Nashawtuc Hill to perpetuate the record of his service to the colony.

From 1659-1671 he lived at Lancaster and later at Groton. Known as the "Kentish soldier" because he used his former military training to good advantage against the Indians, Simon Willard had nine sons and eight daughters, nearly all of whom married; and he and his brother, George Willard, and his sister, Margery Willard Davis, were the progenitors of almost all of those in this country who have borne the Willard name, as well as hundreds of thousands with other surnames.

At St. Margaret's Church in Horsmonden, the 1605 baptismal record of Simon Willard, as well as that of his brother and sister, may still be seen in the old vellum church register that dates back to 1578. Here, too, are the Willard Memorial Window, placed in the ancient church through funds raised by members of the Willard family in America, and the brass plaques honoring Simon Willard and his famous descendant, Frances Elizabeth Willard.

Before leaving England, Simon Willard married his first wife, and after her death, he married the sister of, and later, the cousin of his friend and associate, Henry Dunster, the first President of Harvard University. A number of his descendants served that institution in various capacities.

One of Simon Willard's sons, the Reverend Samuel Willard, was the chief executive of Harvard from 1700-1707. However, regulations at that time required the President to live on the campus, and the minister had to accept the title of Vice President in order to maintain a close relationship with his dearly loved Old South Church in Boston, which he served from 1678-1707. Among the many persons he baptized in this church was the youthful Benjamin Franklin, before he set out for Philadelphia. Another of the Major's descendants, the Reverend Joseph Willard, Samuel Willard's great-grandson, was also President of Harvard University from 1781-1804. Through the years, the Willard family has included Presidents of other colleges, signers of the Declaration of Independence, and eminent persons in many fields of endeavor.

Sara's line of descent from Major Simon Willard may be traced back to his third marriage, to Mary Dunster, cousin of the first President of Harvard. One of their children, Henry (1655-1701), continued to live in Lancaster after his father moved to Groton, and Jacob Willard, a direct descendant of Henry's, became the great-grandfather of Sara. Jacob Willard (1786-1818), who was for many years a member of the Boston bar, and the first postmaster at Fitchburg, Massachusetts, was born in Lancaster and received his B.A. degree from Brown University in 1805 and his M.A. in 1808. In 1810 he married Mary Elizabeth Pitman of Providence, Rhode Island, whose father, the Reverend John Pitman, was a Baptist minister and had served in the Continental Army during the Revolutionary War. The Pitmans were also descended from an early colonist of New England, and many of them were prominent in professional and civic life. Mary Elizabeth Pitman's brother, Judge John Pitman, had the distinction of graduating from Brown University when only fourteen years of age, and upon completing his law training was too young to practice. From 1834 to 1864 he was the United States Judge for the District of Rhode Island.

For a time Jacob and Mary Elizabeth Pitman Willard lived in Marblehead, Massachusetts, and here their second child, George Washington Willard, Sara's maternal grandfather, was born on January 18, 1813.

George Willard was educated at Amherst College, where he roomed with Henry Ward Beecher. One of the most memorable incidents of his college life was the night that he and his roommate slid down knotted sheets that they had hung out the window, and, against regulations, went off elsewhere for the evening. They returned to their room in the same manner, and the college authorities were no wiser.

A man of energy and action, after his college days were over, George Willard founded a trading post where the city of Milwaukee stands today, this region then being in a state of primitive wilderness and without another white man in the territory of Milwaukee County. Here he traded with the Indians for pelts. He moved on later to Cincinnati, and there in 1840 he married Sarah Ann Trevor, of Connellsville, Pennsylvania, whose father, Caleb Trevor, had been born in England and had come to America in 1793.

Religion was important to the Trevor family, and Sarah Ann's grandfather, Samuel Trevor, gave the ground for the First Baptist Church in Connellsville. Sarah Ann Trevor had been named for her own grandmother, Sarah Bond Trevor; and so the first name of the poet really goes back to her great-great-grandmother's name.

In 1834 George Washington Willard settled in Peoria, Illinois, where he engaged in the dry goods business. He bought his first steamboat, the "Ohio Valley," in 1847, and operating this vessel proved so successful a venture and one so congenial to his nature, that he soon bought a fleet of other boats, which plied the Mississippi, Illinois, Ohio, and Missouri Rivers. Within a period of fourteen years he was interested in as many as forty-nine boats, some of them the largest and finest that came to the St. Louis levee, such as the "Hiawatha," "Sunshine," "Albert Pearce," and "Dew Drop," all famous boats in their day. At this time the Mississippi River was the great highway of traffic and travel to New Orleans and the Gulf of Mexico, and St. Louis was a busy and colorful port.

For out of the little log fort with its cluster of crude dwellings, which Pierre Laclède Ligueste, a French trader from New Orleans, had established in 1764 to promote fur trade with the Indians to the northwest, had grown St. Louis, the largest city in Missouri and a leading industrial and commercial center. St. Louis was the great river port of the Central Plains in the middle nineteenth century, and most of its trade was carried on by the paddle-wheeled vessels that moved up and down the Mississippi, transporting goods from both north and south. In those days the river was virtually alive with steamers heavily laden with products and passengers, and all the business of St. Louis was done on the levee, with boats arriving and departing every hour.

In 1848 Captain Willard moved his family to St. Louis, and here, in the thriving river business of the town, he became an important and respected figure. When the clouds of the Civil War arose, he was a determined and consistent Union man, with strong personal sympathies for his friends in the South, and in his boating experiences he was sometimes forced to serve one side as well as the other. In 1861, on his last trip up the Missouri River with the "Sunshine," General Price, of the Confederate Army, took possession of the boat and compelled him to carry a cargo of gunpowder from Jefferson City to Boonville and afterwards to carry recruits to other points on the river. On the return down the river from Council Bluffs, the boat was taken by General Lyon of the Union Army, and used for his purposes in turn. When the "Sunshine" was released, General Lyon gave Captain Willard dispatches of great importance with orders to deliver them to General Fremont, which he did.

These experiences were not agreeable to Captain Willard, who had been accustomed to command, rather than to be commanded, and in 1863, he disposed of his steamboat interests and purchased a large farm near Centralia, Illinois. Here he passed the remainder of his life. Captain Willard had joined the Second Baptist Church in St. Louis in 1848, and in 1850 he and his wife were among those who helped organize the Third Baptist Church of that city. At Centralia, he took an active part in the development of the country and in civic work, and he helped to establish a Baptist church there, also.

Among the Teasdales, too, were ancestors who had distinguished themselves, especially in professional fields. The Teasdale family originally came from the valley of the Tees River, a wild, rugged, and beautiful region in northern England, covered with moorlands and towering hills, near the border between England and Scotland. As the Tees River flows southward and turns to the east, it becomes the boundary line between Yorkshire and Durham, and it is from Durham that Mr. Teasdale's ancestors originally came. The earliest reference to the family is a statement that on September 16, 1749, a license was granted John Teasdale to marry Anne Garthwaite at the Church of St. Margaret's at Durham. Their son, the Reverend Thomas Teasdale (1752-1827), Sara's great-great-grandfather, and his son, Judge Thomas Teasdale (1779-1847), Sara's great-grandfather, were both born in Durham and came to America in 1792. Because he had suffered considerable persecution in his native country after he left the Established Church of England and advocated so earnestly the tenets of the Baptists, the Reverend Thomas Teasdale decided to follow God's work in the new world. He settled his family in the northern part of Sussex County, New Jersey, where he took charge of a church in Hardyston Township that later came to be known as Hamburg Baptist Church. Although he was frequently asked to become the pastor of important city churches, he could not be induced to sever the ties that bound him to his country church, and he served it for over twenty-five years. When he died on April 25, 1827, at the age of seventy-five, he was buried in the grave-yard of the little rural church for which he had such a warm affection.

His son, the Honorable Thomas Teasdale, served as a Captain in the New Jersey Militia in the War of 1812, and later was a member of the State Legislature; he also served as Surrogate for Sussex and Warren Counties, and Judge of the Court of Common Pleas. Judge Teasdale had eleven children, ten of whom reached maturity; two of his sons, John Teasdale and Thomas Cox Teasdale, became eminent Baptist ministers. The Reverend John Teasdale, Sara's grandfather, who was born on November 12, 1806, was only two years older than Dr. Thomas Teasdale, and the brothers were devoted to each other.

John Teasdale, a rather frail young man, engaged for a time in teaching school; and during this period of his life he met a young lady, Susan Losey, who was deeply concerned about his religious beliefs and persuaded him to dedicate his life to God. He, in turn, persuaded his brother, Thomas, to do the same thing, and the two brothers were baptized together on November 20, 1826. For a number of years after this, John studied at a theological seminary in Hamilton, New York, but poor health prevented him from finishing his course. His first ministerial assignment brought him back to the little church at Hamburg where his grandfather had preached for so long.

In May of 1831 he married Susan Losey, and eight children were born of this marriage. Hoping that a southern climate would improve his health, in 1836 Elder John Teasdale left his native state for Virginia, where he was associated for a time with the American Sunday-School Union. From 1836 until 1839 he served as the minister of the Baptist Church of Fredericksburg, Virginia, and it was in this little town that the poet's father, John Warren Teasdale, was born on November 13, 1838. At this time Dr. Thomas Teasdale owned Ferry Farm, George Washington's boyhood home, just across the Rappahannock River from Fredericksburg. He advertised the farm for sale on May 10, 1841, and quite probably the Reverend John Teasdale lived at Ferry Farm during his pastorate of the Fredericksburg Baptist Church and continued to live there and care for the 1,082 acre farm until it was sold in 1842.[1] For he remained in Fredericksburg until then, when he returned to New Jersey as minister of Schooley's Mountain Church.

After spending a number of years in this post, he decided that the West presented the greatest opportunity for further service. He surveyed the field thoroughly, and in 1850 he moved to Alton, Illinois, serving as agent for Alton College and General Agent for the American and Foreign Bible Society, until he was asked to be the pastor of the Third Baptist Church of St. Louis.

He assumed his ministerial duties in St. Louis on April 3, 1854, and had just gotten started in his work there, when his

[1]According to Dr. Oscar H. Darter, of Fredericksburg, Virginia, who has written a history of the Fredericksburg Baptist Church.

untimely death occurred on November 1, 1855. For he was a passenger on an ill-fated (Missouri) Pacific Railroad train, the first to leave St. Louis for Jefferson City, which fell into the Gasconade River. A number of prominent citizens, the Reverend Teasdale among them, had been invited to be the guests of the railroad for this initial trip that ended so disastrously, killing or mortally injuring nearly thirty persons.

The train had moved safely on for more than one hundred miles, when it reached the bridge that was approached by a high embankment, terminating in an abutment of thirty feet or more in height, from which the chasm to the first pier was spanned by a section of one hundred feet. As soon as the train was upon this part of the bridge, and before the engine had reached the first pier, a terrifying crash was heard. The bridge gave way, and nine of the ten cars fell into the chasm below, piling up on each other in a great mass of ruin. Elder Teasdale was heard to exclaim just before his car went down: "Great God! How terrible are thy judgments!" These words were remembered in St. Louis for a long, long time afterwards. His injuries showed that he perished instantly.

Dr. Thomas Teasdale was especially grieved by this loss. He felt as if part of his own life had gone into the tomb with his brother. To Susan Losey Teasdale, he wrote on November 17, 1855:

My sister, what can I say to comfort you? My own heart is bursting with grief. I can scarcely write for falling tears. I feel that *I* need some one to comfort *me*. How, then, can I attempt to comfort *you?* What shall I say? It seems to me that all human utterances, at such a time, are utterly impotent and unavailing.

But, my sister, there are "exceeding great and precious promises," and encouraging Scriptural assurances to which I may refer you for consolation in the time of your deep distress. . . .

You have also the consolation of knowing that your dear husband was one of the best of men. None knew him but to love him; and those who knew him best, always loved him most. To me, he was a very dear brother. I may say, twice a brother. We were so nearly of an age; raised in the same family; slept in the same bed; ate at the same board; studied in the same schools; baptized in the same stream and on the same day, by the same loved minister; licensed and ordained by the same Church; married the same year; and together and apart, preached the same glorious Gospel for twenty-five years, that it seemed to me, we were almost one and inseparable. But he is taken and I am left. How long I may linger behind, I cannot, of course, tell. Oh! that I may be as fully prepared to meet him in that bright land to which he has gone![2]

Not many months before this accident occurred, Dr. Thomas Teasdale had gone to St. Louis to help his brother hold a revival. The visiting minister had been ill then; the weather was uncomfortably hot, and for a number of reasons he did not feel that his part of the revival had been much of a success. And he had often wondered afterwards for what purpose he had been called to St. Louis at that time. But after this tragedy, it seemed to him that God had given the two brothers this final opportunity to be together, for this was the last time that they saw each other.

Dr. Thomas Teasdale, Sara's great-uncle, was as prominent a minister as his brother, and one of the most sought-after speakers of his time, who preached widely throughout the country. He served a Baptist church in Washington, D. C., for some years and knew many important personalities. Among these were Lincoln and Jefferson Davis, and he persuaded them to sign the only document that contained both of their signatures while they were in office. This was a paper permitting cotton to be transported through the lines, the profits of which were to be used for the benefit of the children of dead Confederate soldiers, who were placed in the Mississippi Orphans' Home.

Sara's father, John Warren Teasdale, had intended to study law and follow in the footsteps of his grandfather, Judge Teas-

---

2A Friend, *Elder John Teasdale* (Nashville, Tennessee: Southern Baptist Sabbath-School Union, 1860), pp. 120-121.

dale, but the sudden death of his father, shortly before his seventeenth birthday, changed his plans, and he turned to business instead. He was a courtly gentleman of the old school, kindly, gentle, and essentially chivalrous. In later days he wore a long, flowing white beard and made a well-remembered picture driving through the streets of St. Louis in a carriage drawn by fine horses. For he was very fond of horses, having as many as eight at one time, and even after the automobile became a popular means of transportation, he could not be persuaded to buy one, preferring to use his carriage all of his life. Though his wife was not averse to using the horses when it suited her, she frequently mentioned their expense, as she preferred to spend her money on travel, a comfortable home, and her hobby, Oriental rugs. Knowing how Mr. Teasdale was so often preoccupied with horses, the family still recalls with affection the remark that he made upon seeing his first grandchild. "Mamie," he said to his son's wife, "that's a fine boy! That boy will have a pony when he is ten years old!" He kept his word about this, too, and Willard's pony and pony cart, which also delighted the other children in the family, are still a cherished memory. Mrs. Teasdale, on the other hand, had more practical matters on her mind when her first grandchild was born. She was interested in seeing that the new baby be named after her family, and she suggested that he be called Willard Walsh after the family names of the two grandmothers, which he was.

The poet's mother was born on October 3, 1843, in Peoria, Illinois. She had been a sickly child and was not expected to live to adulthood, but she had a very strong vitality; on her eighteenth birthday she declared that she would reverse the 18 to 81, and she did die in her eighty-first year. Though she was kind and generous in many ways, she was never able to free herself from an inherent Puritanical nature. She was small in stature and an energetic person; of the two parents, she was the more forceful, aggressive, and out-spoken.

*Sara Teasdale
and
her mother*

*Sara Teasdale
as a
young girl*

John Warren Teasdale and Mary Elizabeth Willard met each other at the Third Baptist Church in St. Louis, and they were married at Centralia, Illinois, on October 7, 1863. They returned to St. Louis to live, where Mr. Teasdale had established J. W. Teasdale and Company, wholesale dealers in dried fruit, beans, and pecans. The business prospered, and long before Mr. Teasdale's death in 1921, his older son, George Willard, took over the management of the firm. Other members of the family also worked there at intervals, and even after George Willard's death in 1924, the business was carried on for a while with no Teasdale connections, before it closed. For many years the offices and store were located at 806 Spruce Street in St. Louis.

Because of their ancestry and background, Sara's parents were devout in their religious worship, and it was a disappointment to them that their children were not as absorbed in the church and its teachings as they were. When Mamie Teasdale's husband, Joseph Wheless, wrote a book questioning certain religious beliefs, it caused them no little concern. It was impossible for them to move completely out of the shadow of the Puritanism that was their natural heritage. Sara, too, inherited a bit of this Puritanism, for she was never tempted to live other than according to the strict moral code by which she was reared. She was never really comfortably at home in sophisticated New York society that liked the taste of liquor, nor in the bohemian atmosphere of carelessly free romantic morals that she found in New York and Chicago in the early decades of the twentieth century. Her nature, whose only passion was for beauty, was tempered by a certain Puritan restraint.

For many years, Mr. and Mrs. Teasdale made their home at 3668 Lindell Boulevard, a house that they had built and that had been largely designed and planned by Mrs. Teasdale, with the aid of an architect. For a while their neighbor on the west was Lewis Wallace, author of *Ben-Hur*. On the east at one time lived a young girl named Elly, who played with little Sara. Sara learned to spell the word *icicle* by looking out of the window of her father's room and saying, "I see, I see Elly." In 1909 the Teasdales moved to 38 Kingsbury Place, a large home in a fashionable neighborhood that had also been built according to Mrs. Teasdale's ideas.

Their summers were spent in Michigan, for around the turn of the century, when they were visiting in Charlevoix, they saw a house that especially appealed to them as a summer home; and when Sara was sixteen, they bought the large white house, called Altasand, the back of which faced Lake Michigan. Built on land that rose sharply from the water, it had a particularly enchanting view of the blue lake, and there was a high wooded bank nearby. About forty-five steps led from the house down to the pale gold, sandy beach below.

The house, and also the stable, which was regularly in use, because Mr. Teasdale had his horses shipped to Altasand every summer, were of frame construction; in the latter stayed the coachman who looked after the horses and the carriage, and who was well liked at the stores and offices where he transacted family business. In Charlevoix, also, as in St. Louis, there are residents who still recall Mr. Teasdale, with his long, white beard, a courtly gentleman seated behind his sleek, black horses, riding in the carriage with Mrs. Teasdale, who always shielded herself with a tiny, adjustable black silk sunshade.

Each summer Mrs. Teasdale would ask Mrs. Cook, who lived in Charlevoix, to open the house for her, and to keep an eye on it in the winter. Mrs. Cook's father used to spend much of his time rocking on the porch, and he was the subject of Sara's poem, "The Philosopher," who explained the secret of his ninety-two years in these words:

"I make the most of all that comes,
And the least of all that goes."

Sara's favorite place at Altasand was a small summer house, built on stilts and overlooking the constantly changing and colorful water of Lake Michigan. Here she spent many happy moments, writing poems, answering letters, reading, or talking with her friends. A little footbridge led to this secluded spot.

Altasand is no longer standing today, and alas, for the sands of time and change! The square white barn has long since become a garage. The family used the house every summer until 1921, when Mr. Teasdale died at Altasand. After that, they never stayed there again, and after Mrs. Teasdale's death in 1924, the house was sold.

When Sara was born, her mother was forty, and her father was forty-five. Because of the three older children in the family, all practically grown, the age span between the child and her parents appeared even greater than it was, and the baby seemed almost more like a new grandchild than a new child in the family. Actually, the first grandchild, Willard Walsh, was born only five years after Sara's birth.

Coming into the lives of her parents rather late in life, little Sara was watched over anxiously from the day of her birth. Her early tendency to frailness helped to emphasize this solicitude and perhaps set the pattern for her life, in that she always had to be most careful of her health. She was never strong, was easily fatigued, and was highly susceptible to colds; always, she needed a maximum of rest. For long periods of time, during her life, the poet had a nurse-companion with her; this was not because she was confined to her bed, but merely because the family felt that she was better cared for with someone close by, who could relieve her of some of the burdens of daily living and see that she did not overtax her strength.

In the sheltered atmosphere in which she was reared, Sara was waited on like a princess, surrounded by luxury, indulged in her desires for books, paintings, and music, and never expected to take the least household responsibility. She was never called upon to cook, mend, make her bed, or do any of the other innumerable tasks that must be attended to in a home, nor was she inclined to want to do these things, for domestic chores simply did not interest her. Her friends used to quote, fondly, one of her own lines of poetry as descriptive of herself:

I was the flower amid a toiling world.

Once, when it was her turn to be the hostess for a supper for the St. Louis Artists' Guild, she engaged a caterer and simply left everything to him. But the caterer was late, there was not time to wash the lettuce for the salads properly, and everything was rushed and thrown on the table in haste. Sara was in despair, hid her face in her hands, and moaned comically. In later years this unforgettable fiasco seemed to her to be the perfect illustration of her own inadequacy in regard to culinary arts.

Mrs. Teasdale herself was intensely interested in domestic matters, and it was hard for her to understand why her daughter was not. She often remarked, when Orrick Johns or some other young friend would call to read or discuss poetry with Sara, that it would be more to the point if Sara would learn to bake a good cake and serve it to her young men callers, instead of entertaining them with poetry. Neither Mrs. Teasdale, who was occupied with household matters, nor Mr. Teasdale, who was naturally primarily concerned with his business and his horses, was much given to literary interests and Sara's passion for spiritual beauty and her creative imagination must have seemed interests remote indeed from those of her parents. George Willard, Sara's older brother, and Mamie, her sister, were the two members of the family who were especially interested in Sara's poetic gift.

The child, Sara, was a charming little girl with large brown eyes and titian hair. Since she was the only small child in the family, she was accustomed to being with older people, and talked and thought much as they did. Perhaps, too, this is why she lived, even from childhood, a strong inner life; though she was surrounded by love and care, the lack of other young children in her immediate environment contributed to her shyness and sensitivity. As a little girl, she amused herself with dreams and stories that she herself created. The world of solitude, whose wealth she first discovered at an early age through the life of the imagination, was to become the cherished sanctuary of her spirit for much of her life; its mark was upon her even as a child. Though she ventured from its portals many times over, its magnetism drew her strongly, and it was the refuge that she sought constantly and to which she ultimately returned.

According to her mother, the first word that she ever said was "pretty." Lights, snow, and stars fascinated the small Sara, and early in life she was introduced to the music and enchantment of poetry. Mamie spent much of her time reading to her sister, and she was always especially careful to see that Sara had only the best literature. Like all small children, she loved Mother Goose rhymes and " 'Twas the Night Before Christmas." Before she was old enough to form a sentence, Mamie would stop at the end of a line of poetry and let her say the rhyme word. The poem that Sara herself remembered best from childhood days was Christina Rossetti's "A Christmas Carol," which begins:

> In the bleak mid-winter
>   Frosty winds made moan,
> Earth stood hard as iron,
>   Water like stone;
> Snow had fallen, snow on snow,
>   Snow on snow,
> In the bleak mid-winter
>   Long ago.

The lyrical beauty of these words and the lonely snowscape that they invoked appealed to something in her nature kindred to the poet who wrote them, for they cast a spell over her that was never wholly lost; Christina Rossetti remained one of her major interests until the very end of her life.

Because of the little girl's frailty, her sister taught her at home until she was nine. Then she went to Mrs. Ellen Dean Lockwood's school for small boys and girls, which was on the next block and did not seem too far for her to go alone. By this time she had memorized many verses and stories, and it was apparent that she possessed a gifted and unusual mind. But because of her constant association with adults, she was still very timid about making friends with other children. Mrs. Lockwood, whom the boys and girls loved greatly, was exactly the right kind of person to help the small Sara overcome this difficulty. A capable and understanding teacher, she gave loving and individual attention to each of her little students.

Her school was a place that children remembered with pleasure in later years. She knew how to make her school room attractive with pictures, plants, flowers, and an aquarium, and she believed in stimulating her small scholars to be aware of and to enjoy the wonders of nature. For this purpose she kept a *Sharp Eyes Book;* it was considered a great honor for a child to have his name written in this book when he brought in the first violet of the year, the first maple leaf, buttercup, or pussy willow. After the flower or leaf had been pasted in the book with the honored name of its finder, little stories, pictures, and information about it would follow. Sara, who possessed a creative mind, and who was always sensitive to the moods and expressions of nature, loved to participate in activities of this kind.

Mrs. Lockwood introduced her to Louisa Alcott and other authors whom she enjoyed; and while at this school she started to fill the notebook in which she listed for many years all the books that she had read "from cover to cover," the first ones included being *Little Women, Little Men, Jack and Jill, An Old-Fashioned Girl,* and *Eight Cousins.*

In later years, recalling the days spent under the guidance of Mrs. Lockwood, Sara expressed the deepest gratitude to and affection for this gentle instructor, who understood her disposition so well, and whose patience helped her to overcome her shyness with strangers.

After these happy years were over, Sara attended Mary Institute for the school year 1898-1899, where she was in the fifth academic form, now equivalent to the eighth grade. Her name is still registered in the files as Sadie Trevor Teasdale. Mamie Teasdale had graduated from Mary Institute, one of the finest girls' schools in St. Louis, which had been founded by T. S. Eliot's grandfather and attended by the poet's mother and four sisters, and which was once located next door to his boyhood home.

When Mr. Eliot spoke at Mary Institute's centennial celebration in November of 1959, the *St. Louis Post-Dispatch* carried this report:

"If not for a matter of sex, my brother and I would also have attended Mary Institute," he told a large audience.

Eliot, who became a British citizen in 1927, spent his first sixteen years in a house on Locust Street. Right next door, on the corner of Locust and Beaumont Street, stood the old Mary Institute.

When the girls had left for the week end, he recalled, "Their playground and their gymnasium became mine. Once," he said, "I entered the school yard before the last girls had left. When I looked in a school window and saw a girl looking out at me, I fled out of there in a hurry."

The old school janitor, Uncle Henry Jones, also brought back memories to Eliot. "He was a romantic figure, reputed to be a runaway slave with a mutilated ear, said to have been chewed by bloodhounds. I was also told he had two wives, not in succession, but at the same time."

When he finished reminiscing, he said, "Considering all of this, I consider myself to be an alumnus of Mary Institute. I would say the one and only alumnus."

Sara had expected to graduate from Mary Institute like Mamie, but the street cars going down town were so crowded, and Sara, who tired easily, had to stand up for so much of the time, that after a year, the family decided that it would be wiser to make a change.

The following term found her enrolled at Hosmer Hall, an exclusive private school for girls, which had been established in the year the poet was born, 1884, by Miss Martha Mathews and Miss Clara G. Shepherd. At this time, the school, which was named for Harriet Hosmer, the American sculptor, was located at Washington Boulevard and Pendleton Avenue, and since it was farther out of town than Mary Institute, the street cars were not so crowded.

Established at a time when college education for women was just beginning, Hosmer Hall stressed, from the first, a thorough scholastic background for entry into the leading women's colleges. The basic theory of the school, according to its principal, was that character is developed by the discipline of a trained mind, and the records made by its graduates, who were excused from taking college entrance examinations because of the school's excellent reputation, speak well for the training that it gave its students.

French, German, and Latin were offered, as well as the other subjects required for college preparation. Miss Martha Mathews, who became principal in 1896, was loved and respected by her pupils, as was Miss Louise McNair, a Wellesley graduate, who taught for years at Hosmer Hall and followed Miss Mathews as principal. The instructors were all graduates of leading colleges, and it was a policy of the school to have on its faculty one or two very recent college graduates who would be especially sympathetic with the students' point of view.

Here Sara remained until she graduated on May 28, 1903, at the age of eighteen. The choice of this school seems to have been a wise and satisfactory one, for the young writer was given an education that served to enrich her life, and here, also, she met a group of interesting friends.

At Hosmer Hall Sara first read the poetry of Heine; his lyrical style appealed immensely to her and served as her first important poetic influence. Among the twenty members of her class was Zoë Akins, the late well-known writer who was awarded a Pulitzer Prize in 1935 for her dramatization of Edith Wharton's novelette, *The Old Maid*. Caroline Risque, a talented artist and sculptor, who did not graduate because of illness, and her sister, Aline Brooks Risque, also became friends of Sara's at Hosmer Hall.

The class of 1903 organized a class club in its sophomore year, which was called NPS; since someone had told the members that the club would soon peter out, the initials stood for the Non-Petering Sophomores. The next year they were called the Non-Petering Juniors, and, finally, the Non-Petering Seniors.

One of Sara's classmates still recalls the large house on Lindell Boulevard in which she lived at this time, where one ceiling was intriguingly decorated with murals, cupids, clouds, and garlands. Sometimes, Sara would be driven to school in a carriage, and occasionally she would miss some school activity because her father did not think the horses should be used. She is remembered as a very capable student, a girl with gleaming auburn hair and a delightful sense of humor, who was a little withdrawn and shy. Her friends of these days also recall that she did not have much of the normal teen-age kind of fun enjoyed by every generation of young girls. There were several reasons for this: one, of course, was her health; she was not equal to the usual rounds of entertainment, amusement, athletics, and parties that the average young girl takes part in with enthusiasm. Then, too, her way of life was decidedly different from that of the other young girls, since her parents were older than the average young person's, and she was watched over with especial care by them.

During these years at Hosmer Hall, Sara's literary talent was recognized by her teachers, and Miss Mathews wanted Sara to be on the program for her commencement exercises. But her shyness made her decline, as she did not want to read her work before so many people. Then Miss Mathews decided that for the first time the graduating class should have a class song, and Sara would write the words for it, which she did. Sara's poem was set to music by Ernest Kroeger, a St. Louis musician with an excellent reputation as concert pianist and composer, who conducted music classes at Hosmer Hall.

The *St. Louis Republic* for Thursday, May 28, 1903, described the graduation exercises in detail:

The annual commencement of Hosmer Hall will take place this evening at the Congregational Church, No. 3610 Delmar Avenue.

Twenty members of the class of 1903 have been busily preparing for the event during the last two weeks. Everything is now in readiness, and effort will be made to eclipse previous commencements.

The hundred undergraduates dressed entirely in white will participate in the exercises and will help the graduates sing the class poem, the work of Miss Sadie Trevor Teasdale. Each undergraduate will carry an American Beauty rose, while the seniors, who are to occupy the front row, will carry shower bouquets of green and white.

The exercises will begin promptly at eight o'clock. Miss Aline Brooks Risque is salutatorian. Miss Helen Miles Goddard will deliver the valedictory.

Mr. Richard G. Moulton of the University of Chicago will address the graduates, his subject being "An Eastern Story." He is well known throughout the United States and England as a man of letters, and is the author of *The Modern Reader's Bible.*

After the exercises were over, Sara, carrying her shower bouquet of white and green, stood among friends and relatives, no doubt receiving many compliments on her class poem, her first public creative contribution. Unfortunately, no copy of the words or music exists today. Not a trace of either can be found.

Hosmer Hall was moved in 1917 to Wydown Boulevard and Dartmouth Avenue in Clayton, Missouri, and closed in 1936 after fifty-two years of operation. Some of its graduates achieved recognition for excellent scholarship in colleges throughout the nation, and a number attained success in various fields, but the name of Sara Teasdale is still recalled among the alumnae as perhaps the most distinguished of all its graduates.

Chapter 2

THE POTTERS AND *THE POTTER'S WHEEL*

.

THE St. Louis in which Sara and her friends grew up, in the late nineteenth and early twentieth centuries, contributed a galaxy of famous personalities to the annals of the arts. Besides T. S. Eliot, others outstanding in creative and artistic fields, such as Marianne Moore, Zoë Akins, Fannie Hurst, Orrick Johns, John Myers O'Hara, Hugh Ferriss, Jesse Lynch Williams, Emily Hahn, Alice Corbin Henderson, Paul Tietjens, Fanny Ward, Josephine Johnson, Elizabeth Seifert, Shirley Seifert, Martha Gellhorn, Winston Churchill, and Eugene Field, were born in or were closely associated with the city during those years.

There were a number of factors that made St. Louis a stimulating place for the development of creative talent around the turn of the century. In addition to several fine private schools in the city, Central High School was the large public secondary school of St. Louis, and on its staff were some unusually competent and dedicated teachers. Also, St. Louis University was the first university to be founded west of the Mississippi, and Washington University, which claims five Nobel Prize winners, had been formally established on April 23, 1857, when the old Eliot Seminary was changed to the University. Like Mary Institute, the Eliot Seminary had been founded by T. S. Eliot's grandfather, the Reverend Greenleaf Eliot, D.D., who also founded the first Unitarian Church in the city. These universities offered a college education to young St. Louis citizens without the expense of leaving home—a precious privilege at a time when it was not financially possible for many students to seek a college education elsewhere.

Furthermore, the St. Louis School of Fine Arts was established in 1897, and not only did it offer art classes, but until 1909 it carried on museum activities for the city, also. St. Louis was the first city in the West to establish a school of fine and applied arts, and as early as 1907 it drew pupils from Japan, Mexico, the Sandwich Islands, and seventeen states. Though it was a branch of the University, the School of Fine Arts was a large and completely separate division, with its own building and a highly trained staff. Here all phases of art work were taught: painting, design, sculpturing, book binding, modeling, and ceramics. Each year a group of silver medals and the distinguished Wayman Crow award were presented for the best work, and the winning of any of these was considered an exceptional honor.

One of the most famous of the instructors was George Julian Zolnay, whose bust of Edgar Allan Poe, with his head bowed on his hands, showing the sensitivity, the despair, and the intelligence in the face of the poet, is now at the University of Virginia and is considered a masterpiece of sculpture. So thorough a teacher was he that once when Mr. Zolnay was called upon to make a death mask of Dr. Charles Augustus Bernays, he took his entire modeling class along to show the students this technique. Among the spectators were Caroline Risque, and two of her friends, Nancy Coonsman and Adele Schulenburg, who later became friends of Sara's, also.

As a further encouragement of the love for and the development of art, the City Art Museum of St. Louis grew out of the earlier museum activities of the School of Fine Arts. At the first meeting of the Board, in 1909, Halsey C. Ives, who contributed greatly to the artistic life of St. Louis over a long period of years, as head of the School of Fine Arts, was made Director of the

City Art Museum. Under his guidance, the Museum acquired on permanent loan the collections of works of art that Washington University had accumulated. Two unusual policies were stated in the first Annual Report of the Board, which show how much the Museum intended to do for its own city. One, concerning the many exhibits that would be shown, said: "It is the custom in most art museums to charge a commission on all sales made; but in the Art Museum of St. Louis no commissions are charged, nor will any compensation be accepted, and the services of all the officers and employees of the Museum, and their best judgment in regard to works of art, are at the disposal of the people of St. Louis." The other, pertaining to the purchase of paintings, stated: "It is the intention of the Board, each year, if practicable, to acquire at least one or more pictures painted by St. Louis artists. Too much praise cannot be given to the local artists who have achieved success in spite of the many obstacles that they have encountered, and who are doing thoroughly good work that should and will be recognized and encouraged."

George Sibley Johns, the editor of the *St. Louis Post-Dispatch* for fifty years, and the father of Orrick Johns, helped found the St. Louis Artists' Guild in which such personalities as Kate Chopin, the writer, William Schuyler, the musician and novelist, Thekla Bernays, sister and biographer of the notable surgeon, Charles Augustus Bernays, and other writers, musicians, artists, and architects all participated. Now and then the Guild extended membership to some of the younger artists of the city, giving them a chance to meet and mingle with the more experienced members. George and Carrie Blackman's open house on Sunday nights was another meeting place for the intellectual of St. Louis, where ideas on all phases of fine arts were freely exchanged.

As well as having more than a little interest in the world of art, St. Louis was also highly receptive to the dramatic and musical offerings that were presented in the city from time to time. At the Olympic Theatre, dating from 1866, such actors as Maude Adams and George Arliss appeared, and at the Odeon where a Grand Opera Season was held each year, Caruso sang and Geraldine Farrar held the audience enthralled by her role in *Madame Butterfly*. The outdoor Municipal Theatre in Forest Park was also, then as now, the scene of many operas, musical comedies, and plays; but when the rains came down unexpectedly in the midst of a performance, as they did into the heroine's bedroom when *Arms and the Man* was being presented, the audience had to flee, and the dramatic and opera companies had to begin carrying weather insurance. Sara Bernhardt, Ethel Barrymore, Nazimova, Mary Garden, Olga Nethersole, and Julia Marlowe were among the visiting artists who found an enthusiastic audience in the city.

Another cultural force was the Wednesday Club, a woman's organization of superior intellectual caliber, which was founded in 1887, when a group of earnest young women met weekly to study the works of Shelley. On a far higher plane than the usual woman's club, this organization offered membership by invitation only, and such an invitation was considered a distinct honor and a tribute to one's mental capacities. The Wednesday Club still sponsors what is probably the oldest poetry prize contest in this country, dating from the turn of the century, and open to all poets in the area around St. Louis. Tennessee Williams, known in those days as Thomas Lanier Williams, received his first literary encouragement when he won a twenty-five dollar prize for three sonnets in one of these contests.

The Mercantile Library and the St. Louis Public Library also did their share in encouraging intellectual interests.

Finally, in the world of journalism, there was one man who became the literary legend of St. Louis during the first two decades of the century. This was William Marion Reedy, who was born in 1862 and died in 1920, and whose fame spread first throughout the United States and then to England and the rest of the world. His genius of judgment, his good taste in artistic matters, and his talent for finding and publishing literature of quality attracted universal attention. An enormous man, with deeply luminous eyes and a booming voice, he had a joyful zest for life in all its experiences, and there were two definitely contrasting sides to his personality. On the one hand, he gloried in Rabelaisian bouts, good beer, and fine food; around his name numerous anecdotes grew up concerning his drinking parties and his worldly reputation. On the other hand, he was an insatiable reader, and he possessed the discriminating mind of a scholar that enabled him to write sensitive and telling criticism. His Jesuit education had given him a classical background, and this knowledge of Latin and Greek served as an excellent foundation for his literary career.

He first worked for the *Missouri Republican,* and then served as a reporter on the *Globe-Democrat,* and 1893 found him as City Editor of the *St. Louis Mirror.* When the *Mirror,* then little more than a scandal sheet, was reorganized because of bankruptcy, the new owner made a gift of it to Reedy. Not long after this, it became known as *Reedy's Mirror,* and, gradually, Reedy lifted it, by the sheer power of his critical acumen, into a paper of the first order, with a reputation for introducing literature of quality to the city, the country, and, eventually, the world. In 1920, at the time of his death, his paper listed ten foreign cities in as many European countries where the *Mirror* could be bought regularly, and a number of foreign hotels where it could always be read.

Because of the far and rich horizons of his literary interests, Reedy published the work of a varied assortment of gifted writers who would never have found the public they commanded at that time, had he not sponsored them. The works of Galsworthy, Shaw, Thomas Hardy, Ernest Dowson, Lionel Johnson, Æ, Yeats, and Synge were all reprinted in his paper. And the new American voices—John Hall Wheelock, David Morton, Carl Sandburg, William Rose Benét, Babette Deutsch, Witter Bynner, Maxwell Bodenheim, Vachel Lindsay, and Edna St. Vincent Millay—were also heard there.

Reedy's memory was phenomenal, his critical analyses were penetrating, his vocabulary was rich and unlimited; though he was vitally concerned with local and national politics, he also kept up with the world of fine arts in all its branches; apparently, he read everything, knew everybody, and could converse on any subject with authority.

Unfortunately, he did not leave a book of his own, except for two collections of essays reprinted from the *Iconoclast,* but his influence on the young writers of his period was fabulous, and a story that still remains to be written. Edgar Lee Masters is said to have created his *Spoon River Anthology* poems after Reedy repeatedly turned down the lyrics that Masters submitted for the *Mirror.* Reedy thought they were weak and unworthy of their author, and he told Masters so; he handed Masters a copy of *The Greek Anthology* and advised him to study it and then write of life as he knew it. Challenged, Masters decided to show Reedy that he could be as forceful and realistic as the editor wished, and, primarily for this purpose, he wrote the epitaphs that have become famous. Reedy thought they were excellent, and starting on May 29, 1914, they began to appear regularly in the *Mirror* under the pen name of Webster Ford. Edna St. Vincent Millay's *Aria da Capo* was also originally published in the *Mirror,* as were many of her sonnets, including the one beginning, "Euclid alone has looked on Beauty bare." Among the St. Louis writers whom Reedy first encouraged were Zoë Akins, Fannie Hurst, Orrick Johns, and Sara Teasdale.

Such, then, was the cultural climate that prevailed in St. Louis during the early 1900's. All of these influences combined to make an atmosphere congenial to artistic effort in the city at the time Sara graduated from Hosmer Hall.

In the audience at those commencement exercises on the evening of May 28, 1903, was a girl who was to become closely associated with Sara during the next few years. Williamina Parrish had come to the graduation activities because of two of her friends in the class of 1903: Caroline Risque, who did not gradu-

Sara Teasdale at the age of six

ate because of illness, and her younger sister, Aline Risque. Caroline had often told Williamina (who was called Will, Willie, or William by her closest friends) that she should meet Sara, but Will did not have the opportunity to do so on that particular night. Later in the summer, however, Caroline invited both Will and Sara to her home where they liked each other at once and became the good friends that Caroline had predicted they would be. Because Caroline and Will had a number of mutual friends, all in their teens or early twenties, all unusually gifted in some phase of fine arts, it was not long before Sara met these girls, was included in their group, and began to share with them their parties, discussions, and artistic endeavors.

Though others were invited to join in their fun occasionally, there were eight girls who became fast friends simply because they liked each other immensely and because they were bound by ties of creative interest in music, art, drama, photography, and literature. These eight were Grace and Williamina Parrish, Caroline Risque, Vine Colby, Edna Wahlert, Celia Harris, Petronelle Sombart, and Sara.

Will Parrish and her sister, Grace, who had been educated in what is now Visitation Convent in St. Louis, were entirely different in personality. Grace was a dainty, fastidious "lady" of a girl with conservative views. Will was a born leader, a girl of strong convictions and even stronger will power, and she was never happier than when she was directing some undertaking. Both Grace and Will adored music, and Will played the piano, while Grace played the violin. The versatile and gifted Will, who could produce a superior water color, write a creditable sonnet, take a leading part in a play and carry it off to perfection, and do almost anything else that she seriously attempted, also possessed excellent critical faculties; she never failed to speak her mind, and poor, inefficient work in any medium was sure to call forth comment from her, with directions as to how it could be done better.

While Will and Grace were in their early teens, they had obtained a small Eastman Pocket Kodak and started experimenting with photography. They had no professional training in this field, but by reading all the photography magazines that they could get their hands on, and by collecting all the photographs that especially appealed to them, they gradually acquired a store of knowledge on the subject. They learned to do every bit of their own work, including the fine points of developing their pictures. "We never allowed anyone to 'do the rest' and I really believe that no one can be really sincere in his work and wish to improve who leaves any portion of the work to others," Will once wrote in an article in *Western Camera Notes,* and nothing could be more indicative of her character. "Our greatest move in the right direction," she explained, "was when we resolved to try for ourselves what would happen if we took pictures with the camera pointed at the light, instead of facing the 'victim' to the light as all the little Kodak books eternally preached. It was then that we really commenced to exist artistically." Their efforts produced an original kind of art photography, which added a new dimension of interest to their pictures. By using glass negatives and a combination of skillful brush work plus a partially printed picture, they achieved unique results; and their photographs began to find a public by being reprinted in current camera magazines such as *Browning King Magazine, Photo Era, Camera Craft,* and *Western Camera Notes.*

Caroline Risque posed for a series of especially successful pictures. Maude Adams was then at the height of her popularity as the gypsy girl, Babbie, in Barrie's *The Little Minister.* Will thought that Caroline resembled her, and she dressed her in the Babbie gypsy costume and made a number of arresting and original prints. One of these was shown at the New York Salon and became quietly famous in photography circles. As the years went by, the girls continued their work and became members of the Salon Club of America, exhibiting their photographs all over the United States and also in Europe, receiving many honors and awards for them.

Small, slim, dark-haired, and vivacious, Caroline Risque was perhaps the most highly gifted of all these girls. Never very strong, she had to be careful of her health continually, for she was usually engaged in a great number of creative undertakings that quickly used up her strength. Particularly talented in any phase of art and sculptural work, she was also quite capable of turning out excellent prose or poetry when the mood struck her. Everything that she did had a grace and finish that is not often apparent in the work of a young girl. Temperamental by nature, excitable, animated, exuberant at times, she had a high-strung disposition and was abundantly loved and teased by her friends, especially by Will, who recognized the very great promise of her capabilities and was determined to see that she fulfilled them.

The very soul of loyalty and dependability, Vine Colby, an exceedingly well-rounded girl, possessed an out-going personality and an unselfish and cheerful disposition. A slender brunette, Vine had grown up reading, savoring what she read, and distilling it into good, leisurely talk and delightful essays. Although she was equally active in dramatic productions and tried her hand now and then at artistic projects with interesting results, Vine had a genuine gift for journalism and creative writing. And though she was very much absorbed in music, art, and literature, she also possessed an unusually fine and balanced outlook, which enabled her to recognize the practical side of life as well as the artistic; she could give of herself to either with equal vigor and success.

Edna Wahlert, who was known to her friends as "Ned," had sparkling hazel eyes, very white teeth, and heavy, dark hair, and she was intensely interested in science. She was lively and spirited, had definite likes and dislikes, and would sometimes enter an argument just for the thrill of a battle. In high school she had headed the debating society and had never lost a single debate. Her creative ability lay especially in the literary field; she wrote poems, plays, and strong stories of protest presented objectively.

Celia Harris, a lovely girl with fair skin, a sprinkling of freckles, and pale, rippling, gold hair, was especially deeply drawn to and influenced by the Celtic Renaissance. She had a low, delightfully modulated voice, frank, boyish ways, and a rather square jaw that emphasized the strength and integrity of her character. Her gift, too, lay in the field of creative writing, and her versatile talent could produce plays, stories, poems, or sketches.

A tall brunette, who was more silent and reserved than the others, Petronelle Sombart was a girl of strong will power with much hidden fire within her. Her bearing gave the impression of stateliness. There were many facets to her abilities, for she had a variety of talents. One was a fine voice, which she was most interested in developing; she was also drawn to the theatre and frequently took part in dramatic productions; and also, she had a genuine gift for artistic work, especially for painting in water color.

The Sara whom these girls knew had an eager, responsive nature. One of her most endearing traits was her delightful sense of humor, which is not at all apparent in her poems, but which was a very definite and characteristic part of her personality. She could apply it to herself or to the life around her with equal enjoyment. Because of her rest and hours of solitude, the most important part of her existence was her rich, inner life, which nourished her dreams, her ideals, and her poetry. It was almost impossible for Sara to write without invoking the image of a make-believe lover; as she once told Celia Harris, she wished it were otherwise, but her poetry simply came to her that way.

At times she was possessed by intense enthusiasms, as in the case of her admiration for Eleonora Duse and Sappho. Her romantic nature led her to idealize people—not only those unknown to her personally like the actress, Duse, but also others such as her friend, Bessie Brey, to whom she wrote "Faults" and "I Saw a Ship."

Williamina Parrish
1909

Photographs by
Grace Parrish

Music, art, and literature were all important to Sara. No doubt Mamie Teasdale's interest in and love for art influenced her younger sister. For Mamie had intended studying at the St. Louis School of Fine Arts, but because she was born with one eye very weak, her doctor did not advise her to take up painting. This was a deep disappointment to her, but as a compensation, she filled her life with lovely pictures and visited art galleries often. Sara, too, loved beautiful works of art, and in her room were reproductions of some of her favorite paintings and of figures from the Parthenon frieze.

Vine Colby, in writing about the Sara of those days, said:

Her delicate health was not a shadow or drawback in her daily life, as far as her friends were concerned. She did not indulge in self-pity; she practically never referred to feeling ill, even when she had a trained nurse living with her for long periods. Whenever we met, she was overflowing with high spirits, fun, a keen interest in everything. At the time, I took this healthy-mindedness for granted. Now, looking back, I can see that it was heroic and admirable. It must have cost a great deal. It implied exceptional courage.

Sara was not sentimental, but she was extremely romantic. She lived so much in dreams that it was impossible for me to visualize her as a wife or mother. Her spirit remained fixed at the stage of romantic love. One could no more imagine her otherwise than one could imagine Isolde planning Tristan's dinner or getting the children off to school. She lived and breathed poetry. The world of strife and struggle and practical affairs was as unreal and remote to her as *her* world would be remote and unreal to, say, the president of the Chamber of Commerce.

There was a quaintly old-fashioned side to Sara. She never cared a thing about fashion or style, but serenely followed her own preferences. She wore her hair with sidecombs long after sidecombs were passé. She wore high-buttoned shoes, long sleeves, high necks—perhaps because of her sensitiveness to chills and colds, but also because she did not care what was in fashion. As a girl she lived in Peter Thompson dresses, which she loved.

Her feeling for nature was an adoration, especially for the sea and stars. Her poetry is saturated with worship of the sea and stars, not because they are stock poetical properties, but because she truly gloried in their beauty and mystery to the greatest extent.

Though she had no technical knowledge of music or of painting, she cared deeply about music and surrounded herself with reproductions of great works of art. At one time she had obtained an Aeolian harp—this must have been during her Sappho enthusiasm—and she once played for me a record of a nightingale's song.

Sara was honest, genuine, frank, but reserved, except to a very few.

Ned and Vine had known each other at Central High School; later, Vine, Ned, and Celia studied at Washington University; and also, at one time or another, Caroline, Petronelle, Will, Grace, and Vine studied at the St. Louis School of Fine Arts.

One of the very first festivities enjoyed by this group of friends was an Alice-in-Wonderland party, at which time each girl was given a name out of Wonderland, and for a number of years after this, they were affectionately referred to by their make-believe names. Will was the Hatter, Caroline was the March Hare, Celia was the Dormouse, Grace was Alice, Sara was the Carpenter, Vine was the Red Queen, Ned was the Duchess, and Petronelle was the White Knight.

On a memorable day in 1904, six of the girls had gathered together in one of their favorite meeting places, the home of Mrs. Charles Harris on Thornby Place. Mrs. Harris was a member of the Wednesday Club and one of a number of the older generation sympathetic to their activities and ideas whom the girls called the "Olympians"—probably because this name was synonymous with "adults" in Kenneth Grahame's *Dream Days* and *The Golden Age,* and also because these women seemed powerful in their accomplishments and their abilities. A warmly interested and active worker in civic undertakings, Mrs. Harris liked people young and old; but especially did she enjoy and believe in the possibilities of young people with a fine gift on the way to development. And she had a genuine affection for and interest in each one of these girls.

On this particular day the girls were eagerly discussing the dazzling heights they might reach by trying their artistic wings. Finally, their hostess, Celia Harris, suggested that if they were really serious about improving their creative talents, they should form a club for mutual help, criticism, and accomplishment. The idea won instant enthusiastic response, and thus, the Potters, an organization that was to become a footnote to American literary history, was born. Caroline Risque suggested that the club be given this name, and its significance is easily understood, as the girls thought of themselves as creating something of enduring quality through their own industry. Mrs. Harris became their official sponsor and was referred to fondly as "Mater Pottorum." Until its sale in 1906, her home on Thornby Place was often used as a meeting place for the group.

Ned and Petronelle, who were not at the first meeting, joined the group later, and though others were invited to share in their activities from time to time, these eight remained the original Potters.

From the very beginning, there was no argument whatever among the various club members as to who would take charge of them and run things. The undisputed power of the group was Williamina Parrish, a born organizer and executive, an accomplished musician and artist, who was blessed with an unerring sense of good taste, and who had the drive and forcefulness to wring from her followers the creative results that she wanted. When a suggestion was made that the girls bring out a monthly magazine, so that their creative work would have a means of presentation to the public, even through private publication, Will Parrish, with no opposition, elected herself Editor, and a masterful Editor she proved to be.

For though the Potters were active in many cultural fields, their most enduring accomplishment as a group remains the hand printed and illustrated monthly magazine that they brought out faithfully, from November, 1904, through October, 1907. Called *The Potter's Wheel,* it was made up entirely of original literary and artistic creations of its members, except for a sprinkling of quotations that especially appealed to them. Just one copy of each issue was put together and brought out on the first Friday of each month. The material was supposed to be turned over to the Editor on the last Friday of the preceding month, or drastic consequences could be expected. Every Potter was required to complete at least one contribution for each issue, and Will ruthlessly kept at her staff until the material came in. "I simply go and camp at their homes," she was reported to have said, "and I make their lives miserable, but the *Wheel* always comes out."

Put together with painstaking care, these little volumes still speak eloquently of the varied talents of the Potters. Originally eight by ten inches, the *Wheels* were composed of heavy art paper pages, in tones of beige, tan, brown, and gray, each with a decorated cover, suitable to the season, of heavier paper. After the first year, they were enlarged to ten by twelve inches. Every smallest detail in them was done by hand: the binding, the colorful covers, and the printing, which frequently made use of letters gracefully interlaced or illuminated in old manuscript style. Within their covers were found original poems, essays, stories, sketches, and plays, all by the Potters.

In these pages Sara Teasdale's poems appeared for the first time in print, her initial contribution being "Translations from German Lyric Poets." In the first number of the *Wheel*, the poet signed her work S.T.T., but in the August, 1905, issue, after she had come back from a trip to Egypt and other lands abroad, there appeared this announcement:

This similitude of an Egyptian scarab will henceforth be the signature of S.T.T.

And this was followed by her initials enclosed in such a scarab. Many of her songs, sonnets, and lyrics that were originally printed in the *Wheel* helped to make up the contents of her first volume of poetry.

The variety of artistic work to be found in the pages of the *Wheels* is as interesting as the written contributions. Water colors of taste and quality were included, such as Will Parrish's stained glass window effects, Caroline Risque's illustrations for children's verse, and Petronelle Sombart's designs for curtains and for wall paper borders. Original photographs by Will and Grace were shown, with a series of portraits of the various Potters appearing in different issues. One such group is listed in the Table of Contents for March, 1906, as "Portraits of Grace Parrish, the second of which was hung in the American Salon, 1905-1906—by Williamina Parrish." Other types of art work like Grace's "Design for Curtains for a Library Door," Vine and Will's collaboration on a peacock "Design for a Fan," a stencil motif for a silk scarf by Petronelle, lamp shade designs by Will, and photographs of clay objects modeled by Caroline illustrate the wide diversity of talent among the girls.

The work in poetry, as well as in prose, reveals a very real gift for literary expression among the group. Will Parrish wrote a series of quatrains called "The Rubaiyat of Friendship," from which the following are taken:

> As all the doors of life have but one key,
> And all the rivers flow into one sea,
>   And all the sands are on one desert laid—
> So, friend, do I begin and end in thee.
>
> The desert path is dry and hot and wide,
> And shifting ever is the desert tide,
>   But with glad heart I join the caravan,
> For art thou not to journey at my side?
>
> When in the market place I wander round,
> And see how, not for love, all men are bound,
>   Each to his trade, but gain and greed their aim—
> Ah, then I know what treasure I have found.

The children's poems by Caroline Risque that are scattered throughout the pages of the *Wheels,* reminiscent of Stevenson's verses and bewitchingly illustrated by the author, would still delight a child's heart today. One of her most memorable contributions is a brief poem called "Thanatos," which she printed in the May, 1905, issue:

> Where was a heart
> Is dust.
> Weep not, for soon
> Thou must
> Lie silent there,
> And Earth that seemed so fair
> Be naught to thee,
> As, wrapped in that great cloak
> Of slumber deep
> Thou, too, shalt lay thee down
> To dreamless sleep.
> And thy little green cell shall be
> Locked with a Master-key
> That none may break thy rest
> Nor trouble thee.
> Thou in thy little turn
> Shall learn what all must learn.
> Then wherefore weep?

Ned Wahlert wrote many a provocative story for the *Wheel,* but occasionally she contributed a poem, such as "To Him," which still has a fresh, youthful quality about it, and which was used many years later by Sara in her anthology, *The Answering Voice.*

> I have wandered to a spring in the forest
>   green and dim,
> The sweet quiet stirs about me—
> The water twinkles at me,
> As I stoop to dip my cup,
>   As I stoop to drink—to him.

True, I'm only half in earnest—I touch the
    cool, wet brim—
He'd laugh if he could see me—
I'm glad he doesn't see me,
As alone with my queer gladness,
    I stoop to drink—to him.

Vine Colby, who translated the songs of Horace for the *Wheel*,
was equally adept at writing stories, sketches, plays, and poems
for the magazine, and was the author of this little lyric entitled
"Sympathy":

I would have opened wide my doors
And filled my house with light and song,
But I lay sleepless in the dark
Because for you the night was long.

Whatever pain you have to bear
Some instinct helps me to divine;
And if your eyes are wet with tears,
I know—by those that rise in mine.

Of Sara's poems that were printed in the *Wheel*, her sonnets,
especially those to Eleonora Duse, were outstanding. Once in a
while she wrote a prose piece like "An Appreciation of Tristan
and Iseult" or the brief sketch entitled "The Crystal Cup," but
the majority of her contributions were lyrics, songs, and sonnets,
some of which she printed by hand, and some of which Will
printed for her.

Sara had no actual contact with Eleonora Duse, and, in fact,
never even saw her, but she was deeply impressed by her charm
and dramatic strength, and several pictures of the actress, which
Julia Marlowe was instrumental in getting for her, inspired her
to write a number of sonnets. The world of ancient Greece sym-
bolized for Sara the supreme age of beauty through the centuries, and her heart turned back to it with joy; this influence
was an important part of her development. It led her to an

abiding love for Grecian art and literature. Because she especially liked the picture of Eleonora Duse in the play, *The Dead City,* she wrote the following sonnet to this picture and printed it herself in the March, 1906, *Wheel,* with a reproduction of the photograph:

> Carved in the silence by the hand of Pain,
>   And made more perfect by the gift of Peace,
>   Than if Delight had bid your sorrow cease,
> And set a smile upon your lips again,
> And brought the dawn to where the dark has lain;
>   Oh strong and noble! tho' your woes increase,
>   The gods shall hear no crying for release,
> Nor see the tremble that your lips restrain.
>
> Alone as all the chosen are alone,
>   Yet one with all the beauty of the past,
> A sister to the noblest that we know,
> The Venus carved in Melos long ago.
> Yea, speak to her, and at your lightest tone,
>   Her lips would part, and words would come at last.

Sappho's influence on Sara, too, is recorded in the *Wheel,* for Sara loved every line of exquisite singing that the Grecian poet left to the world. She considered the Sapphic fragments and the statue of Venus de Milo supreme examples of the purest and most sublime expressions of creative artistry that the world has ever known. Though her enthusiasm for Eleonora Duse faded with the years, she never lost her interest in Sappho, and much of her early work was concerned with her. Sara chose to disregard the erotic legends that have grown up around the poet's name; instead, she felt a spiritual affinity with this lyricist of ancient times who sang of love and beauty; the echoes of her fragmentary songs, blown down the years, spoke compellingly to Sara's heart. Sappho was the

> Impassioned singer of the happy time
> When all the world was waking into morn. . . .

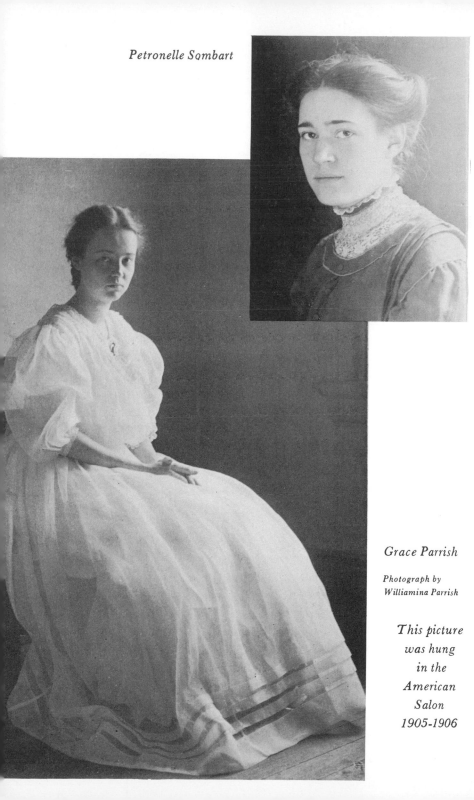

Petronelle Sombart

Grace Parrish

Photograph by
Williamina Parrish

*This picture
was hung
in the
American
Salon
1905-1906*

Perhaps because a number of Sappho's fragments were discovered on papyrus in Egypt around 1900, Sara wrote in another poem to Sappho, first printed in the *Wheel:*

> Oh tell us we shall find beside the Nile,
> Held fast in some Egyptian's dusty hand,
> Deep covered by the centuries of sand,
> The songs long written that were lost awhile—
> Sole perfect singer that the world has heard,
> Let fall from that far heaven of thine
> This golden word.

When an issue of the *Wheel* was completed, it was carefully passed around among the friends and relatives of the Potters; since so much loving care, time, and thought went into each number, it was considered an honor to be allowed to examine the contents. Among the Potters themselves, a little book with blank pages was circulated after each issue of the *Wheel* was "published." In this little book the members wrote down very frankly their criticism, both good and bad, of the magazine's contents. Their critical remarks were always taken in the spirit in which they were intended; no one ever got her feelings hurt by them, as each girl knew that only through constructive criticism could improvement be made, and improvement of their various arts was their aim. Someone made up a gay little poem that applied to the books of criticism:

> Hot cross criticisms, hot cross criticisms!
> One a month, two a month,
> Hot cross criticisms!
> If the pepper makes you sneeze, reply in stinging witticisms—
> One a month, two a month, hot cross criticisms!

One of the most attractive *Wheels* is the issue of December, 1905, for which the book of criticism has fortunately been preserved, though only Will, Sara, and Ned left their comments in it. The Table of Contents reads as follows:

Cover Designs	Caroline Risque
Contents Page Design	C. Risque
Calendar for December	W. Parrish
Christmas Verse	Celia Harris
Triolets	Sara Teasdale
Window Design	W. Parrish
To-Day	Edna Wahlert
Portraits of E.H.W.	Grace Parrish
Inscription	Vine Colby
Clay Sketches	Caroline Risque
A Cottage	Edna Wahlert
Decoration for Song	W. Parrish
To Joy—A Sonnet	Sara Teasdale
Translations from the Latin	V. Colby
Stencil Designs	C. Risque
The Last Day	Celia Harris
Designs for Lamp Shades	W. Parrish
Dedication	Sara Teasdale

The cover of this number was a Christmas scene of shepherds watching the sky; the contents page was decorated with carol singers. On the inside of the cover was a stained glass window design of the Christ Child. Will was pleased with this work, writing in the little book:

Now here's a truly cover, even if our artist did overstep the bounds of decency and order, and produce it a week after the day it was due. She has saved her honor this time, by so noble a set of contribs as the cover, back and front, and the contents page. They are among her very best work—and speaking unbiasedly I must say they are far, far above the Guild work that competed for the $150.00 *Post-Dispatch* prize and [was] printed with gusto in the Paper today. Why are mediocre and bad things always given a showing (and money) while the good go unseen and unheard of? Just contemplate the same subject handled by M. Stoddard, Artist, and C. Risque (also artist, you bet!). In color, feeling, design, placing, method, which is the better? "The rest may reason and welcome, 'tis we the *Potters* know."

Sara, too, was enthusiastic over this particular *Wheel.*

We never had a more ampial *Wheel* (excuse the Parrishism). Note the contents page. Everything—every kind of thing, I mean, that has ever been in the *Wheel* is in this month. All except some of the lovely colored photographs. Let us hope for more soon.

C.R.'s cover is *great.* W. P. is right in preferring it to the P.D. covers. It hath an olden look—as tho' it were done by an old master long ago. I could wish that the Shepherds' heads did not make so even a line. The flap, contents page, and back are all too good to be true—almost.

Celia Harris's little Christmas poem listed in the Table of Contents was later published in the *Globe-Democrat:*

PRAYER FOR A CHILD ON CHRISTMAS EVE

Little Christ, look down tonight!
   Everywhere
Children's stockings, new and worn,
Wait with mine Thy birthday morn.
I shall find mine plump and tight
   As I always do.
   Fill the others, too.
Leave no empty stocking there.
Little Christ, look down tonight.
   Hear my prayer.

But somehow it never did get printed to go into this *Wheel,* and Will wrote in the book of criticism:

. . . Her little Christmas Prayer is not to be matched for childish sweetness and directness and simplicity. It is not yet printed, but I cry "mea culpa"—and also "Barbarae Culpa." She is to do the picture, but you see 'tis the holy Christmas time.

Sara's "Triolets," which told of offering a prayer and a gift of green bay to the Goddess of Love, were later printed in her first book, *Sonnets to Duse.* These lines brought forth this comment from Will:

. . . I am o'er much fond of the little verses, they are simple, direct, and have that quaint singing quality that we find in all of Sara's dear little songs. Of course, "goddess" and "distress" are not the most pleasing rhyme, but "bodice" is about all that one could find otherwise. I do not quite like "I told about my prayer," it isn't Greek, but I cannot suggest a substitute.

When "Triolets" appeared in her first book, Sara changed this line to "I sang of answered prayer."

The Window Design by Will was a stained glass Madonna in water color; she held a child in one arm and a lily in the other, and at her feet lilies were growing. Will wrote of her own handiwork:

The poor Mother of God! but light coming thro' that window would give a warm, comfortable, shut-in feeling that would be pleasant, and that is one of the requisites of a window of stained-glass, methinks.

Sara also liked this painting, and wrote:

If I knew more about designing, I should say more about the window. There is something very charming about it. The madonna is certainly Celtic. I agree with what I believe C.R. said, that the lilies would be better if there were more of them. Of course the color is lovely because W.P. did it. I wish, tho', that the glass at the bottom of the window were different. I don't like the mixture of rose and blue.

At Ned's hands, Will fared worse, for Ned wrote:

William's window-mater is stiff. Even a glass woman doesn't have to stand like a sentinel with a lily stalk straight against her arm—she ought to be bendier. . . .

The results of the photographs of Ned taken by Grace in this series of portraits of the Potters did not wholly please the girls. Will expressed her sentiments in this way:

Celia Harris

Edna Wahlert

ographs by

amina and Grace Parrish

It is too bad something grand and worthy could not have been done by Grace in the portrait line, with the good model she had. But when people are afraid of being taken, and have very seldom submitted to the operation, what is a poor artist to do about it? Two out of 26 is a discouraging result. These two are good, especially the three-quarters. But a profile is so desirable to add to the collection. Maybe in a few years, when this set begins to be taken over again (we having grown and improved so vastly in every way that we inspire the artist with this desire), our brother Ned may have become so callous to the lime light that she can face it unflinchingly and naturally.

Ned was even more definite on the subject:

If Edna *ever* has an expression on her face like that shown in the top portrait, she deserves to go about the world for the rest of her living existence with a false face on, and to not be a Potter. It is too sadly objectionable for *anything*.

Vine's poem in this issue brought nothing but praise:

An Inscription
(For a book of Stevenson's to be given to a friend)

O friend, may days of cloud and shine,
Shrill tempest and still peace be thine.
And may thy life not lack its share
Of grief and tumult and despair,
And all the vexing small mishaps
That mad-cap life throws in our laps.
Ever thy wakeful spirit be
Instinct with curiosity
To learn of touch and tones and looks
The kindly wisdom not in books. . . .
Yet this book is both wise and gay,
Fit comrade for a toiling way;
In bleakest days it glows, a friend,
Like inn-lights at a journey's end
Where kittens by the hearthside purr
And sheets are sweet with lavender!

Of this poem Sara wrote:

The "Inscription" is a love of mine. It is really good enough for R.L.S. Could one say more? Are not the last three lines *fully* up to the dearest Josephine Preston Peabody?

However, in printing this poem, Vine had had to erase one word, which left a gap in that particular line. Will commented:

The "Inscription" would be a most joyous addition to a Stevenson collection—why limit it to *a* book? It is too bad that the tooth was extracted for the printing has such a clear, strong look, and such mistakes are maddening (far be it from me to insinuate that the Artist isn't *just* as mad as the others).

Will's water colors, illustrating lines from Stephen Phillips's "Song" from his *Sin of David*, were greatly admired. Sara offered Ned some technical points on her poem, "To-Day," and the other contributions were all remarked upon at length.

Of Caroline's clay sketches, which Will had photographed, one of them being of a friend of theirs, Susan Williams, holding a little boy, the Editor wrote:

The clay sketches are great, particularly the Little Boy Blue— didst ever see so dear a boy? No Benny about him![1] It is a wonderfully easy, natural pose and arrangement; every line is properly managed. I can't see how those old fossils at Art School don't go wild over the work of our Barbara-Potter.

Sara's "Dedication" in this issue was a little poem taken from a small book of her verse that she had printed by hand in the fall of 1905 for her sister, Mamie, who had married Joseph Wheless in 1904. Called *A Sonnet of Songs,* it was bound in soft brown leather and included fourteen songs and two sonnets. Sara printed in the little volume: "This edition of *A Sonnet of Songs* is limited to one copy printed for M.T.W. by Sara Teasdale at the sign of the 'Brown Desk.' "

---

[1] A standing joke among the Potters was Will's opinion that any little boy named Benny could not help but be extremely effeminate.

Ned wrote about the poem, "Dedication": "I wish I could produce things as careful and neat as Sara's. Don't her pages always look clean? I like your 'Dedication,' Sara, I really do." And Will added her opinion: "Sara's 'Dedication' is as sweet and simple as the dear little songs it is dedicating."

But of Sara's contributions to this issue, the "Sonnet to Joy" was by far the most superior, and the Editor recognized this:

The "Sonnet to Joy" is quite an achievement—it is in a way impersonal, and that was what Sara strove after. I call it a good, good thing, and I like every line of it—personally, I think it is as good as the Rossettis and Brownings and such, but that is rank heresy. I prefer so many Potter things to the great ones of the earth.

Through such artistic and creative effort as the examples from this *Wheel* show, and by the critical analyses, complimentary and otherwise, which the girls offered each other in all honesty, the *Wheel* flourished. Under Will's forceful editorship, thirty-six numbers were put together. When the group finally disbanded, each girl was given several of the *Wheels* to keep permanently. The three that were Sara's are now in the Yale University Library's Collection of American Literature; others are in the Missouri Historical Society's care; some were lost or destroyed over the years, and a few are still lovingly cherished by friends or relatives of the Potters.

Chapter 3

A TRIP ABROAD

•

EARLY in 1905, Sara was absent from the world of Potters for a time, as she and her mother made a tour of the Holy Lands, Egypt, and a part of Europe for three months. Mrs. Teasdale, who liked to travel herself, thought it would be a rich and stimulating experience for Sara to see some of the places about which she had read and studied, and this tour seemed particularly suitable for them. The Biblical Lands appealed to Mrs. Teasdale, and the itinerary included Greece, Italy, and England, whose artistic and literary associations especially interested Sara. They sailed on the S.S. *Arabic* on Thursday, February 2, with over six hundred passengers, many of whom were ministers.

Although she sent back a stream of post cards to her friends and family, Sara did not have time to write many letters on this trip; for she spent every possible spare minute reading her Baedeker, and she also kept a detailed diary of her travels.

From the very first, the sea's changing beauty, which she soon came to know intimately, and which she was to mention so often in her poetry, fascinated her; on February 7, she wrote in her diary:

The blue of the ocean is deeper than that of Lake Michigan, I think—more of a peacock blue and far more magnificent, for the waves are veritable mountains. You can have no idea of the sea until you are in the midst of it. I have never seen a marine picture that gave a real idea of it. It is more restless, passionate and powerful than any painting can be. The foam on the great waves that break upon the ship is like lace laid over sea-foam green satin, only how *much* more beautiful! The foam goes in myriads of little half ovals and covers the whole of the broken waves with its network. "The Iceland Fisherman" gives one a little idea of the sea, but not the most lovely side of its disposition.

The ship first landed at Madeira, and the sight of the city in the distance thrilled Sara, and she wrote of it:

Madeira looked lovely even before breakfast, and the nearer we came the more beautiful it was. It rises from the blue sea like a great mountain of emerald dotted over with pearly white houses. The clouds covered the highest tips of the island, and the faint haze made the ravines a deep violet. Such a beautiful sight I have seldom seen.

While in Spain, the tourists also visited Seville. Sara fell in love with this city and especially with the great cathedral there:

I can hardly speak of it. It is much the most satisfying building I ever saw. So glorious it is in the beauty of coloring, proportion, solemnity and grandeur that no idea can be gotten of it from words. The whole thing is made of light tan colored stone magnificently carved inside and out. There are 37 chapels! The organs are enormous. How I'd love to hear them played upon! The stained glass windows are up about a hundred and fifty or two hundred feet above your head. There are not a great many of them—at least it doesn't seem as though there are, although I believe the number is 97— but they are large and made of bright and not dingy colored glass, and therefore make a great deal of light. Of course the cathedral is not light like a church. It is about twilight. The glorious reds, greens, and blues of the windows—many of them are figures of saints—make the most exquisite effect in the grey wall. There are a number of Murillo's pictures in the cathedral. They are behind great gates which a sexton opens with keys. He had a great key ring so heavy with keys that I could hardly hold it. The bell tower is very old and was built by the Moors as the tower for their mosque, which stood where the cathedral stands now. Of course its architecture is very different from the Gothic architecture of the church. We climbed up the winding incline plane to the top. It was an awful climb, and going down was almost as hard as climbing up, but I'm not sorry I went because the view of Seville and the Cathedral was grand.

Of Murillo's paintings, Sara wrote:

... the picture which I liked best was one of Christ on the cross leaning down to comfort St. Anthony who stood beneath him and a little to his right. The grey brown part of the saint contrasted with the magnificently modeled and colored part of Christ was a thing never to be forgotten. You will hardly be able to see how a Crucifixion could be sensuously beautiful, but it was, for the figure of Jesus was not emaciated, and the expression of the face was divine—no less. The left arm was still nailed to the cross, so that the body had to curve in order that Christ's arm could be round the beautiful saint beneath him. The sweep of the curved body was lovely.

While in Seville the travelers also visited the Alcazar, a famous old Moorish palace, whose exquisitely carved and colored interior decorations impressed Sara as "a veritable Arabian Night's dream of loveliness." The grounds around the palace also enchanted Sara:

The gardens of the Alcazar are a dream. Such palms, trees, green hedges, mossy old fountains, strange grey turreted walls, and funny "surprise waterworks which are apt to sprinkle the unwary tourist" (as the guide-book says) are not found outside of fairyland. Well, the whole case is that Seville *is* fairy land.

After their sight-seeing in Spain, the passengers returned to the *Arabic* to continue their journey. Though many of them suffered from sea-sickness on the voyage, Sara and Mrs. Teasdale escaped this discomfort. But their stateroom was so continually cold—only forty-nine degrees the first morning on board—that Sara's throat soon began to trouble her. And it was not long before she had a temperature because of it. Unfortunately, she was quite ill just as the ship was about to land at Piraeus, the seaport for Athens, and she was deeply disappointed at the prospect of not being able to visit Greece. She confided to her diary:

Dr. Craster (isn't that a nice English name?) has been in once, and is coming again in a little while to paint my throat with some horrible bitter stuff. But the worst of it is that I shall probably have to miss Athens entirely—at any rate, I shall consider myself fortunate if I get even a glimpse of it. How can I bear it? To be so near—in the very harbor—only a few miles from the city, which is inland—and yet perhaps go to my grave without laying eyes upon it! The city where so many glorious things are—the place of all places on the cruise, except Rome, that I'd most love to see. God knows best. I should be glad of what I've had. As usual, my fever will not go down right away, and my throat is still bad. I am sorry to have Mother miss Athens. She will not leave me.—A few minutes ago I stood up for a second until I turned out the electricity to rest my eyes, and found a thread of bright light on the cabinet. You cannot see real things, sometimes, until the glare of unreal ones has been taken away. When I stood up, I saw all the glory of the full moon on the water.

The next day, Sara recorded:

Like Moses I have been in sight of the promised land, for I have spent about five hours on the deck drinking in the exquisite beauty of Athens from "afar off." What a terrible disappointment! But I suppose it is for my own good. . . . But how thankful I am to get even on deck, after being cooped up in my stateroom! And what a magnificent color scheme I saw before me! The deep blue sky against the mountains—many of them entirely covered with snow— and the city at their feet, with the Acropolis like the crown of it all, standing high, high above the city, her glorious Parthenon glistening yellow in the sunshine.

Perhaps the ancient gods of Greece intervened in Sara's behalf, for two days later the doctor told her that she could go ashore for three hours. And though she felt weak and shaky, for she still had a temperature, she and her mother ventured to Athens. There were many things that Sara was eager to see, but the Acropolis was the place above all others where she wanted to spend her precious time. And she wrote of her experience there:

It is a steep hill, almost a mountain that rises in the most beautiful way from the narrow plain between the mountain and the sea. The Greeks knew exactly how to do things. They put the Parthenon on the finest site for a temple that you can imagine. The top of the Acropolis is level and besides the P., there is a small beautiful Ionic temple to Wingless Victory that is in very good preservation, the Erechtheum of combined Doric and Ionic architecture, and the magnificent Propylaea or gateway to the temples behind it. The marble of all these buildings has been mellowed by time into an exquisite golden color. When we had driven as far as we could go up the A. we got out and looked down on the Theatre of Herod Atticus, an enormous place with marble seats around it in a semicircle. . . . I was crazy to go to the top of the A., so we had two Greeks make a basket of their hands and I was carried to the very top. How glorious it was! The view was superb, but it was more interesting to walk among the ruins and to think how many many feet had pressed the same stones before. . . . On getting back to the ship I went to bed, too excited and thrilled with beautiful memories to rest, but oh so thankful to have seen it, even if so hurriedly.

Though this exertion satisfied Sara's spirit, it did the condition of her throat no good, and since her stateroom stubbornly stayed at a sixty-degree temperature in the day and fifty or below at night, the doctor decided that she would recover more quickly in the ship's hospital. And there she spent the next several days. She was sorry to miss seeing the Church of St. Sophia in Constantinople, but she was moved to reflect, with her characteristic sense of humor, that

The principal decoration inside is mosaics against a gold ground. Many of them have been painted out with white-wash because they were Christian symbols. There is a head of Christ which is said to miraculously reappear thro' the white-wash every twenty-five years.

How many miracles of this kind go on all the time in our cellar, which is white-washed a good deal oftener than that!

By the time the ship reached Joppa in Palestine, Sara was well enough to go ashore and see some of the points of interest. Soon afterwards the tourists went on to Jerusalem; Sara's sensitive heart was touched by the beggars, the mud huts, the diseased natives, and the pitiful condition of the country as a whole, which was so much in evidence. She wrote: "Poverty all through Palestine is so prevalent that it makes you heart-sick all the time."

Their first night in Jerusalem was an experience that neither Sara nor her mother ever forgot; and Sara left a vivid record of their arrival there.

There is noise and confusion everywhere. When the wind blows, the dust is awful. The city is very dirty, so that you have the pleasure of knowing that you are being powdered by something quite different from the clean dust of Charlevoix County. Jerusalem is a modern Babel, there are forty languages spoken in the city. We were told to go to the Notre Dame, a very large convent that has accommodation for more people than any hotel in Jerusalem, I imagine. It was sunset when we came into the city. When we got to Notre Dame we found it perfectly enormous, made of stone inside and out, and as cheerless as a tomb. I was still weak from being in bed, and my throat not yet well, so that when I had been dragged up to the third story (the ceilings are *terribly* high) and assigned a cell-like room, my spirits were at their lowest ebb. Added to this, on our way up the stairs we had met one of our party, who was wrapped in a big shawl to keep warm, who told us even if our room *was* cold, not to have a brazier (they are open charcoal stoves) because two ladies from the *Arabic* had been asphyxiated by one the night before (I have since found out that they are alive). When we were convinced that staying in Notre Dame would be the last of us, too, we told our dragoman to take us to another place. The remembrance of our first night in Jerusalem will always be one of the most terrible in my memory, we were so tired and cold and *so* homesick for America. We finally found it necessary to stay all night at the fourth place, although our room was the very worst I have ever slept in. This is the coldest season in Jerusalem. The summers are so intensely hot that all the hotels are made with very high ceilings, stone hallways, and so forth.

In spite of the cold and the discomfort, though, the next morning Sara and her mother managed to see a number of interesting things, such as the Mosque of Omar where Mohammet was supposed to have ascended into Heaven, a distant view of the Mount of Olives and the Garden of Gethsemane, and Solomon's Stables. The other hours, too, were well filled with sight-seeing.

Our day in Jerusalem was dark, chilly, and rather windy. The hotel halls were like ice. . . . In the after-noon we started at half-past two in carriages for Bethlehem, returning about five o'clock. The roads are fairly good, but the drive was a dreary one. We saw the black dome on Mount Zion where David is said to be buried, the well where the Magi saw the reflection of the star after they had lost sight of it, the tomb of Rachel, the fields where Ruth gleaned, the pasture where the Angel appeared to the Shepherds, and a number of other traditional spots. Finally we came to Bethlehem. The place is the most absolutely abject and heartbreaking thing that I have ever seen. The streets are so narrow that we ran into walls twice. The dirt and squalor are awful. This is said to be the most promising town in Palestine! The words of Phillips Brooks' song: "O little town of Bethlehem, How still we see thee lie . . ." kept coming back into my mind while we were winding through these alleys. What a strange place for "The hopes and fears of all the years" to meet in! Christ never seemed so real nor so dear to me before. Surely he must have seen much of human suffering if Nazareth was as full of sorrow in his time as Bethlehem seems to be.

Sara bought a crucifix on a necklace made of olive stones for Williamina Parrish while she was in Palestine. After the visit to the Holy Lands, the passengers next landed at Alexandria and went on to Cairo, where they saw the pyramids and the Sphinx, which seemed to Sara very much like their pictures.

Returning from this trip, she and her mother rode on camels, and Sara said of hers:

Mine was a good tempered one—thank fortune. They hate to get down for you to get on and off. It takes quite a while for them to fold up their various sets of legs and all the while you are wondering whether you'll reach the ground safely.

The freezing weather in Jerusalem had not helped Sara's bad throat, and while in Egypt she consulted a doctor about it. He gave her some medicine and advised her to rest. But this was impossible, for the tour was constantly moving on. One day the travelers drove to Heliopolis, six miles from Cairo, and were disappointed not to find any ruins there. However, Sara did not feel that the trip had been in vain.

But the obelisk that stands there—erected 4,000 years ago in the time of Abraham—fully repays a visit. It is a shaft of red granite carved on its four sides with pictures of birds and other things which have been translated into words and show when and by whom it was erected. These hieroglyphics are identical on the four sides. They are exquisitely done and the stone has lasted so well that it is impossible to believe that when Jeremiah sat beneath it, it was already ancient. Plato sat beneath it too, and there Joseph met Asenath. I wonder what will be left of our monuments in the year of Our Lord 5905. Anything? Poor old Egyptians, with their loves and their hates and their mummy makings, and yet, I'd rather be my own humble self than that black, broken old piece of stuff that used to be the greatest ruler of his time, Rameses II. Since I've been in those countries I've almost felt as though God has forgotten about them, and so many, many have suffered and died and gone back to earth with so little knowledge of Him, and so much knowledge of pain and disease and sin.

One afternoon, the tourists were taken to see the Temple of Karnak, the largest and most impressive ruins in Egypt. Of this sight Sara wrote:

You can form absolutely no idea of them either from words or photographs. They are a series of temples, rather than one, and it took 2,800 years to build them. They were started 4,000 years ago! ... While the ruins are grand and magnificent, they are not at all beautiful according to my ideas of beauty.... Then, too, the color of the stone is that of dust, while the Athenian ruins are a lovely golden color. The Greeks wanted to build something as beautiful as they possibly could. The Egyptians wanted to prove what wonderful people they were. There are literally *hundreds* of representations of Rameses II in Luxor and Karnak.... You might read about it from now till doom's day and see pictures, too, but you'd never be able to imagine the effect produced by the carving, carving, carving on countless roofs, walls, and columns. One can understand how in 2,800 years the work was not finished. While these walls are the most interesting things I have seen in my life—yes, I can almost say they are, for by "things" I do not mean people—partly because of their antiquity, partly because nothing about them is meaningless—they are not beautiful. The heaviness and stiffness of Egyptian art would become intolerable if one had to see a great deal of it.

After Egypt, the next stop for the *Arabic* was Naples, and from there the travelers went on to Rome to spend three days, much to Sara's delight. Of the Sistine Chapel, one of the first places they visited, Sara wrote:

I was somewhat disappointed in Michelangelo's "Last Judgment" —it has been much damaged by time. The celebrated ceiling deserved an hour's time and I could give it but about a minute. It fairly hurt me to leave. It is a magnificent thing. It strikes me that Michelangelo's work is the very pinnacle of the masculine principle of art—if one can so express oneself—and Raphael's art is the highest expression of the feminine.

St. Peter's Church brought forth this comment from Sara:

I think that Gothic architecture is far better and more solemn than the Renaissance architecture. All the churches in Rome are in the latter style. I like the Seville Cathedral better than any church in Rome—even St. Peter's. Renaissance style is too ornate to be sincerely religious.

The only thing that marred their stay in Rome was the continual rain, and Sara concluded that "Rome must be a very damp place, for moss clings to every old wall and roof. Poor Keats! What a bad place to bring him to cure consumption!"

One afternoon a group of the tourists were taken for a ride along the Appian Way. They saw many notable landmarks, such as the ruins of the Palace of the Caesars, but one place that Sara would have loved to stop and see was not visited.

We passed the Protestant Cemetery where John Keats and the heart of Shelley (his body was burned) and John Addington Symonds are buried. I have always said to myself that if I ever went to Rome, I should go to visit their graves, and I felt very badly that I could not. I should so love to have put some flowers upon them. Theirs are the first graves that I have ever really cared to visit. It was getting late and cold and of course I could not stop because all the rest of the party would so much rather not. I doubt if one of them—except my mother whom I told of it—knew that Keats and Shelley were buried there. . . . The cemetery is very beautiful, for it is full of trees—many of them cypress—and the ground is carpeted with violets. I am so glad that Keats' body is lying in a place full of beauty, for he loved pure beauty more than any other English poet, I think.

When the tourists arrived in Paris, their next stop, the city was celebrating one of its many festive days, and an atmosphere of unrestrained gaiety prevailed. Sara was captivated by the magical spell of the French capital, and wrote:

I am in love with this city. It is what a city should be, for it is more fond of beauty than of money. . . . Confetti vendors were everywhere and the streets and the pavements were so paved with it that they looked as though the rainbow had been powdered up and fallen upon them.

In Paris, for the first time, Sara and her mother were free from the guided tours arranged for the group, and they reveled in being able to go about where and when they wished. One of the first places they visited was the Louvre, where Sara found many old and dearly loved friends in the form of original paintings, whose reproductions she had admired for a long time. Speaking of the Salon Carré, she wrote:

In it are a number of things that I have loved all my life. . . .
From that one room one could learn enough about Italian art to be unashamed all his life. It seemed to me that Raphael excelled in sentiment, Leonardo in intellectual depth, Tintoretto in vigor and impassioned drawing, Correggio in beauty of faces and beauty of *everything*—composition and coloring, Murillo . . . in exquisite coloring, and Rubens in the glorious amber light which he sheds upon everything.

Sara had always been deeply responsive to color, and stained glass windows invariably drew her attention. One of the places in Paris that made a lasting impression upon her was described as

. . . the most exquisitely beautiful church I ever saw. I have never felt the beauty of color so forcibly as when I stood within it. . . . It is a tiny little chapel built by St. Louis and is in the court of the Palais de Justice. It is called Ste Chapelle, and is a purely Gothic structure, so richly carved and delicately conceived that I have never seen anything to compare with it. The beauty of the interior is in its perfect proportions and stained glass windows. It is all stained glass—that is, the narrow buttresses are all that separate the windows from each other. All the windows are alike in that the glass is all— or almost all—in primary colors (there is however, a little green, purple and a very little pink used)—and the windows are divided into various sections so that about thirty different pictures are seen on one window. The figures in the different scenes are no more than a foot high. The beauty of the windows is not in the designs, but the glorious color. They look as tho' they were made of rubies, emeralds, sapphires, and amethysts. You forget everything in looking at them with the sun behind them.

At the Luxembourg Sara was especially delighted with the pictures by Henner, but it was to the Louvre that she returned with overwhelming joy a few days after her first visit there. This time she saw one of the things she had come all the way from St. Louis to look upon, and it did not disappoint her.

We went down-stairs next, and when we got to the door, I looked to the end of the long, long corridor and way at the end of it, against a dark red curtain, beautifully lighted, stood the most beautiful thing in the world—the Venus de Milo. Oh, I could hardly contain myself, her beauty made me so happy. She is so far, far more lovely than any reproduction that I ever saw. The nearer I came to her, the more I loved her. Yes, I really love her—almost as one loves a real person. I can understand how Pygmalion loved Galatea. I cannot express the pleasure one has in being near this glorious woman. You are glad, as was Théophile Gautier, that her arms are gone, because they might hide her body. I have never seen so noble and pure and unconscious a woman as this Venus. The marble is so magnificently carved that it looks like flesh. I have left the loveliest thing until the last. It is her mouth. In no reproduction is it at all like the original. It is so very near a smile, and yet so full of repose. I don't believe that the exact reproduction will ever be caught by anyone. The lips are the most beautiful shape—you can tell from them that she is the goddess of love, but it is a spiritual love.

On a third visit to the Louvre, on another day, Sara saw a group of landscapes painted in the nineteenth century; two artists enchanted her, and she wrote:

Some of the Corots are too lovely, as well as some of the Duprés. I like these artists the best of them all. Corot is like Shelley, and Dupré is like Keats. The latter has more glorious wealth of color and the other a silvery fairy-like poetic quality that reminds me of "Alastor.". . . It seems to me that the landscapes of Corot and his friends will never be superceded. I thought the same thing the other night when I heard "The Valkyrie." It seemed to me that Wagner had reached the pinnacle of operatic composition.

Wagner's opera was an exciting experience for the young traveler; but an even more thrilling evening was in store for her when she heard "Tristan und Isolde" for the first time. Before she attended this opera, she wrote:

I have been reading a libretto of "Tristan and Iseult." Of course it was in French and I couldn't understand it very well, but I could get the idea pretty clearly. It is magnificent—Wagner was a great poet as well as a great musician.

Though the part of the diary that described this memorable evening is lost, Sara often told her friends how deeply this music moved her.

Eleonora Duse was performing in Paris at this time, and Sara hoped to see her in "La Dame aux Camélias," but she was not able to do so.

The days in France flew by all too swiftly, and in late April Sara and Mrs. Teasdale went to England. Sara left this first impression of the country that was to become so beloved by her:

I never saw such perfectly charming houses and such care and neatness and beauty everywhere. The season here is almost a month later than in France. Of course the country will be much lovelier in a month or even a few weeks. But the hedges were green and so were the meadows. Little lambs were everywhere. I saw more sheep than in my whole life put together. The furze is in blossom and so are the primroses. It is easy to believe that I am in England, for things are just as they are in books.

Not even the dingy face of London that was first presented to her could quell her soaring spirits.

At about six P.M. we pulled into the great Charing Cross station. What a hub-bub was there! How dark and dreary London is after

Sara Teasdale's home
38 Kingsbury Place, St. Louis

Mr. and Mrs. John Warren Teasdale,
Sara Teasdale's parents,
with Mrs. Alice Teasdale in the background

Paris! All the houses in Paris are of light colored stone but here everything is grimy. However, it is the greatest city in the world, and lots of people I love have lived here, so I am content.

One of the first things that Sara did after reaching London was to look in the telephone directory for Swinburne's name and address.

Imagine my joy when I finally saw his name in the alphabetical list of northern suburbs as living in Putney, and found his name next to his friend's Theodore Watts-Dunton's as living together at No. 11.

Soon after they were settled in their hotel, the Teasdales went on a shopping trip. Sara had not bought any clothes in Paris, as the exaggerated French fashions did not appeal to her, but at Liberty's in London she found a dress that was a treasure, the first of many of a similar style that she wore with grace.

It is an artistic dress—one of the few I have ever seen. I don't think that a dress can be artistic if its lines are not beautiful. And if it has a great deal of trimming it is so cut up as to be ugly, no matter how "handsome" it may be, or how beautiful its color scheme is. It is entirely one color—there is nothing to cut it up into a checker-board. There is no trimming at all except the loveliest smocking I ever saw. It is dark blue Tyrian silk—a sort of greyish blue.

While in London, the travelers saw many, many things of interest, but none made Sara happier than a trip to a certain doorway that she had longed to gaze upon for many years. Writing of her visit to Elizabeth Barrett Browning's old home, she said:

I have done nothing since I left home which gave me so much pleasure except perhaps hearing "Tristan and Isolde" or "Hamlet." We took a Bayswater 'bus and told the conductor to let us off as near as he could to Wimpole Street. They are wonderfully careful and kind about directing you in London. We had to go thro' a sort of arch, then thro' a funny little street about three hundred feet long. When we had done that, we found ourselves in the most quiet, reserved, aristocratic old street that can be imagined. Every door plate shone like gold and everything looked as tho' only the most dignified of middle-aged people had set foot there. I felt very unworthy to be there, not on account of dignity, however. I could believe that the stones upon which I stood had been there when Browning hurried over them. We walked for several squares before we came to No. 50. It was much as I had expected to find it. I had a feeling that it would face the north and have its front door on the left—all of which was true. . . . We then walked up Marylebone Road. Close by is Marylebone Church where they were married on September 12, 1846. They were having evensong at the church so we went in. . . . I should have walked up to the altar-rail, if so many of the people had not remained after the service.

Another famous home that Sara glimpsed briefly was Swinburne's, on Putney Hill. Putney Hill, Sara found, was not a hill:

It proved to be a street leading up to a gentle incline from the bridge—a rather pretty place for a home, but not what one would imagine a poet would want, for Putney is not poetic at all except that it is on the Thames. Like every place near London, it seems too full of people. Swinburne's house is a three-story brick, detached on the right, but on the left attached to the house next it. There is a fence in front and a small front yard with bushes on it. The whole place has a very citified appearance. How I longed for the front door to open and S. to come out!

Sara was constantly charmed by the picturesque English countryside, and of its waters she wrote:

English rivers are so different from American ones that they resemble canals more than they do our rivers. . . . They are all quiet, slow-flowing, comfortable looking streams, uniformly lovely because of their lovely green shores. They all flow on top of the ground. . . . English rivers are too well bred to overflow their banks.

In the British Museum Sara was especially interested in the Elgin marbles that Lord Elgin had taken from the Parthenon. She and her mother spent a pleasant and enlightening day at Oxford University; but their time was so crowded that the one thing Sara regretted not seeing there was Pembroke College, which was founded in 1624 by Thomas Teasdale, and where Samuel Johnson had once been a student. In the Bodleian Library Sara saw a ring with some of Keats's hair in it, some locks of Shelley's hair, and some Shelley manuscripts.

One day Sara and Mrs. Teasdale went to Keble College to see the painting, "The Light of the World." One wonders if Sara knew at that time that Christina Rossetti was among those who posed for Holman Hunt for the head of Christ in it. She did not mention this in her diary, but wrote:

I had always expected to find it a life-sized figure, but it is only about four feet high. It is a very beautiful thing—wonderfully impressive and painted with true Pre-Raphaelite care. On the whole, it is the most perfect representation of Christ that I have ever seen.

Shakespeare's home, of course, had to be visited, and on the way to Stratford-on-Avon, another wish of Sara's was granted.

I told our driver to be sure to show me a lark if we saw one. How happy I was when we saw it—and heard it too. I never appreciated Shelley's "Skylark" as I did then. The bird was soaring, soaring until he was a mere speck against the blue sky—and twittering in the loveliest way all the time. The notes were like silver raindrops falling from heaven. A little farther on we heard a nightingale! I was so happy that I could hardly sit still and listen. Of course the notes are longer and more beautiful at night, but it is a mistake to think that nightingales never sing in daylight. Such a lovely tender sad song I have never heard a bird sing before. . . . A nightingale has twelve distinct notes. Some are exquisitely beautiful. He kept on singing until we were out of hearing—the notes were golden and full of music—real music. We could not see him for which I was sorry.

Sara was duly impressed with Shakespeare's home, but she had to confess to her diary:

Stratford was much as I expected to find it—quaint and quiet—a fit place for hero-worshipping. I am quite sure that I appreciate Shakespeare as much as most people, but I cannot help admitting that the sight of 50 Wimpole Street, London, moved me more than all the various shrines of Stratford put together.

But even at Stratford, Sara found something to remind her of Wimpole Street, for in the house where Shakespeare was born, she noticed that the walls were covered with the names of long-ago visitors. A guide pointed out the signatures of Carlyle and Scott, which were a little hard to find.

But on one of the oaken rafters "R. Browning" was easily made out. It was written rather laboriously as one would naturally write when the thing was above one's head. After it was the date "1837." He must have been 25.

One of the last things the travelers saw before sailing for home was the Walker Gallery in Liverpool. Here Sara was most interested in Rossetti's painting, "Dante's Dream," although she felt that it had been reproduced too much. Another picture also captured her interest.

Next to Rossetti was a picture by Millais painted when he was a Pre-Raphaelite of the Pre-Raphaelites. He was only twenty when he did it. It is far more olden and Botticelli-ish than any other Pre-R. thing I ever saw. To my mind it is a great picture. One cannot help thinking that in doing such stuff as "The Northwest Passage" he had allowed public taste and not art to guide him.

On May 10, 1905, the travelers started on their homeward voyage across the Atlantic, and Sara concluded her record:

Here endeth the diary—carried on for so long and laid aside with something akin to joy. What is more lovely than to be going home?
S.T.T.

Chapter 4

THE POTTERS' *LOG*

•

WHILE Sara was abroad, the Potters had continued with their magazine and their good times, and on her return, she joined the group again. From time to time different friends of the members drifted in and out of their meetings. Bessie Brey, a tall slender girl with finely chiselled features and golden hair, one of Sara's good friends, came occasionally. Guida Richey, a neighbor and intimate friend of the Parrishes as well as a close friend of Celia's, was invited now and then; Guida, who was talented as a photographer, was a gifted mimic, full of wit and inspired clowning. For her Wonderland name, she was christened the Walrus.

Another friend who was included in many of their early activities was Inez Dutro, and she was given the name of the White Queen. Inez was engaged at this time to Francis Crary George, and she soon moved out of the horizons of the Potters, for she became Mrs. George on March 17, 1906, and went to live in Kansas City, Missouri.

As the first happy and successful year of the existence of the Potters was nearing its close, Will decided that it would be a good idea to have a Scribe who would keep a *Log* for the group. She appointed Vine for this task and presented her with a large book full of blank pages. In this, as in almost everything else, the Editor showed her usual fine judgment, since a happier selection as Scribe of the Potters could not possibly have been made. For Vine possessed a distinctively fine and easily readable handwriting; she was immensely observant, letting little escape her attention;

she had a style of her own that was detailed, discriminating, and humorous. She knew all the little personal characteristics of each Potter that endeared her to the others, and she was a very conscientious young person who reported fully on what had happened at their meetings and usually did so promptly. Her records are still a joy to read for those who want a more vivid picture of the Potters. And the little pencil sketches made by Caroline Risque in the *Log* are a delight to see.

But unless one were familiar with the private code of the Potters, much of what Vine wrote would be a mystery. For throughout the *Log,* the various Potters are sometimes called by their Wonderland names. Caroline, who was very small and dearly loved by all of them, was given several nicknames; she was referred to occasionally as the March Hare or the Deserted Village; but most often she was called simply Barbara, since she was the "Babbie" from Barrie's *The Little Minister* of the successful Parrish photographs. Bohemia was the Potters' name for Caroline's studio workroom at her home, where she modeled her clay figures and did her other art work. Arden was the imaginative home that the Potters sometime hoped to have for their own. Will had drawn up a blueprint for Arden, including in it a music room, workroom, library, dining room, kitchen, conservatory, modeling room, porch, and a long hall with an organ at one end and a fountain in the center. For the Potters were very, very fond of fountains.

Vine inscribed the first entry in the *Log* on October 13, 1905; a section of it follows, which establishes the tone and mood—half-serious, half-hilarious—that characterized many Potter meetings:

William suggested that I write a chronicle of events for the Potters. I think I should like to do this for myself; and perhaps, after years and years, others of the Potters may like to turn back to the records to find their old faces and voices. Well, this day we met at Bohemia, since Mrs. Harris was too ill to have us come. Celia is undergoing Osteopathy and was not allowed to join us. Our housewifely Inez, who ought certainly to wear a big bunch of keys at her girdle, baked for the young Harris a birthday cake when the event occurred. This proceeding is quite like the White Queen, only I suppose she should have sent the cake before the birthday instead of afterwards to be quite consistent.

Almost all of us were in a rather croaky state this day of the days.[1] William had a cold—also a high horse—Sara had laryngitis, Barbara was trying to determine whether she had caught tonsilitis from Sara or from Ethel, and the Scribe was laid low by a combination of cough and cold. Grace failed to come. . . .

. . . When the Scribe arrived, encased in two jackets, Inez was already there, sitting on the floor by the bed, and William was in a rocker at work on a contrib, a book-cover for "Masters of Art." It was destined to be finished in the blue leather which hung over Barbara's screen. The Editor was wroth—at her work and at the October *Wheel* and at two of the unhappy contributors, one of whom was skulking behind her chair and daring to show one eye, which, however, was extraordinar' wickit-lookin'. Meekness, in the opinion of the Scribe, is at best but a cultivated virtue on the part of the March Hare. She has been observed to agree in a servile manner to the law of the Editor, and then to make ribald remarks and screwed up faces behind the editorial back.

It is a pity that William can't be a warrior queen; she gets ripping so magnificently. First her cheeks fire up, then she snorts, her nostrils quiver and her eye flashes forked lightning. And her vocabulary is of a richness and thumpingness and fearlessness not to be matched.

The Scribe was introduced to Plarnish and to Barbara's other turtle and to the gold-fishes—also the stones, souvenirs of the travellings of Barbara and Company. As the Scribe expressed a desire to feed the turtles, Barbara and the Editor obligingly went on a fly-hunt, Barbara armed with her Bread-and-Butterfly Net, the Editor with a glass. Then was there racing and chasing on Canaby Lea! From chair to chair the nimble Editor heaved his bulk, but the fly was still more nimble. At length the disappointed and breathless gentleman gave over the chase, loudly declaring that Barbara had wilfully scared the game with her net, so that the animals refused to sit.

[1]The day the contributions for the *Wheel* were due.

By this time Ned, the chraoibhiu eno (cluster of nuts—brown-haired girl) and Sara in her admired blue dress, had arrived. Will exhibited a set of pictures of Petronelle, which quite fascinated Sara, Inez, and me. Barbara offered to decoy Petronelle to pose so that we might see her.

We talked much of Petronelle and of Sue Williams and step-mothers and things. This was afterwards when all hands went below deck to have chocolate. The Editor rapped the table with a spoon (which it had been cast at her as a missile, by the way) and said, "The difference between Petronelle and Sue Williams is that I could *use* Petronelle as my wife. I could say, 'Petronelle, get my breakfast.' " (Barbara, out of order, told the Editor to go to, for Petronelle would say, "Get your own breakfast!") "But if I married Sue, it would be *I* who would get *her* breakfast!" Can't you see William, in sweet humility, bringing on the muffins and saying, "Yes, ma'am, anything more, ma'am?" Well, you are not to suppose that William was permitted to expound her views in peace. The March Hare's whiskers were twitching to break in; Ned was talking, using her hand as a megaphone; and Sara and the Scribe broke in, burbled and brabbled "continual." The little feasts of the Potters are always as jolly as possible, and generally argumentative. Beer and skittles, in this case represented by three helpings of chocolate in the Japanese cups, and chocolate cakes, seem to have an exhilarating effect upon us.

What did we fight about? Oh yes—one thing was Women Who Paint, not landscapes but themselves. The Editor explained that to test the genuineness of a complexion you press your finger deep into the cheek. If a white mark appears and then becomes the same color again, the complexion is real. This is extremely ingenious, but it is something like belling the cat, for who would dare to try it? Ned, of course, took the negative side from sheer love of combat, saying that there was no reason why one should object to painted women.

* * *

"They all trooped out" after they could contain no more of the viands, and all trooped upstairs. Will's Celia Calendar was lovingly displayed by Barbara to those of the Potter tribe who had not yet seen it. Ned thereupon urged Will to make covers for magazines, a request to which the March Hare added her Amen in a voice like that of a gnat in the railway journey of Alice.

Among Barbara's quarries, Sara discovered a blue stone which matched her dress. The owner immediately proffered the stone as a gift, and proposed that Sara wear it around her neck. . . .

It was discussed in common council where to hang the Mona Lisa.

* * *

At about a quarter to six, Ned and the Scribe began to gravitate towards their wraps. Barbara protested that the clock was wrong. The Scribe, however, knows her duty to her home beefsteak, and resolutely donned her hat and two jackets and gathered together her books and pencils and lunch-boxes.

A conference concerning *Il Pagliacci* was held between the stair-rails by the departing ones and the March Hare.

And so endeth the first chronicle.

Sometimes the girls met at the home of Mrs. Harris, and at other times they met at the homes of the various members. One particularly enjoyable meeting was held at Sara's house on January 2, 1906:

The Scribe is sitting in the attic while a rain of the best quality is rushing against the window-pane. The sky has been in a very bad temper most of the day. But what care the merry, merry Potters? What ho, my cup-bearer, "pour out more generously the four-year-old Falernian wine from the Sabian jar! The gods make everything hard for the dry!!" — Well, we could scarcely be called dry when we got to Sara's today. Grace was the only one with an umbrella, and that was her Mother's sole treasure, to the stones of Vichy be it said. As for me I might have been the Nickleman of the Sunken Bell just rising out of the well—"a demned, damp, moist, unpleasant body."

The company was: Sara, Will, Barbara, Petronelle, Grace, Bessie Brey, and me. We were in Sara's room, all over the floor of it for the maist part. My pen runs to the unwieldy Scots tongue, for Sara would not descend to plain Anglo-Saxon at all. She out-Barried Barrie and out-Ian Maclarened Ian Maclaren. The Editor is as usual petting a single phrase to death. It was till very recently "Far be it from me." Now the venerable gent has gone daft, absolutely daft over a mongrel, half Scotch collie and half German dachshund, to wit, "muckle schön." This handy phrase he blushes not to apply impartially to Monna Vanna and to gold-fishes.

Speaking of gold-fish—the gold-fish we have always with us. Six or eight, appertaining to Barbara, Petronelle, and Will were having a good time in Sara's wash-bowl. Those of Barbara were carried home in a vase which Sara fell in love with at the age of four. Those for the Mother Parrish were put into a tin pail and wrapped around with paper nabkins.

Sara had a Lit'r'ry Digest with a picture of William Sharp. Spread out on the couch were a number of lovely books, those Sara had just bought. We sat up on our haunches and looked at Sara's Egyptian pictures.

Sara and Bessie opened a trap-door and disappeared below, to come up again with plates of ice-cream and angel food. Unhappily, the spoons did not come simultaneously, and we sat chilling our fingers and watching the ice melt. The tantalization of Tantalus was nothing in comparison.

After the ladies had retired, we sat and drank wine. It was an orjy. Will says it ought to be called orjy for that sounds so much more hilarious. (This joke was made under the influence of the fiery fluid.) Someone remarked, "They call the Potters intellectual young ladies! Oh if they could see us now!" Barbara and Will were overcome first and sank ingloriously below the table. I say *below* the table, for if there had been a table they would have sunk below it. Barbara got very wild indeed and talked of "Wine-bibbers, vine-bibbers—I know what I'm trying to say! I mean—."

We drank toasts, beginning with Will's "To the *Wheel*." Barbara followed with "To the Editor." Then Sara proposed, "To Celia." Bessie followed with "To the Potters." By this time Grace began to pray that the wine would run out before her turn came. I gave, "Goldfish"; Grace, "To all of us," and Petronelle, "To Sue Williams."

Hurrah! Three cheers, my bully boys.

Then we tried with might and main and matches (to be alliterative) to make wine burn on an inverted saucer. It would not, but a light we would have; so Sara got alcohol, and a lovely white-blue flame shot up and we were tickled to death and did it some more. We named the flames. One was Fiona Macleod, one was Eleonora Duse, and one was Maude Adams.

Because they were so deeply interested in art, music, drama, and literature, the Potters, though all different in personality, shared many of the same burning enthusiasms. Eleonora Duse, Julia Marlowe, Olga Nethersole, and Maude Adams were favorites who came in for a great deal of discussion and comment. The pale, romantic rays of the Celtic Renaissance cast a lovely light over the Potters, and they were passionate devotees of the young Yeats and Fiona Macleod.

Joseph F. Sheehan, an Irish tenor of the Castle Square Opera Company, which played several long seasons in St. Louis, also appealed to them strongly, particularly to Will and Grace, who had met him personally and photographed him. In the *Log* he was referred to as J.F.S.

In St. Louis, too, there were a number of people for whom they felt a special affection. One was Jennie Marie Antoinette Jones, a teacher of English at Central High School. Tall, pale, grey-eyed, and aloof and dream-haunted in manner, she was said to have aspired at one time to be an actress, and she was extremely impressive in her reading of poetry and Shakespearean drama to her classes. Her voice had a melody and peculiar timbre that fascinated her listeners as she interpreted Greek tragedy for them. Usually, she seemed to the Potters like a tragic heroine or a legendary lady who had stepped out of Celtic poetry. She took a particular interest in the Potters and their activities, and in the *Log* she was referred to as J.M.A.J.

Two other teachers of Central High School, Miss Isabel Wilcox (later Mrs. Janni) and Miss Jennie Chase, were also especially respected and loved by the girls, and were mentioned occasionally by the Scribe.

Still another person to whom the Potters gave their unreserved devotion was Susan Creighton Williams, the sister of Jesse Lynch Williams, who won the first Pulitzer Prize for drama in 1917 with *Why Marry?*, a dramatization of his novel, *And So They Were Married*. Susan Williams had been educated at Mary Institute in St. Louis, and the essay that she read when she graduated on "The Poets of Canada" so impressed the audience that it was remembered and spoken of for a long time afterwards in the city. A strikingly lovely person, with a gift for drama, she had once met Yeats, and she recited his poetry and that of other Celtic poets with taste and feeling. She was born of a prominent family, her father being a retired Presbyterian minister, who read Greek and Hebrew and owned and edited a religious weekly, *The Mid-Continent*, in St. Louis. Intensely interested in the cultural life of the city, Susan Creighton Williams was the youngest member ever to be admitted to the Wednesday Club, which was considered a signal honor among the intellectual women of St. Louis. She had taken the part of Margret in Celia Harris's "Prose Play in Rhythm," a Celtic play published in the first issue of the *Wheel* and later presented by the Potters. An excerpt from the *Log*, describing a meeting held at Sara's house, will illustrate the pleasure that Susan Williams brought the Potters and the high regard they had for her.

November 10, 1905

The Editor, who was buttling for Sara, opened the door for Ned and the Scribe. The Editor was black and blue and looked good enough to eat. This is the first time that I remember seeing the Editor in a blue gown. She reminded one of those rather hackneyed lines, "Du bist wie eine Blume, so schön und hold und rein."—(You are like a flower, so fair and sweet and pure). That is one of the first things that impress you in the Editor, her amazing, almost uncanny air of spotlessness. And this appeals especially to such grubby chimney-sweeps, such inky Caddy Jellybys as we are, Ned and I.

Every one was there with the exception of Celia—which was how great a pity! for Sue Williams came. Before she came, however, we fought a pitched battle about the size of the *Wheel*. The trouble was our Gracie. She knew it would be dog's-eared and skinny and flippy-floppy like the *Ladies' Home Journal*. It was a pretentious-looking thing; it would not sit down comfortably on your lap. The designs would be sprawly and every fault would glare. It is lucky that Grace can't be a member of Parliament, for she is so conservative that they would never succeed in repealing that law about marrying the deceased wife's sister, when *she* was opposing such an innovation. . . . The November *Wheel* in all its offensive bigness was there, all but the cover. This was due to the fact that William would not accept the Knight cover which Barbara made. Grace reported that the Editor came home one night last week, swelling like a turkey-cock. Grace merely waited, feeling sure that Vesuvius would erupt pretty soon. And sure enough the Editor gave vent to this enigmatical expression, "That STINKIN' little friend of mine!"

* * *

Besides Sue Williams, Sara's friend Bessie Brey was with us. Barbara showed us just how Sue sat to pose for the clay statue. Of course we begged the lady to recite for us. Do you remember how she stood swaying with the long portieres, and seeing visions away off? It is lovely to feel yourself yielding to witch-craft and enchantment, as you do when she whispers, "My souls are nine," or "Dalua," or the fragments from Moira O'Neill. We each had our favorites and made her do them all. Grace and I claim the same one, the one by Moira O'Neill but Grace wavers between that and "The Little Black Rose." I'm no saying, mon, but what "The Little Black Rose" is a bonny thing, but then they all are. And in fact she could take "Innery ory, ickory an" and with that wonderful voice make a romance or a tragedy out of it.

It is always hard to get down to an every-day mood after Sue's voice trails off into silence at the end of something exquisitely pathetic. Nobody wants to speak. Today she entered the prosy regions herself by an easier transition. She spoke of Fiona and Mr. Yeats and of a friend of Mr. Yeats who met Dalua in the woods. . . .

Sue has given us something for Arden—a white gravelled path, bordered by red and white carnations and extending so far that it vanishes in a point at the horizon. . . .

Recalling that enchanted time when she had entertained Yeats in her own home, Susan Creighton Williams wrote many years later:

He lectured to the Wednesday Club in St. Louis, and after the lecture our small Poetics Section entertained him in a small room. We listened to that twilight voice, we were attentive to his strange chanting way of delivering his poems, and we watched the long straight lock of black hair that fell constantly down over a high white forehead. . . . In appearance, voice and manner, he was what a poet, *this* poet, should be. He talked easily, read any poem asked for, and made us feel that he was not at all bored.

That evening William Schuyler, a musician who was a friend of mine, brought Mr. Yeats to my house. He was delightful. He talked readily about the Abbey Theatre, and described settings and costumes of his own play, *The Shadowy Waters.* "All blue-green and green-blue with ornaments and weapons in copper." I was tongue-tied, but all alive to what was happening. Yeats was here in the room sitting by the fire! Will Schuyler and I had been experimenting with reading to music, and now he went to the piano and urged, over-urged me to try something. It was miserable. I knew that Yeats had given much time to reading poetry to the psaltery—and here I was fumbling with word and voice. "She was plumb scared," Will told him, as they went away, and Yeats answered ruefully, "They always are." But it wasn't that I was scared; it was that I was wasting moments that might have given me more tones of that voice.

On February 23, 1906, the idea of dedicating the various issues of the *Wheel* was discussed at another meeting at Sara's home and duly recorded by the Scribe:

There was some misunderstanding as to whether we were to have a dressed-up tea-party at Sara's or not. Sara was of the opinion that we were. William was supposed to have notified everyone, but somehow nobody was very certain, so that some were in rags and some in velvet gowns. The idea was that we wanted for once to see each other in our festa clothes wi' crunklin' underclaethes. But then, Cinderella did not really need glass slippers and shining dresses to set off her natural superiority, ye ken.

*   *   *

The Editor brought the February mag under his wing. The cover was done by himself in a state of distrust that his friend would produce one. However, he left the space for the name of the month blank; very fortunately, as it turned out, for Barbara actually disappointed all the prophets by turning up with a fine Knight cover, one of the very best we have had. Then she retired upstairs for a space and on returning cast a further sop to Cerberus in the form of a child-verse. And now who so bland and genial as the Editor, in Nottinghamshire? Just butter the Editor's parsnips for him and you will find him a very pleasant-spoken fellow, oh very tractable indeed, ma'am.

We have a new idea about the mag. Each number is to be dedicated to a dedikee to be chosen, turn and turn about, by the Potters. We decided that the first dedikee should be our mother, Mrs. Harris. After that, selection ran wild among the constellations. Sara's vocabulary was reduced to the magic syllables "Duse"; Will glibly recited a list of musical celebrities; someone said Maude Adams. Will thought that the one containing Andrew Lang's ballad might be dedicated to Miss Wilcox.

Grace was very enthusiastic over the idea until someone suggested that the dedicator be compelled to write a dedication to the dedikee.

Among those to whom future issues of the *Wheel* were dedicated after this decision was Susan Creighton Williams. For her issue of February, 1907, Will printed Susan's name in white ink on the dedication page, which was grey, and made a suitable little design. Among the contributions were a photograph of Susan as the Celtic maid, Margret, taken in her grey costume with long white sleeves, and enlarged by Grace for this number, a little lyric by Sara, which was originally written in a book of Celtic verse that she gave to Will, and a Celtic border design and illustration of two quotations from Fiona Macleod by Will. Susan was delighted with the honor bestowed upon her, and she wrote a note to tell the girls so, addressing it to Will, whom she always called Jean, after Will took the part of Jean in Celia's play.

3945 Delmar Avenue

Dear Jean and Others:

I've been hoping to see you tomorrow, but in case I do not, let me tell you—no, but how can I tell you how much pleasure you have given me and how I love being associated—in white letters on gray paper—with what I think the best thing in all St. Louis. I try not to be too proud, but every one who comes to the house looks at it, and then at me, with new respect. I don't know how I have been fortunate enough to win your friendship—and really I don't deserve it at all—but it's a very sweet thing to me, and has put a new color into the town for my thought.[2]

Warmly yours,
Susan Creighton Williams

Monday

Oh and incidentally:—The little sister's enlargement of the Margret pictures pleases my family so much that they've set their hearts on having some. Would it be possible—professionally?

Another friend of the Potters and perhaps the one that exerted the greatest outside influence on them was Lillie Rose Ernst, a botany teacher at Central High School, who was destined to become one of the city's most eminent citizens. A person of the highest intellectual and moral integrity, Miss Ernst had been born in 1870 and at this time was in her thirties. She possessed a strong and individual personality, and was business-like in appearance; she wore glasses, and her golden hair was pulled straight back. Often she was seen carrying an ivory-headed umbrella, and she was partial to starched shirtwaists. An outstanding educator and civic leader, later selected as one of St. Louis's ten leading women, she devoted her entire life to her native city, which was richly rewarded by her services. After her education at Central

_____

[2]Susan Williams was in mourning for her father at this time.

Lillie Rose Ernst

Susan Creighton Williams
as Margret
in "Prose Play in Rhythm"
by Celia Harris

ncy Coonsman in "Ye Comet's Tail"
1908

Photographs by
Williamina and Grace Parrish

High School, she had graduated from Washington University and later was the recipient of an honorary Master's Degree and Phi Beta Kappa membership from the University. She started her teaching career at Central High School, was principal of the Cote Brilliante, Mark Twain, and Blewett High Schools, and also served as Assistant Superintendent of Instruction for St. Louis.

Her far-reaching influence that was first felt in the classrooms of Central High School, where she made a multitude of intimate and life-long friends of numerous young people, guiding and encouraging them to better their lives, was later extended widely throughout the city in a variety of activities. She was associated with the Board of the St. Louis Children's Hospital, the Urban League of St. Louis, the Wednesday Club, the League of Women Voters, the St. Louis Bird Club, and various other educational and civic organizations. Even the Alpine Club of Canada claimed her as a member, for she was an ardent mountain climber.

The Potters who had been students at Central High School had first come under Miss Ernst's spell there, and it was not long before the other members of their group also came to know her well. She was intensely interested in their organization and encouraged them to put forth their very best effort in the *Wheel*. Among her admirers, it would be hard to say who was the most ardent. Ned felt particularly close to her because they shared a scientific interest in and deep love for all growing things; Caroline also loved her especially and was frequently to be found presenting some of her work, modeled in clay, to her idol. Vine and Will, also, found her an endlessly fascinating and stimulating conversationalist and a wonderful friend. Even Sara, who was a little shyer than the others about expressing her affection in exuberant terms, wrote a sonnet to Miss Ernst that appeared first in a *Wheel* and later in her book, *Sonnets to Duse and Other Poems:*

To L.R.E.

When first I saw you—felt you take my hand,
I could not speak for happiness to find

How more than all they said your heart was kind,
How strong you were, and quick to understand—
I dared not say: "I who am least of those
Who call you friend,—I love you, and I crave
A little love that I may be more brave
Because one watches me who cares and knows."
So, silent, long ago I used to look
High up along the shelves at one great book,
And longed to see its contents, childishwise,
And now I know it for my Poet's own,—
So sometime shall I know you and be known,
And looking upward, I shall find your eyes.

From the very first, Lillie Rose Ernst was a welcome guest at
all their meetings. Though she was frequently referred to as
L.R.E. in the *Log,* the Potters also christened her The White
Rabbit as her name from Wonderland, and at various times she
was also called The Desired Article and The Causa Honoris.

In only the second number of the *Wheel* of December, 1904,
one of the most attractive of all the magazines, which was built
around the theme of friendship, there is a page with this poem
printed on it:

To The Potters

Aye, try that Potter's wheel!
What tho' its halting whirl
Does turn the clay to but a doubtful shape!
The hand must *grow* to skill—
The heart must spiral up to the ideal.
A steadfast purpose must make true
The motion of the wheel
Before the cup can fill itself with meaning.
But every thought, sincere in that it aims
At truth, howe'er remote or vague,
And every sympathetic touch
That seeks to make that truth a little plain
Will leave its impress on the clay. And so
Again I say, "Try—try that Potter's wheel."

On the back of this page is a note that reads:

The verse on the opposite page is inscribed on the back of a report on "Educational Organization in the British Isles" with this note, "Verse Libre—written while waiting for the band concert. With apologies to the magazine writers." Although the author has sought to conceal her identity behind the respectable covering of "Educational Organization in the British Isles," we think we can detect the hand of our good friend and good teaser, Miss Ernst.

Occasionally, when she could spare the time, Miss Ernst would invite the Potters to meet with her at her home at 3513 Halliday Avenue. One such glorious occasion was recorded in the summer of 1906 by the Scribe; Sara was at Charlevoix during the summer months, and so she was not included in this very typical meeting.

July 6, 1906

This is a red letter day in Potter history. The "toot and tumble" was invited to come to the house of their beloved L.R.E. They took their Alfreddavids that they would meet at three at the middle entrance of Tower Grove Park, whence they would be led to the House by the V.C. and Barbara, the only ones who are not laggards in love and dastards in war, and who consequently deserve the hand of the fair Ellen of 3513 Halliday Avenue. The Editorial party, consisting of the fair Editor, Grace, Barbara, and Petronelle, was late of course. It's a failing of theirs. The V.C. was on time. That is a failing of hers. Also Ned, Adele, Eleanor Foote, and Dorothy[3] were on time more or less. The V.C. had a lovely fern draped over her waistcoat but was deprived of it by Ned whose love of Botany and the Fauna and Flora of Missouri is so extremely incipient as to be scarcely visible to the naked eye.

We advanced up Miss Ernst Avenue in maiden meditation each clasping some article, except Petronelle and Ned, I think. Dorothy had an umbrella, a quail wishbone (gift of Miss Chase) and a tiny copy of *Henry V*. Adele had her candle-stick carefully packed, by the V.C., in doll-blankets. Barbara had the Mowgli ink-stand in a Busy Bee box. Grace and William had the fragments of the two

[3]Dorothy Colby was Vine's sister.

new *Wheels*. Eleanor had a large package of empty bottles for L.R.E. I had a volume of R.L.S., and my *Francesca da Rimini* which Adele had just returned to me. We certainly circulate literature a good deal.

The poor Editor had a bad headache from overworking to get the *Wheels* done. ("By the Great Horned Spoon, I will get them done!" W.P.) but you never could have told it from his air, which was buoyant as a lark—a nice lark in a pongee dress with a red neck-tie. The Editor has such a 'earty way of saying, "Come tuck your left fin under my larboard flipper!" . . .

L.R.E. was at the door and gave each a real L.R.E. handshake. (If Barbara had rheumatism in her hand this time, *I* say, serves her right.) Mowgli was produced and given to his future owner, who declared, when the candle stick was put next to him (Mowgli), that Adele was absolutely not in it. Poor Barbara is afflicted, however, that everyone thinks her candlesticks and inkstands much too lovely to be really used. They are, in fact, just "pawlor ornaments" and have no traffic with tallow or ink. In the course of the afternoon, a blue and white book, *The Isle of Dreams*, was given to Barbara, who thereupon put on most insufferable airs, and strutted if ever any woman did. Ask her to recite the inscription! When the March Hare is very happy and triumphant, she lifts one foot up, screws up one eye, and clasps her treasure to her bosom, uttering the while little snorts and sniffs and scrittlings in her throat. O you *har* a hartful dodger, Barbara Risque Esquire! I know your tricks and your manners, you small—you small—nice child, you!

We sat in a sort of a circle, like the audiences in Schiller's ballads, and held our regular simultaneous-combustion conversation. It may not be as elegant as the Salon of Madame Rambouillet, or as peaceful as the Douma, but we like it tip-top. Our visitors do not get acclimated to it very easily. They cannot shuffle off the mortal coils of convention and politeness, and because they wait to speak until some one gives symptoms of being about to finish, never get it said. . . .

We made ourselves entirely at home, fell upon the book-case and borrowed freely. The V.C. had the cheek to lend one of the books on her own responsibility. Miss Ernst immediately gave this audacity a legal air by declaring that any of her possessions were at the disposal of the Potters. So Barbara proceeded to take a Japanese print from the wall, and try it upside down.

We talked over our darling project of going down to Saxton's for a week, "the whole bawnch," as Signor Janni says. . . . Also we talked of our darling scheme, which is a Potter house. Miss Ernst said she had an eligible third story with a side entrance and a winding stair. We thought she was telling fairy tales, and proposed an outside stair-case, a ladder up which we could mount at night with lanterns to our enskyed abode. Wouldn't it be jolly? Oh wouldn't it just!

Barbara put Miss Ernst through a catechism in regard to most of the articles of the Potter creed. It runs something like this: "Dost thou love cats? And dogs? And Julia Marlowe? And Sue Williams? And the Golden Age?" etc. Probably if she had been catechising any one else, the third article of the creed would have been called L.R.E. Well, Miss Ernst survived this scorching ordeal, although on some points she is an awfu' heretic. Not to like cats! Barbara's eyes expanded and her mouth drooped. Not to like J.F.S.! William groaned and declined to discuss the subject at all.

They spread a table for us and we brought in our chairs and fell to. . . . We talked about so many things at table that I cannot write them all—Heaven, Joseph Sheehan, Barbara's book of child verses, the Potter home, our culinary accomplishments (I *can* make delicious biscuits and if any knave dare say I can't, I'll prove it on his caitiff carcass!) At about six o'clock the Editor pulled out his watch, with a sort of White Rabbit dear-dear-I-shall-be-late expression, and the party broke up and ran for its bonnets and plumes and umbrellas and books and other impedimenta. And our Miss Ernst took us down to the corner where we got our car. In four weeks we are to meet again on Miss Ernst Avenue, and at that time the Editor must produce pictures of all the Potters thus far photographed, to adorn the wall of 3513 (Miss Ernst Avenue).

A very happy day, my children, nicht wahr? And how much we wish all the Potters could have been there.

Now and then there was friendly rivalry among the girls for the time and attention of Miss Ernst. Vine once admitted in the *Log:*

I am commonly agreed to be a very fortunate person. Barbara and Sara consider me a selfish pig in regard to Miss Ernst. To be sure there is no reason why *I* should be permitted to take walks with this well beloved Olympian, and be introduced to her friends, the trees, any more than Barbara and Sara and the rest. But I do not take Miss Ernst into a corner and eat her up and make insulting gestures to Barbara and Sara and the rest as they hang over the fence. I take the good the gods provide, with a properly humble and chastened spirit and an eager desire to share it with others.

The Potters liked nothing more than to leave St. Louis for a week end or, even better, a week, and spend the time at an old farmhouse called Saxton's. Sometimes they persuaded Miss Ernst to go with them, and since she was such an enthusiastic lover of nature, she would share with the girls her wealth of information about plants, birds, flowers, and other outdoor life.

Saxton's was at Sulphur Springs, which was a short trip by train from St. Louis. Mr. Saxton's widow used to take paying guests to make a living. In the old-fashioned parlor was an oil painting of the late Mr. Saxton, done by some boarder who could not pay his board otherwise. The girls irreverently christened his portrait "Ashes-of-Noses," because of the ashy color of the large nose. The house had a number of attic bedrooms with dormer windows, which were under a sloping roof, and it was without any comforts except good substantial food. But the Potters were in the house only for meals. The rest of their time was spent in roving through the fields and woods; late in the evening they would come home, and in the fall their arms would be filled with great branches of fiery red and yellow autumn leaves. Sometimes they made a big bonfire.

In the colorful surroundings of this serene Missouri country-side, Miss Ernst proved the best of companions imaginable, and she freely showered on her young friends her fascinating knowledge of botany and bird life.

Remembering the beauty of Saxton's and all it once meant to her, in later years Sara wrote:

Places I love come back to me like music,
 Hush me and heal me when I am very tired;
I see the oak woods at Saxton's flaming
 In a flare of crimson by the frost newly fired. . . .

Another poem by Sara, which referred to this lovely place and was reprinted in a little memorial booklet to Miss Ernst, is called "Redbirds," and ends with these lines:

Redbirds, redbirds,
 Are you singing still
As you sang one May day
 On Saxton's Hill?

Under this poem in the tribute to Miss Ernst is written:

Yes, Sara Teasdale, redbirds still sing on Saxton's Hill, sing for others as they did for you and Miss Ernst that May day. We agree. A day of birding with L. R. Ernst was a day for poetry, for song rich as "Redbirds"!

Chapter 5

A BEGINNING AND AN END

•

WITH the fame of *The Potter's Wheel* spreading far and wide throughout St. Louis, for the chosen people who saw it spoke highly of the magazine, it was inevitable that William Marion Reedy, who was always interested in new talent, should hear of it. Reedy's attention was first drawn to the *Wheel* and the Potters through Frances Porcher, who had seen the magazine, was quite impressed, and was preparing to do an article on the Potters for the *Mirror*. Mrs. Porcher's husband operated a book store where Sara and some of the other girls purchased volumes dear to their hearts, and both Mr. and Mrs. Porcher were interested in literary matters.

The first reference to Mr. Reedy and his notice of the Potters was very casually inserted in the following *Log* report on December 15, 1905:

The gallant Harris of Thornby was forcibly detained at home by his mother. Otherwise, every chieftain rallied to the banner. Sara drove up in a coach and four (wheels) just as Ned and the Scribe arrived on foot. We thought it might be Celia; but catching a glimpse of a bonnet and plume of white chiffon and feathers, we concluded that it was only a bloated aristocrat and disdained to stare. At least, the Scribe did. I can't answer for Ned. But the lady in the carriage turned out to be just Sara. She was ready to apologize for all the pomp and circumstance on the grounds that she had to go to a tea. The Editor said something very impolite and strongly masculine on the subject of teas.—Anything unusual in the way of raiment is sure to call forth comment from the Potters. "Oh she has a train!" cried one. "Is that the English dress?" said another. The Editor, who always knows when a contrib has been tampered with or tinkered up after it has been handed in, now exclaimed, "Ha! Was that pink piping there before? No? I *thought* it looked nicer than before."

The Potters heard to-day of the loss of one of their friends among the writers, Fiona Macleod. This bad news rather blackened the day for some of us to whom Fiona was especially loved.

Celia is to have some photographs taken soon, with her hair in the plaited coronal which we all like so much. Will says, "She looks like a regular Princess in an old tale, you know, and she ought to wear one of those long slim things that er—go in when they get there." This is very descriptive when helped out by hands, though I fear a dressmaker would not know when "it" got "there.". . .

* * *

The December *Wheel* was on view and was liberally admired. Mr. Reedy is to see some of the *Wheels* at Mrs. Porcher's house some time.

* * *

Sara says she wished she had known Will in the days when Will was practicing exercises on the piano. Grace drew the veil upon Will's tricks and manners at this "epic" of her existence (as Ned says). It seems that Will was in the habit of kicking the piano and pounding the keys to hurt their feelings and trying to pry off the ivory tops. Will says she only used to bite her own finger and then bang the note with it. . . .

On February 2, 1906, the Scribe further recorded that:

Some of the *Wheels* have been shown to a publisher. The publisher pored and pored over them. Then he came back and pored some more. All the *Wheels* were at Sara's today and we were trying to decide which ones should go to Mr. Reedy.

On February 9, 1906, the Scribe made this notation:

Mr. Reedy has seen the *Wheels* and he not only pored—he rolled. He rolled, he pored, and he has given an order for two covers for the *Mirror*.

Mrs. Porcher's article entitled "The Potters and the Potter's Wheel," which had been eagerly anticipated by the girls, was published on April 5, 1906, and served as an excellent introduction to the public of their work. After telling how the group organized and the magazine started, she characterized each Potter. She spoke of Will as being

... the very soul of the organization and a girl of such genuine and versatile talent that one wonders why she was not put in an art school years ago and that she is not in Paris now.

Scarcely less talented is her younger sister, Grace, and both girls have done wonderful work in photography, work of international reputation. (Late medals from Vienna attest to this.) Grace does her finest work in photographic portraiture, although her color work is excellent. In portraiture, however, she rises above even the artist photographer and is the psychologist *en rapport* with her subject. She does not pose her model, she catches the fleeting glimpse of soul at the psychological moment and some of her results are marvelous.

Caroline Risque, a delicate girl of high nervous temperament, is *par excellence,* the genius of the Potters. She writes almost as well as she paints and if she were more painstaking and less impulsive in her work could rise to almost any height as either artist or sculptor. Given a stronger physique and incentive for continuous effort, we will yet see great things from this girl of the Potters.

Sara Teasdale, too, will be heard from or I lose my guess. Hers is the perfect literary spirit, sonnets, lyrics, and translations being now her line of work, and Vine Colby has the natural born instinct of the journalist combined with a talent for artistic design that promises much for her future if she wills to go in wider fields, up steeper grades.

Celia Harris is surcharged with the literary dramatic spirit and shows at her best in lyrics and plays. A one-act "Prose Play in Rhythm" of Miss Harris's has been successfully performed; this same little play is one of the finest and best contributions to *The Potter's Wheel,* appearing in the first issue.

Mrs. Porcher spoke, also, of "Miss Sombart with a peculiar handling of color schemes that makes the little she has done so far extremely noticeable, and E.W. who does fine literary work."

After describing the *Wheel* and quoting many selections from it, Mrs. Porcher concluded her article:

It is rare to find a set of girls so nearly equal in their work or so thoroughly in harmony, and in the light of what they have accomplished solely for their own amusement and the development of their own special lines of talent, it is no prophetic spirit which sees that they have almost reached the parting of the ways where they will be more—or less. They cannot hold out their hands to the stars as toys any longer. Untrained effort and pure, but selfish, joy of the eye and intellect among themselves, is growing into something that belongs to the world and their fellows. Three of them are in Art School now; already there is the stir of the growing soul in the others. The lure of printer's ink will call bye and bye so loudly that it must be heard and then—the Potters will go their ways, up rocky heights, maybe, but ever I trust towards the eternal Heavens. If one could only hope that they might bear with them their ideals of friendship and that humility of soul, that divine dissatisfaction that leaves the heart pure and the brain clear; that nerves the hands and soul to do something worth while, not for ambition's sake alone, but for God and humanity.

The harmony and friendship among the Potters that was so apparent to Mrs. Porcher was a very important reason why the girls accomplished so much and worked together so well. From time to time, various honors came to members of their group; there was never any jealousy among them; each was genuinely glad and thrilled for the recipient when good fortune came to any one of them. The sincere good will and joy in their friendship that existed among them was briefly touched upon in an entry in the *Log* made by the Scribe about a month before Mrs. Porcher's article appeared:

Grace, Guida, Ned, and I were downstairs at Sara's, while Sara, Barbara, Petronelle, and Will were in my lady's chamber, putting the finishing touches on the new *Wheel.* Sara and I were the only ones who paid our luncheon call on Mrs. Marshall. We were in consequence inordinately self-satisfied. Guida, with the frankness of a Rousseau, revealed *her* method of conducting party calls. You call up the victim and ask, "Is Mrs. So and So at home?" If the answer is yes, you say in a professional tone, "I should like to get her subscription to the Amalgamated Ice Fund." If the answer is no, you hasten to go and leave your square of white cardboard, and everyone concerned is happy ever after. But one shudders to think of the hollowness of society and social forms. That is one especially nice thing about us—we no longer need to behave with propriety to each other. Every one of us knows that we are always glad to see each other, even if it is not convenient to call. Our social order belongs to the golden age when gloves and calling cards were unknown.

The *Log* does not reveal what the girls thought of Mrs. Porcher's article, but evidently they were pleased with it, for Vine wrote on April 6, the day after it was published:

We agreed not to read the article in the *Mirror* until we were all together at Mrs. Harris's this afternoon, but I think no one kept her promise. If I can induce one of the Potters to give up her write-up, I shall put it here in the *Log.* It is time that the *Log* was diversified by something other than sheer Loggery. Celia's letter and Inez's are going in. We ought to have, too, a printed copy of Celia's last poem and the *Globe-Democrat* references to her play. We have a new institution, named by Sara, Miss Jeannette McGargle. She is our press committee. If any Potter is hectored and cornered by any reporter, all she has to do is refer the reporter to "our press committee, Miss Jeannette McGargle," who is always out of the city.

* * *

Sara has made her Duse sonnets into a sehr hübsch little brown book. It starts on its journey towards a certain Palazzo tonight.

Sara was trying to make an adjective from the word vanity. I have forgotten for what she wanted to use it, but at any rate, "vanitious" was the best she could think of. I suggested "vain," and she quite beamed with relief, for Sara has the passion for the right word, and would no more say a "curran" people when "hantle" was the proper term, than T. Sandys would.

It was William Marion Reedy who actually introduced Sara's work to the world through his paper. In the March, 1906, issue of the *Wheel* was a little prose sketch by Sara, which happened to catch Mr. Reedy's eye, as he looked over the magazines. He liked it so well that he printed it in the *Mirror* on May 17, 1907. Sara was delighted, and when, in addition to the honor, Mr. Reedy sent her a check, her joy knew no bounds. In *The Potter's Wheel,* Sara used these words from Ernest Dowson as an introduction to her fable:

> She knows us not, nor recks if she enthrall
> With voice and eyes and fashion of her hair,
> A little, passionately, not at all!
>
> . . .
>
> We pass and go: but she shall not recall
> What men we were, nor all she made us bear.

But when Mr. Reedy printed it, he used another quotation for the introduction.

THE CRYSTAL CUP

Under the leaf of many a fable lies
The truth for those who look for it.
If thou wouldst look behind and find the Fruit,
Have thy desire.

—JAMI

There was once a man who possessed a wonderful cup of crystal. So cunningly was it fashioned that it seemed sometimes to be the red of the flame, and anon it was blue, or, maybe a green like the sea where it is shallow at the shore.

The man knew that the cup was a priceless treasure, and he longed to fill it with wine. In the hot golden sunshine he went from vineyard to vineyard where the girls were gathering the honey-sweet grapes, and from the warmth of the sun he passed into the chill of gray wine-cellars to taste and see what was good.

One virtue of the cup was this: the greater number of rare wines that were mixed within it, the more valuable the cup became. For the crystal shone more brightly as the wine mounted within it. When at last it was full, the man was happy. He longed to be alone so that he might dream over the beauty of the cup and very slowly drink the wine.

He turned away from the grape gatherers, and, as he turned, he saw a woman coming toward him. She walked beside the stone wall of the vineyard, now in the sun and now in the shadow, for there were tall trees above her. Her hair was mixed with the sun, like gold that the goldsmith has worked over lovingly. When she came quite close to the man, having nothing else to give her, he handed her the crystal cup. She drank the wine without looking into his eyes. Then she set the empty cup down roughly on the stone wall, and passed on. The man's eyes followed her. He turned to take the empty cup because she had held it in her hands. But it was broken into a thousand pieces, each stained faintly by the wine.

· · ·

And the man went his way empty handed and full of sorrow.

A year later, on May 30, 1907, Reedy printed Sara's long poem in blank verse called "Guenevere," which attracted considerable attention and was widely reprinted. This was followed by other of her poems, and as the *Mirror* was extensively read, her reputation as a poet of achievement and promise began to be established.

Meanwhile, in the spring of 1906, the Potters were sorry indeed to learn that Mrs. Harris would no longer be able to let them meet at her home, since she was planning to move. Vine dutifully wrote of this sad news in the *Log* on April 6, 1906:

Mrs. Harris is planning to give up the house in Thornby Place in May; and while of course we know that this is wise, we cannot help regretting it on account of the happy times we associate with that particular roof. I am afraid the next occupants may hear the ghosts of Potters go wailing around the library. But we need not feel homeless, for are *we* not really the walls of our house and the roof thereof, wherever the house is? Besides, half the time we live in Arden. If you start up the white path bordered by red carnations, which leads to Arden, you are almost sure to fall in with the Potters who are going to or coming from the beautiful gates of the place.

Though the girls had discussed a house of their own with Miss Ernst, no definite plans were made until Mr. and Mrs. Parrish told them that they could use the little building in their yard for a club house. The Parrishes once had a large number of cats, and since the family was very musical, each cat was named in honor of an opera; there were the Aïda cat, Fra Diavolo, Mimi, and many other fine feline specimens. Mr. Parrish finally got tired of having so many cats continually underfoot, and he built a little house for them in the garden. One morning, for some mysterious reason, all of the cats were found dead; it was never discovered who or what had helped them leave this world. Since the dwelling had lost its occupants, and since the Potters were so eager to have a place of their own, the Parrishes thought they might be able to fix the little house over and use it. The Potters were overjoyed, and their plans were described fully by Vine:

September 25, 1906

We have a house, a Potter house. The dream of our hearts is even now being nailed into solid fact by a carpenter. It was a week ago Wednesday when we met—Everybody and Miss Ernst—in Tower Grove Park, that the scheme was unfolded. Oh dear, if only all the Potters were here to take a hand in the excitement and add to the number of contested points. The house is in the backyard of House-of-Parrish. It has a yard of its own, which already blooms in our mind's eye with many flowers. A fountain plays (I mean it will play) into a cemented basin of fish and water hyacinths. In the garden is to be placed Barbara's Faun. A peach-tree is there, and will be surrounded by a circular seat à la Robin Hood. We have chosen Saint Francis of Assisi for a patron saint. B. is to do a statuette of him, and insists on placing it beneath a bowl of goldfish so that if St. Francis is seized with a desire to preach to the fishes in the night-time, why he *can*.

There will be a red gravel path leading up to the front door, which, by the way, is in five glass panels to be decorated in a stained glass effect with pictures of the Potters in silk. The Dormouse is to be at the top.[1] We shall have a swinging signboard—"The Potter's House." We are going to shingle the walls inside, ourselves. The new windows have been put in. We see them with red geraniums and white curtains blowing in and out. Tomorrow we are all to appear with hammers to nail on the tar-paper. There will be a shelf on which we shall have books of Theatre pictures, Maxfield Parrish's, the *Log*, etc. Grace is going to have her Burne-Jones "Hope" and the "Beata Beatrix" Miss Wilcox gave her, framed for the Potter House walls. There are also to be portraits of all the Potters. Probably a big chair will be built into the wall. The Causa Honoris will look very decorative in it.

Fortunately, Will and Grace took the inevitable photographs of the girls shingling the inside of the small house. The card of the carpenter who helped them (*C. G. Hory—Carpenter and Joiner*) is still to be seen in the *Log*, too, with this note beside it: *Sara was too ill to lend her aid*, referring, of course, to the fact that the Carpenter was Sara's Wonderland name.

A stubborn little iron stove was installed in the Potter House to use on cool days and evenings. This was given the name of Lady Kitty Ashe, because, like the wife in the then recently published *Marriage of William Ashe* by Mrs. Humphrey Ward, it "demanded so much attention."

In appreciation of this wonderful gift, the Potters printed this inscription in the *Wheel* for January, 1907:

---

[1]Celia had gone west for her health at this time, and the Potters wanted her to know that she was not forgotten.

Vine Colby

Caroline Risque

Photograph by
Williamina and Grace Parrish

Dedicated to A. C. and D. L. Parrish, who made our Dream of a Potter House a Reality.

When the Potter House was completed, the girls held a house-warming, but since Vine was unable to attend, there is no record of it. From time to time, various friends of the Potters contributed gifts to the little house. Mrs. Harris sent a book with which to start the Potter Library, J.M.A.J. sent a calendar of Walter A. Clark's *Canterbury Pilgrims,* and Miss Chase sent a fern basket as an Easter gift in 1907.

Sara, whose throat had given her continual trouble ever since her trip abroad, spent some time with her sister, Mamie, at Colorado Springs in the summer of 1906, hoping that the dry western air would completely cure her. Her friends kept her posted, of course, on the plans for the Potter House, and she sent an incense burner as her housewarming gift, which was used on many future festive occasions. On Sunday, March 10, 1907, there is this notation in the *Log:*

We had a spur of the moment party, in the Potter-house....
The house was darkened—no candles even. We filled the incense-burner with alcohol and lit it. A beautiful flame sprang up. We were sorry Sara could not see it.

Being strongly interested in the dramatic and make-believe, and always ready to have a good time, the Potters, besides putting on plays, giving musicals, painting, sculpturing, writing, taking and developing pictures, and getting out their magazine, loved to dress up and have parties. Shortly before Inez's marriage, a Mrs. Marshall gave a party in her honor, and of that occasion Vine wrote:

...Perhaps Mrs. Marshall is not used to having her guests lay their ears to the table to peer at the effect of a green sleeve through a blue bowl. But happily people expect the Potters to be a bit queer—eccentric but amiable genii. The wit rolled around the table in balls like the thunder at Alice's party....

The raiment deserves a chapter all to itself but it won't get it. Suffice it to say that Grace stepped out of Cranford, and Sara wore green woven water and William golden brown woven water.[2] Inez played the Symphony in Red by special request. Guida was happed up in white and lace; Petronelle's noble form was draped in a pale brown toga, a sort of Whistler's "Arrangement in Brown and Gold Bracelet," and the March Hare wore inwisible blue. The March Hare obligingly favored the company with another representation of Mr. Yeats, this time with the addition of a long, lean lock of black hair in one eye. Mr. Yeats did have March hair, you know. It was as mad as mad could be. Also a March Neck'rchiff. It is said that Barbara weighed eighty-seven when she began on the oysters, and ninety when we got to the ice-cream hearts. But she is still a small affair that can slip through an eight-inch crack with great ease.

Another gay, good time that was long remembered occurred on February 27, 1907:

I was met at the door by Melisande-Maeterlinck in a red gown and with pearls twined through her hair. Eugene, the Poet, was at the head of the stairs, basking in the frowns of a bewitching dancing-girl in red and yellow. An innocent and very buxom child of six in a white French dress, pink sash, very pink calves and white socks came down the stairs. As my readers have no doubt guessed, these shady characters were no other than—(hold your breath!)—Petronelle, Guida, Grace and William. Petronelle was magnifique. It is a shame that the state of the streets and public opinion would not permit her to go around in a red garment that goes in when it gets there. . . .

I was getting into my Kate Greenaway dress while Barbara was being hectored into her Babbie costume by the Editor. Such language! The poet and Grace had to be sent from the room. Sara had a very picturesque Assyrian dress, with a black veil which

---

[2]"Woven water" refers to these lines from one of Sara's sonnets to Eleonora Duse:

I think your snowy tunic must have hung
As now your gown does—wave on wave a mass
Of woven water.

covered the face up to the eyes. We all tried it on afterward to see if we could look cowed and enslaved and brow-beaten. Ned put on a Dutch costume with handsome but very cumbrous sabots.

We had our photographs taken by two's, and then we wished to try a group. The front porch was the only available place. Judge of the joy and amazement of the howling populace of small boys! They thought us an excellent target for snow-balls. We stood it until some one of them shouted a remark about Guida's costume netherwards. Then we beat a hasty retreat.

In bringing the *Log* up to date on New Year's Day, 1907, Vine described, among other things, another memorable dress-up party:

It is a pity that no record was kept of our numerous Saxton trips. Do you remember "Little Journey to the House of Beethoven"[3] and Will's complaint that there was no sheet-music there? Also how hysterical the V.C. became over William's "Do you know you are occupewing my pie?" Then there was the Julia Marlowe week when we all lived at the Garrick and were all, in the Gracie's phrase, molten masses about the lovely Julia. 'Member the night we carried off L.R.E., and Will and Barbara and the V.C. sat on her chest till 3 a.m. in sweet converse about ships and sealing-wax and cabbages and kings? Of course you do, but it is nice to remind you of it. Then there was the house-warming of the Potter House, which I had to miss. And there was the grand tea-party in celebration of the birthdays of Grace and Barbara and the *Wheel*. Oh how muckle schön that was! Grace dressed as an old-fashioned little maid in pantalettes, and Barbara as an old-fashioned little boy. They spoke moral pieces, hand in hand, and played "the latest thing, *Juanita*," on the violin! The Christmas party: We all came as children. William was in a white French dress (frocks, they call them at that stage, do they not?) with a pink sash and socks; Grace had a white frock with a loose black leather belt, and terminated in white legs and white socks and sandals; Petronelle was a very handsome boy of eleven, in a Knickerbocker suit of dark red sateen, turn down collar, and a most remarkable blond wig made by herself, out of rope—plain ordinary garden rope. Ned looked very handsome in

<hr>

[3]This refers to Elbert Hubbard's book by that name.

a brown suit with tan legs and a short brown wig. Our poor sick Sara couldn't come but sent word that we were not to sit down suddenly on any vacant spot, for she was going to project her astral body into our midst. Barbara was in a blue and white sailor-suit made by her lady-mother. She was an even smaller little boy than she is a little girl. The V.C. came as Alice in Wonderland. . . . It wore a light blue dress, white apron, white stockings, and black slippers. L.R.E. came in citizen's clothes, but the fact is that with the best of intentions she might find it difficult to look like a child of eight. At it was, E.H.W., P.S., and G.P. looked stalky.

Will photographed the children as they appeared. Then she and Petronelle—oh let us even sit down a minute and tell their names: Barbara was Master Charles Risque, Petronelle was at first Peter Sombart, changed later to Pierre because P. Sombart hates the name Peter; Ned, of course, was Master Ned Wahlert. Now let us even proceed. I had better mention that "even" is the latest pet of W. and G. Parrish. They use it as hilariously as the Elizabethans used "withal"; in fact, they are hardly able to frame a sentence without sticking in an "even" somewhere—and as I am a faithful scribe, I must even do so, too. W.P. and Master Pierre went out to the Potter House to light the tree, and the rest of the children followed soon. The Potter House looked charming with red bells hung in the windows: poinsettias sitting on the shelves; the little lighted cedar tree in the midst, with huge sticks of peppermint candy and little models of Santa Claus in front of a lighted lamp in Saint Francis's niche; a splendid Captain Kidd done by Pierre Sombart after Howard Pyle, on the wall; and a waste-basket sent by Celia and overflowing with the presents that were to be distributed later.

L.R.E. had not yet arrived and the prospect was gloomy. Her family said darkly that she had gone downtown. We did not want to begin the festivities without her, but as the moments passed, and the rain pattered on the roof, and the wind soughed, and we gloomily sucked our peppermint sticks, the Editor's brow grew blacker and blacker and finally she announced that she would abandon that woman to her own devices; that if she did not turn up, after having been fairly *threatened* with invitations—huh! you bet we wouldn't go to *her* old party! We took hands and galloped

SOME OF THE POTTERS IN THEIR PARTY COSTUMES WITH THE SCRIBE'S COMMENTS FROM THE "LOG"

etronelle Sombart
ARDS AND YARDS OF
, SOMBART

illiamina Parrish

*aroline Risque as
Babbie" from the
otograph by Grace and
illiamina Parrish*

d (Edna) Wahlert
HIS IS THE BEST STUFF.

*ine Colby as
Alice-in-Wonderland*

race Parrish
BEANSTALK. (See Rule 42: "Persons over one mile high not
lowed in the Potter House.)

around the tree till we were out of breath, and the 500 hair-pins in Barbara's bobbed hair began to leave their moorings. Then we cursed the evil fate that kept L.R.E. away—I mean the literal Potter curse which is employed only on momentous occasions, and in concert with a stamp of the foot each time. Then Barbara and the V.C. in desperation tried the efficacy of prayer. We prayed vigorously for two minutes—Ned counted the seconds—and wonderful to relate, in about a minute more the door fell in with L.R.E. and her umbrella. B. made a wild inarticulate dash and embraced the answered prayer with arms and legs. The Almighty's reputation rose visibly. Then when we had pealed off L.R.E.'s shells and got at the kernel, Master Sombart distributed paper dirks which we were to pin, blindfolded, to the place where Captain Kidd's dirk was indicated. The Deserted Village came nearest and received a Mother Goose book as a reward. Grace got another "pitcher-book" for being by popular vote the sweetest child of all. Everyone had contrived some humorous gift for everyone else, and of course, there were a great many subtle jokes. . . .

L.R.E. kissed her adopted children all around, when she left. . . .

Because all of the Potters had other intimate friends of their own who were sometimes invited to join in their gay times, the girls decided that they would create the title of Associate Potters; the Associates were to be included in their trips to Saxton's, their plays, their theatre parties, and other festivities, but would not be expected to contribute to the *Wheel.*

Dorothy Colby, for instance, was Vine's sister, and she knew the other Potters well, and now and then had been included in some of their activities.

Nancy Coonsman, who had dark, wavy hair, radiant blue eyes, and a sunny disposition, was a young artist and sculptor already making a name for herself in St. Louis. She had graduated from Central High School, completed the first year of her course at the School of Fine Arts, and her portrait busts were even then winning local fame. Both Nancy and Adele Schulenberg, who was not an Associate Potter, but who frequently joined the others in their fun, studied under George Julian Zolnay and were considered two of his ablest students. In later years Nancy and Adele shared a studio.

Adele Garrels, an attractive blond, had gone to school at Central High and Washington University, and was a special friend of both Vine's and Ned's.

Gussie Isaacs, whose orange-red hair, green eyes, and very fair skin made her striking in appearance, was another good friend, loved by the Potters and enjoyed because of her wit and intellect.

On Sunday, June 16, 1907, Will wrote out and attached to the wall of the Potter House a document saying that these four girls had been elected to the "Degree of Associate Potters, thereby enjoying all the privileges of the Potter House and any other Nice Thing that may come to the Potters."

Sara's signature was not included among the others on this declaration, for very probably she had already gone with her family to their summer home in Michigan. She had been ill for much of the time in 1907 and had not been able to attend many of the Potter meetings, but she still sent in her contributions to the *Wheel*.

Though she did not meet him in person until they were both guests at a dinner in April of 1909, Mr. Reedy had successfully launched Sara's literary career, and in the summer of 1907 word came that *Poet Lore* had accepted one of her sonnets called "Silence," written to Eleonora Duse. With Will's help, meanwhile, she had arranged her poems for publication, and the Poet Lore Company had accepted the little book. Since the sonnets honoring Eleonora Duse made up the first and most impressive part of the volume, she called her book *Sonnets to Duse and Other Poems*.

Much of her time during the summer of 1907 at Altasand was spent in reading the proofs; and on July 11, she wrote Vine:

... the last few days I've been threshing over my proofs for the third, and I hope, the last, time. If it is this much bother to get out a little volume of poetry, what *would* a three volume novel be? I weep for Dickens and Thackeray when I think of it.

I have such a dear Maltese kitten to heal my heart, broken by the death of Stelio. I've named her "Fosca" after the heroine of *The Flame of Life*,[4] the beloved of Stelio, you know. I should have named her Eleonora out and out, but Papa was so disgusted with the length and magnificence of it—said that the name would kill her as Stelio's did him—that I desisted.

Like so many other poets and authors who have to sponsor their first publication, she paid the Poet Lore Company $290 for printing 1,000 copies of her book, though some of these were unbound. Today, the little volume is a collector's item. It was dedicated to her father and mother who, because of her long illness in 1907, were glad to pay for something that would bring her pleasure. But it was Will Parrish who had worked long and hard with Sara, helping her in the selection of the poems and in changing certain lines and words, to whom Sara felt most deeply indebted. Vine was visiting Sara at Charlevoix in September of 1907 when the little books arrived, and Sara, of course, delightedly gave Vine a copy lovingly inscribed. But the very first volume that was given to anyone was sent to Will with this inscription:

To William—without whom as all dedications say but this one *truly* —this book would never have been written—
from her
Sara—
Sept. 12—1907
The first copy sent to anybody goes to the most beloved of W.P.'s.
S.T.T.

Sara knew how much Arthur Symons admired Eleonora Duse. She sent the English author one of her little volumes, and on October 5, 1907, Symons reviewed it for *The Saturday Review* of London, saying:

---

[4]La Foscarina. in D'Annunzio's novel of 1899, was supposed to represent Duse, and the novel was apparently the story of the actress and D'Annunzio.

In this little American book there is poetry, a voice singing to itself and to a great woman, a woman's homage to Eleonora Duse. The sonnets to Madame Duse are hardly the best part of the book, for they speak and the lyrics sing; but they speak with a reverence which is filled with both tenderness and just admiration.

After quoting some lines from the lyrics, Mr. Symons added:

There are little songs for children, or about them, as lovely as these, and with a quaint humor of their own. The book is a small, delightful thing, which one is not tempted to say much about, but to welcome.

The Potters were as elated as Sara over the publication of her book and this favorable review in an important periodical.

Meanwhile, however, things were not going as smoothly with their own magazine as with Sara's literary career. For the Editor seemed to be having trouble with her staff. The last entry in the *Log* is dated March 26, 1907, and reads as follows:

William has made a proclamation and attached it to the Potter House wall. It concerns the *Wheel* and should certainly be read by every Potter who has the interests of the *Wheel* at heart.

The ominous note sounded by this statement was indeed emphasized by Will's message, written in both black and red ink to attract attention and with a great many words underlined:

PROCLAMATION!!!

To Whom It *Does* Concern:

Witness, that the Undersigned, Editor of the Magazine entitled The Potter's Wheel, in view of the *Laziness, Ingratitude,* and *General Lack of Interest* of the Members of this Organization, has *Firmly Decided* to resign from Editorship of said Magazine, if the following Rules and Regulations are not Complied with *To The Letter,* and *Sworn* to by Each Potter upon his Sacred Oath—To-Wit:—

1. That Each Active Member Accept and *Fulfill* a portion of Labor

assigned him (thus making the Duty and Responsibility of the Nerve-Wracked Editor less) as follows:

Here the Editor listed the various members and what was expected of each one in getting an issue of the magazine ready. And she added:

That all Potters take an *Active Interest* in the Magazine, the Potter House, the Potter Yard and Garden, and pay Weekly dues, 5 cents, and not leave all these Things for the Editor, to Increase his Grey Hairs.

At the conclusion she signed her name and gave the others an opportunity to sign under these words:

We, the Undersigned, accept *all* the above Conditions Upon Our Solemn and Sacred Oath, as Witness our Sign and Seal:

Evidently, the Editor pulled her staff together for another six months of publishing, for the *Wheel* continued to come out through October, 1907. By this time the girls were nearly all through their formal schooling, and various interests began to carry them away from Potter activities.

One of the last things that they undertook as a group was a presentation of a play called "Ye Comet's Tail or As You Say," a Shakespearean farce in three acts by Will and Vine, given on the lawn of Miss Ernst's home late in September of 1908. Will and Grace, as usual, took a number of excellent pictures of the cast.

Elsa Maxwell, who was interested in acting at this time, read the Prologue and the Epilogue and took a small part in the play. The Parrishes had become acquainted with Miss Maxwell, who was with the Constance Crawley Company, when they photographed the Crawley players. After the Crawley enterprise failed, Miss Maxwell took a part in Marie Doro's Company, and she invited the Potters backstage to meet Miss Doro in her dressing room.

Some twenty-five years later, Will made by hand three books, including in each the text of the play, the pictures of the participants in their costumes, and pictures of each of the Potters and their Associates. She sent one to Lillie Rose Ernst with this note:

Christmas 1933

Dearest L.R.E.—

I thought you might be amused with a copy of the famous *Comet's Tail,* so I made you this while making one for V.C. and myself—putting into them the only copies of the photographs now in existence, the negatives having long since disappeared. I had great fun making them, and remembering those hilarious days when you were so good to us and so one of us—our Causa Honoris! The Potters were a lucky bunch of "youngsters"!

My love to you—

Always affectionately

Willie

In each of the books Will also pasted a picture of Miss Ernst, and under the picture in L.R.E.'s book, she wrote:

The Causa Honoris
Whose Back Yard was our Battle Ground

The wonderful days of Potterdom were at an end. Although the members who had become attached to each other still retained their bonds of friendship, the time had now come for the individual girls to scatter far and wide, seeking their personal destinies and careers. The seeds of training that they acquired under Will's direction, however, continued to bear fruit for a number of them in their own creative work.

Will and Grace eventually went to Europe and remained there for many years, continuing to maintain their interest in photography. Guida Richey also went to Europe and studied photography.

Vine went abroad for one summer and returned home to a position as Editorial Assistant and Secretary to the Board of

Publication of Washington University; she won a scholarship to the Missouri School of Social Work, of Washington University, but did not accept it, as she decided to marry. Her poetry and prose were published in the *Mirror, Theatre Magazine,* and other periodicals, and she was the first St. Louis author to have a short story included in the O'Brien annual anthology of the best magazine stories of the year.

Caroline spent two years in Paris studying at the Colorossi Academy under Paul Bartlett and Injalbert. In Paris she exhibited many pieces of work in the Salon, a design for a fountain among them, and sold much of her work. One of her pieces was bought for the Museum of New Orleans, and another went into the home of an Ambassador. On returning home, she opened her own studio, married, and was head of the Art Department of John Burroughs School in St. Louis for many years.

Petronelle's family moved to Long Island, and she made many trips abroad, spending much of her time in Milan, studying music, before she married.

After spending a year with her mother on a ranch in New Mexico, Celia graduated from the University of Nebraska. She taught at Mary Institute, worked briefly for the *Lincoln* (Nebraska) *Evening News,* and later for New York City's Charity Organization Society. One of her poems, "Witch-Woman," was set to music by Deems Taylor.

Inez Dutro George died in Hutchinson, Kansas, in 1909, after the birth of her second child.

Ned Wahlert went to Europe and returned home to marry a scientist. Meanwhile, her work appeared in many publications, including *Poetry, Reedy's Mirror, The Smart Set, The Seven Arts, The Dial, Poet Lore,* and O'Brien's anthologies of short stories.

Nancy Coonsman, who married Mannel Hahn, the brother of Emily Hahn, completed her four years at the St. Louis School of Fine Arts, graduating with honors, and later studying with Gutzon Borglum in New York. She was selected, over a number of competitors, to design the charming fountain for the Kincaid Memorial, which is located in the sunken garden behind the St. Louis Public Library. The City Art Museum of St. Louis bought her bronze head called "Maidenhood," whose model was Georgia Cady, a girlhood friend of some of the Potters; it also purchased Nancy's bronze head of William Marion Reedy, both of which are still in the museum. Nancy also won a competitive commission to design a monument to American soldiers who fell in France during the first World War, and she went abroad to supervise the installation of this monument. She has also designed a Pick Memorial in Chicago and the large Dough Boy in Overton Park, Memphis, Tennessee, which is a D.A.R. Memorial of World War II, in addition to modeling numerous portraits of children in bronze.

Because of the great interest in Irish culture that her meeting with Yeats had aroused, Susan Creighton Williams, who married a St. Louis lawyer, began to study Irish mythology; she made an extensive collection of translations of old manuscripts as well as modern adaptations of Celtic prose and poetry. Using her wealth of knowledge and material, she acquired a reputation as a story teller of distinction; recounting the long sagas of Cuchulain and Finn MacCool, she delighted her audiences as long ago she had charmed the Potters by her recitations of Celtic poetry. She has been much in demand as an interpreter of the legends of ancient Ireland both on the east and west coasts, and she has appeared at the Students' International Union in Geneva, the Anthroposophical Group in New York, and before schools, colleges, clubs, and benefits throughout this country and abroad. She has also made a long-playing record utilizing this material.

Lillie Rose Ernst lived until 1943, spending her last days in a little house connected with her family home, which she built in the place that the garden had occupied. Miss Ernst and the golden memories that she left them were never forgotten by the Potters. In 1934 she received a letter from Williamina Parrish, dated January 9, and enclosing a note written by Vine about L.R.E.:

Carved in the silence by the hand of Pain,
  And made more perfect by the gift of Peace,
  Than if Delight had bid your sorrow cease,
And set a smile upon your lips again,
And brought the dawn to where the dark
          has lain;
  Oh strong and noble! tho' your woes increase,
  The gods shall hear no crying for release,
Nor see the tremble that your lips restrain.

Alone as all the chosen are alone,
  Yet one with all the beauty of the past,
A sister to the noblest that we know,
The Venus carved in Melos long ago.
Yea, speak to her, and at your lightest tone,
  Her lips would part, and words would come
          at last.

Sonnet to Eleonora Duse printed by Sara Teasdale in THE POTTER'S WHEEL

Proclamation !!!

To Whom it Does Concern :—

Witness, that the Undersigned, Editor of
the Magazine entitled The Potter's Wheel,
in view of the Laziness, Ingratitude and
general Lack of Interest of the Members of
this Organization, has Firmly Decided to
resign from Editorship of said Magazine, if
the following Rules and Regulations are
not Complied with To the Letter, and
borne to by Each Potter upon his Sacred
Oath—— To-wit:—
— That Each Active Member Accept and
fulfill a portion of Labor assigned him
thus making the Duty and Responsibility
of the Never-Wracked Editor less.) as follows

PROCLAMATION

by Williamina Parrish
March 26, 1907

Williamina Parrish
shingling the Potter House

Tell her I still think of her as one of the best I ever knew, a really great Gal, and that I keep on being grateful for what she put into our lives when we were puppies. I'd like to think of her as unchanged, every golden hair where it was, and in a starched shirtwaist and that turban with a pheasant-breast, or whatever it was, it *was* L.R.E.! And say I hope to meet her in Heaven if not in St. Looie, carrying that ivory-headed umbrella. The lovely photograph of her in my copy of "The Comet's Tail" is a great satisfaction, sorta like having a piece of the Oak Tree you grew up under!

V.C.

Will's own letter reads as follows:

Dearest LRE—

Just a note—in pencil!—to enclose this testimonial from V.C. which I know will afford you a chuckle—as well as warm the cockles of your heart!—V.C. is still the Scribe of the Log—forgetting no details!—

What a lovely time we had that night in your Sanctum, beside the old Log-fire (even if it *didn't* log-fire to *your* expectations—to me it was heavenly—a real Hearth-Stone—)—I loved everything in your little Retreat, & I loved all over again its Moving Spirit— (that means *you* in case you are a bit mystified as to my metaphors!) —The *same* LRE!!—I hope we deserved it!—I think perhaps we did, though—for you had no more staunch admirers—I might say, Lovers—than the Potters, one and all. A few of us came nearer to you than the rest—me, f'rinstance!—Also CR—& Edna, in her funny aloof way—But I think each one of us shared in your generous interest—no?

I was pleased to see your sisters—and see them so little changed. Give my affectionate regards to them.

Also, I was *deeply* impressed by your Doctor Friend and your Mountain Climbing with her—Great Gals, both of you (as V.C. so ribaldly called *you*—Shame on her! But she didn't think I'd report her verbatim!)

My love to you always, my dear—though you might not think it from my long silences! You are one of my very few Ideals—

Affectionately
and
admiringly
Your
Willie—

In later years, the individual Potters realized more and more how much Will had contributed to their group and to them individually with her drive for perfection and her excellent critical judgment. For Will had an intense interest in discovering and developing inherent talent. The people who appealed to her were those who had a spark of creative ability in them, and it was her particular joy and genius to serve, cherish, and bring to light such gifts.

Grace Parrish wrote of her sister after her death: "William dominated the Potters—and if they persisted at all—it was due to her. William had a *gift* for bringing out the best in other people, and I can name five or six people who owe her more than they can repay. In literature, sculpture, music, painting, photography—it made no difference—it was success that she worked for—in any medium."

Sara never forgot how much Will had helped and encouraged her. In thinking over those early days when she first knew Sara, Will once wrote that among Sara's friends, "I was given the honored place of 'literary confessor,' as she called me. And each newborn brain-child of hers was first read to me for approval— or disapproval, for she said, 'I could never really care for a poem of mine unless you approved of it.' But few were the disapproved of, for she had, from the beginning, a rarely sure knowledge of the technique of her art, and her thoughts formed themselves inevitably into a clear-cut perfection from their inception."

In a gift copy of *Rivers to the Sea,* Sara's third book, and the first one to be published after her marriage, the author inscribed this tribute to her friend:

To Willie the god-mother of these poems, October 1915.

In later years, Will, reminiscing about the Potters and her early association with Sara, wrote:

Her father was a tall, patriarchal old gentleman, with a long white beard and courtly manners, and a gentle voice. As he took my hand in greeting, his kindly eyes twinkled as he bowed in his courtly way, and I saw where Sara's twinkling eyes had come from. Sara adored her father, who was really more like her grandfather to her, so great was their difference in years. I think he was also quite a bit older than her mother. She was a small, bustling little body, quite the opposite from her quiet husband. I think both of them were quite mystified by their youngest offspring, as well they might be! For Sara was an innovation in the staid Teasdale family, into which she had been born after the other children were grown-up. She was "Sadie" to them and to all her school friends, and it was I who re-christened her Sara, after she became one of the little group of talented girls called The Potters. I insisted that a Poet could not be named Sadie. Bit by bit, the more dignified name Sara became her title, even with her family. We also decided that the spelling, Sara, was more fitting and more star-like than the Biblical Sarah. Sara Trevor Teasdale was her full name and S.T.T. was her first short signature, later changed to simple S.T. In jocular moods we were "Miss Sadie" and "Miss Willie" to each other. She had a habit of referring to herself in the third person which was piquant and engaging.

At that time Sara lived in a fine old white stone-front house on Lindell Boulevard, near Grand Avenue. I remember only her room, though the house boasted many rooms. It was as quiet as a tomb. Her room was in the southwest corner on the second floor, and had a sort of bay in the west wall with windows that looked north and south, and from the north window she could see a small strip of Lindell Boulevard, where at one time she would watch for the passing of Charles Galloway, the organist, for whom she had a romantic fancy. I remember that she had me take a picture of her seated on the wide sill of this window, clad in "virgin white" and flanked with Easter lilies. "Make Miss Sadie as virginal and chaste and beautiful as you possibly can, for she wants to impress him." Who this "him" was I do not remember. But there was always some special "him" around whom her poetic fancy was weaving a dream—and an exquisite lyric. I would tease her about these "flames" and we called them "Pegs for Pegasus." How many "Pegs for Pegasus" could I name, as I go through her first books of poetry! However, when I first met her, her "Flame" was a young girl, Bessie Brey. For not until several years later did Sara meet and know any men, and her romantic and sensuous nature had need of an outlet, and B.B. was the Peg for Pegasus of that period.

For many years she and I had a rendezvous every Friday morning in the dear old St. Louis Mercantile Library, where we sat in a secluded window-niche and talked of "shoes and ships and sealing wax, of cabbages and kings"—and then we would browse among the tempting shelves of books, always seeking new nourishment for our eager young minds. Sara had a keen interest in the work of her fellow singers, especially Keats and Shelley and Swinburne and the Rossettis—but perhaps most of all, the Brownings, whose *Letters* were to her a never-ending joy. In a way, she resembled Elizabeth Barrett Browning both physically and spiritually, and I think she herself was aware of this resemblance. I know that when she went to London for the first time, she made a loving pilgrimage to 50 Wimpole Street, the romantic background of the Browning courtship. At the end of our all-too-short hour or so in the Library, Sara, with an armful of books, would be driven carefully to her father's house in the family carriage, drawn by two beautiful prancing horses— for those were the days of leisurely elegance.

Perhaps those who feel that they know the real soul of Sara Teasdale as revealed in her books will be surprised to learn that her sense of humor was as exquisite as her singing beauty. In her poems one can look in vain for a spark of humor—though now and then one comes across a vein of gentle irony concerning love and the lover, for Sara was never cocksure of either, being a wise young person. But I, who stood in the wings and heard her off-stage comments on her performance, know how unfailing was her quick reaction to the humorous side of things, especially about herself. Though she took her lyric gift very seriously, never content until each line and word and all punctuation were chiselled to perfection, yet she could and did poke gentle fun at herself, calling herself *Miss Sadie*. "Here is Miss Sadie whining again!" she would say,

Sara Teasdale
1909

Sara Teasdale
as a
young woman

as she read me another gem-cut lyric. She had an equally piquant phrase regarding her lovely Greek poems. "Miss Sadie is swimming in Greece again!"

About her own quiet, unworldly self she was equally witty. Describing herself at some social gathering, she said, "And there sat Miss Sadie like a well-behaved tabby cat by the fire with a bow on her neck and her paws neatly folded." Could any portrait be more quaintly interpretive?

I remember also that when she read me for the first time her sonnet "Crowned" (later printed in *Rivers to the Sea*), before she began the reading of it, she said with a mirthful twinkle in her eyes, "This poem is entitled 'Crowned,' but its real name is 'The Door-mat'!"

It was at Sara's house in Kingsbury Place that I first met her father and mother and her sister, Mamie, who had married in the meantime. But even there I saw practically nothing of her family, for Sara's family and friends were never mixed, as they are in most families. It was as though she lived all alone in this neat Tudor dwelling in Kingsbury Place, so exclusive with its bronze fountain at the entrance gate. In this house Sara had her own suite of rooms, also in the SW corner on the second floor, with doors that were always closed off from the rest of the house. One could not, or did not, drop in on her casually, as one did with other friends, for Sara lived the austere life of a nun, each hour having its fixed and set task—hours of rest, hours of work on her poetry, hours when friends were expected by appointment. I had a fixed day and hour weekly with her, and I was very careful to appear on the exact minute and to leave on the exact minute she had set as the permitted length of our visit—no such thing with her as lingering on until all subjects had been exhausted. This was understood by all her friends, as a concession to her frail health. She said that only in this way could she conserve her small strength and be able to do all she wanted to do. This was wisdom on her part, though many thought it selfishness.

So well do I remember being ushered into the large, dim parlor at the left of the front door by the maid, who would go up and announce my arrival quite as though I were visiting royalty, and in a few moments I would hear a door close and steps on the stair, and then the clear, firm whistling of the love music of Siegmund and Sieglinde, which was a great favorite with her, and the whistling, twinkling-eyed Sara would appear to greet me, and to launch forth on the many enthralling topics we had to discuss. Sometimes she had the maid tell me to come up, and when I would enter the room, the shades would be drawn and she would be on her bed with (Oh, unpoetic habit!) a pair of stockings bound around her brow that had covered her eyes to keep out the light as she took her afternoon nap. Sara was nothing if not practical. The absolute perfection of every line of hers is the reflection of herself—nothing in disorder or at loose ends. Her family was very indulgent with her and humored all her whims—quite as a duck family would humor a swan in their midst, to use a humble simile. Sara lived the life of a Princess in her Tower, as far as I could see. Nothing was lacking to her except vigorous health. Anent which, she once said to me, "I often wonder if I had been born into a family with no means if I would have better health." I often wondered this myself—for in the hours I was with her she did not seem frail or weak, and she burned up energy at a break-neck speed in her enthusiasms. What an infectious enthusiasm she had! Though her interest was limited to things of art and beauty, in that range she was omniverous. I do not think that people—just people in the abstract—interested her. But the few chosen ones who did interest her, interested her overwhelmingly. In the scheme of life she had carved out for herself, many people could not possibly fit—she never allowed herself to burn *her* candles at both ends. This was of the essence to her. She could not have changed, no matter what the temptations from the outside. Her life was a fixed and ordered entity, into which other lives had to fit, if they entered hers at all. It never entered her head to fit herself to others. This, of course, was a strength as well as a weakness. Perhaps because of this we can now enjoy and treasure her books. Perhaps because of this, she is the only one of the Potters who achieved Fame and a lasting Fame. For in the beginning, each of these girls had a talent as promising as Sara's. But only hers will endure.

Chapter 6

IN SEARCH OF HEALTH

·

BECAUSE Sara's health had been very poor during 1907, she went south to San Antonio for a while during February of 1908, seeking the therapeutic aid of a warmer climate; and soon after this, the family decided that a stay at a private hospital in Connecticut might be of some benefit to her. March of 1908 found Sara settled there, where rules about diet and rest were strictly enforced. Her room, which was on the second floor, was the only one that had a porch of its own. Her meals were served in her room where she ate alone; and every night, as soon as dinner was over, she would go out on the little porch and watch the stars take their appointed places in the sky. The moon, too, seemed like an intimate and beloved friend, and the music of the wind in the trees, while starlight and moonlight made the world incredibly lovely, was an unfailing source of pleasure to her.

A basic idea in the treatment at this place seems to have been that the patients should not expend their energy in any way. At first Sara was allowed to write letters for twenty minutes a day, then for ten, and finally not at all, except a weekly letter to her parents. She was also prohibited from receiving any mail for a while, as the doctor thought it excited her too much. For Sara, to whom correspondence meant so much, these rules were hard to bear. Once, a nurse told Sara that her trouble was that she was too full of joy, which was bad for her. (One remembers the poet's own line: "It was myself that sang in me.") But this seemed like a strange diagnosis to the patient who had never thought of her capacity for spiritual exuberance as a liability.

So that she would be completely cut off from outside stimulation, Sara was soon moved into a tiny cottage apart from the main building, about seven feet square, which had been built in the midst of an orchard. Here she spent six weeks with only her nurse and some friendly spiders for company. Not long after this move, she sprained both her ankles, and the days that followed were not very happy or very comfortable ones.

After her long period of complete rest, her doctor suggested that the seashore might help Sara. She left Connecticut with her nurse in July and went to Tabitha Inn, at Fairhaven, Massachusetts, for a while. August found them in Newport, Rhode Island, which Sara had visited as a child, and which she remembered as an enchanted land of tall buildings near the ocean. Then they went on to Gloucester, Massachusetts, where they went out into the harbor in a launch, and Sara, who never failed to respond to the sea, loved the wind, the waves, and the spray blowing in her face.

One day the two travelers ventured into Boston and on the walls of a room in the Public Library saw the mural of the "Quest of the Holy Grail," painted by Edwin Austin Abbey. The girl who was hiding her face in her arms in the section, "Galahad in the Castle with the Maidens," appealed to Sara tremendously, and from this experience came the sonnet written to her, which was included in *Helen of Troy*.

When she finally returned home, after her long absence, she wrote another sonnet called "The Return," which describes the poet's entering her room, where she noticed that her beloved pictures had not even missed her, nor were they aware that she had come back again:

> But Giorgione's Venus did not deign
> To lift her lids, nor did the subtle smile
> Of Mona Lisa deepen. Madeleine
> Still wept against the glory of her hair,

Nor did the lovers part their lips the while,
But kissed unheeding that I watched them there.

In September of 1908, when Sara arrived in St. Louis, the
Teasdales were in the process of building their new home in
Kingsbury Place, an exclusive residential section of the city. One
of the first things that she did was to go to see how the new
house was progressing. At the Lindell Boulevard home she had
a room and bath of her own, but in the new home she was to
have a whole suite of rooms, and, immediately, she began to plan
how she would decorate them. Because she wanted the sun to
pour into her windows, her rooms had been planned for the back
of the second floor, facing the south and west.

Very soon after she returned, also, near the end of September,
Sara went to Attica, Indiana, to visit her friend, Bessie Brey,
who had married a minister. Coming back on the train to St.
Louis, she spent most of the three hours of the trip writing her
long poem, "Helen of Troy."

The next few weeks passed happily in reading, writing, and
resting. As her doctor thought it would do his patient good to be
out in the air daily, Sara went for a drive every morning; she
had her own little phaeton, with her insignia on the side, and her
own horse named Lady Clare. To drive out beyond the city into
the rolling countryside where the sumac was blooming and the
trees were brilliant with autumn colors filled her heart with great
joy.

She started to take private French lessons, which added a new
interest to her pattern of daily living, and her correspondence,
which always played an important part in her life, was becoming
increasingly absorbing.

Before Sara had left for Connecticut, she had sent a letter to
John Myers O'Hara, a poet who was as devoted to Greek literature and life as she was, asking him where she could obtain a
copy of his privately printed *Sappho,* which she had seen reviewed in *The Papyrus.* O'Hara, who had been born in St. Louis,

was working in Chicago. Since Sara had never met him and did not know how to get in touch with him, she put the letter away for some time without mailing it. Finally, however, it occurred to her that Mr. Reedy could give her O'Hara's address, which he did. Mr. O'Hara immediately made Sara a gift of his book, and she, in turn, sent him a copy of *Sonnets to Duse,* and for a number of years after this they continued to write to each other, although it was some time before they actually met.

Influenced by John Myers O'Hara, Sara had become interested in Lafcadio Hearn's writings, and just by chance, when she was staying at the Pomeroy Cottage in Gloucester, in September of 1908, she found one of Hearn's books on Japan and read it. The idea of Japanese incense had always intrigued her, and one of her most appealing little lyrics in *Sonnets to Duse* speaks of it:

> And here beneath an alien sky
> Your breath ascends,
> A column delicate and grey
> That waves and bends,

> And lifts a scent of sandal-wood,
> Devoid of prayer,
> To seek an ancient Eastern god
> Through Western air.

Now this land of cherry blossoms, tinkling wind chimes, and strange and colorful temples began to hold an even greater fascination for her. Her mother bought her a small ivory Japanese girl with a sunshade over her head, which she treasured greatly.

On the day that Sara learned of her first acceptance from the *Atlantic Monthly,* Nancy Coonsman happened to be at her home visiting her. Sara was so happy that she wanted to celebrate this occasion in true Japanese style, and her visitor recalled in later years: "When I arrived, she had me taken upstairs to her own quarters in her lovely home. The room was darkened, and in the middle of the room Japanese floor lanterns were placed around a floor tea table, and Sara greeted me with a positively glowing face and told me the good news that the *Atlantic* had written her just that day; she waved the letter and check gaily—she was just bubbling over. So she gave me a kimono to dress up in and she, of course, did the same; we sat ourselves down on the floor, and she proceeded to pour tea. It is so long ago now—we were like children in our enjoyment of the moment. But the thing that comes through most clearly is the memory of her glowing face and the quality of her voice, a throaty and rich voice. We drank little cup after little cup of tea, toasting her happiness in being 'accepted'; we were really in another world that afternoon long ago."

Mr. O'Hara soon sent Sara a second copy of his *Sappho* to give to another friend, whom she had met only by mail, and who loved the work of the Grecian lyricist as much as she did. This was Marion Cummings Stanley, a poet, and a teacher of philosophy at the University of Arizona.

Sara had become acquainted with Marion Cummings Stanley through Fred Macaulay, a student of Mrs. Stanley's. Mr. Macaulay knew Sara personally and admired her poetry very much. He lent his copy of *Sonnets to Duse* to Marion, and this prompted Marion to send a letter to Sara, in which she said:

I have thought of you so much these last weeks since I discovered you that you have grown to be almost as real a presence in my house of life, as is your friend Mr. Macaulay—and that is very real indeed, for you must know I see him always three times a week at college in philosophy and at least twice a week here at home. However I had really met you before Mr. Macaulay came. It was one day when I was reading the verse in some back numbers of *Poet Lore*. I was in a critical mood and could find nothing that seemed to me really magnificent—until I came to your sonnet on "Silence." I read that carefully and said to myself—This at last is the real thing, and then I remember distinctly (for it was something so unusual) dreaming over the name for a while, and wondering, "Who can Sara Teasdale be and where is she?"

So you see when in the course of our first conversation Mr. Macaulay mentioned your name, I realized we had something in common even more exciting than philosophy. . . .I feel that I must tell you how delighted I am to know your work—and how very happy it would make me if I could know you, too—for I have felt perfectly sure from the first that I should love you.

* * *

There are so many things I should love to tell you and to talk to you about. I should tell you all about Tucson—I know you would be interested in the picturesque flat-roofed adobes of the Mexican quarter—and the quaint old Mission that is almost as old as American independence, and best of all to me, the wide free sweep of the mesa all around us. It stretches out straight from my back door, away and away to the bright blue shadowed masses of the Santa Catalina Mountains. Then I should talk to you about Rossetti—and Gautier—and *The Letters of a Portuguese Nun*—and D'Annunzio, (O how I love *Francesca da Rimini!*) . . . .

As a result of the stimulating correspondence that followed this letter and served to develop the congeniality of the two poets, Marion suggested in late October that Sara come to Tucson to spend the winter, for she felt that this change to a dry and sunny climate would be excellent for Sara's health.

After some persuasion, Mr. and Mrs. Teasdale agreed for Sara to go, and they made plans to send along with her one of their house maids, Mary, in the capacity of nurse, cook, and companion.

At that time Marion and her husband were living in a flat-roofed, white stucco house, which seemed like a miniature Greek temple. Only a short distance from the University of Arizona, it stood on the edge of the desert, not far from the innumerable little tents where tubercular patients lived alone, many of them penniless, eking out a hand-to-mouth existence, while hoping that the desert sunshine would work a miracle for them. Marion, who possessed a deeply compassionate soul and a sweet and lovely face, would frequently go among these poor sufferers, cheering them by her words of encouragement and, even more, by her radiant presence.

It had been arranged for Sara to live in a small cottage about one hundred yards away from that of the Stanleys', which they had built in 1905. The cottage was on the corner of Mountain Avenue and Speedway, three blocks north of the dining hall of the University.

Sara was enchanted with the little house and with the desert; the radiant sunsets, the deep purple of the mountains, and the brilliant stars all struck a responsive chord in her heart. One night she spent outdoors, but she slept very little, as the coyotes baying in the mountains frightened her, and the dazzling starry heavens kept her awake with their disturbing beauty. A poem by Marion called "The Question" described such an experience:

Goaded by the Eternal Question
My restless soul drove me forth into the night.
Out into the desert I wandered,
Alone with the silence, alone with the dark, alone with
    the watching eyes of all the stars.

I felt the earth rock on the deeps of the Infinite
As a little boat tossed on the tides of a boundless sea.
I felt the quiver of time's restless leap, from calm to calm
    of two eternities.

And I cried aloud to the night and to the silence, to
    Time and to Eternity,
And to all the watching eyes of the stars I cried aloud,
"Whence? Whither? What? A word, but a single word
    of the Secret!"

Then all the night was filled with troubled yearning,
And slowly back from the earth and the sky,
Back from the silence and the desert and the infinite
    night

Came the question.
The Eternal Mystery beat upon me insistently from the
    burning eyes of the stars,—
Pricked my soul with points of pain that grew intolerable
Even as excess of light and sound becomes at last
    intolerable to the outwearied senses.

Then I fled away from the desert and the night,
Back to a narrow room—back to the little laughter and
    chatter of men and women;
I fled away that I might hide my soul from the wonder
    of the desert and the night,
That I might hide my Darkness from the Question in
    the eyes of the burning stars.

Sara and Marion were greatly amused when the Tucson paper
announced that "Mrs. Sarah Tisdell, the noted verse writer of
St. Louis, has rented a cottage for the winter on East Speedway
with her maid." It was a new and exciting experience for Sara
to manage a little house all her own. For the first time, however,
she realized how costly the maintaining of a home can be, and
frequently she had to write to her father to send more money
for household expenses.

The days in Arizona passed happily for Sara; she had a kitten
that was much company for her, and her maid, Mary, had an
endless store of Irish folk lore at her finger tips. While Sara was
eating her dinner alone, Mary would sit down and entertain
her with fascinating stories of Celtic superstitions. Marion, who
was busy with her University duties, saw as much of Sara as she
possibly could and had lunch with her every day. Every night,
too, she would walk the short distance from her home to have a
talk with Sara before she went to bed. The devoted Mary called
Sara "Baby," and it was not long before Marion, too, started
calling Sara by this affectionate term.

Early in December, Mamie's husband, Joseph Wheless, stopped
by to see Sara on his way to Mexico. He found her well and

happy, and since she dearly loved to have someone read aloud to her, he entertained her by reading from the *Odyssey*.

The two and a half months that Sara stayed in Tucson proved to be a very rich interval in her life. Marion, who was beloved by all who knew her, became a devoted and cherished friend, as well as a dependable critic of Sara's poetry. Because Tucson, though thinly settled at that time, was a very popular health resort, and because the University was located there, authors, critics, and other interesting personalities were present in the little town from time to time. The contacts with these teachers and writers were all enjoyable to Sara. Dr. Ernest Sutherland Bates, American biographer, historian, and critic, had become a Professor of English at the University shortly before Sara's arrival, and he became a close friend of Marion's. Michael Williams, founder and first editor of *The Commonweal*, and author of *The Book of the High Romance*, also visited Tucson with his wife, Margaret, and they, too, became closely associated with and fond of Marion.

It is easy to understand why Marion Stanley attracted loyal and devoted friends. A highly gifted individual, with an excellent mind cast in a prophetic mould, she was poet, philosopher, and scholar, and possessed a spirit that was altogether generous and unselfish. She was eight years older than Sara, having been born on February 15, 1876, in San José, California, where her early life had not been easy. Christened Alice Marion, she was called Alice by her father and Marion by her mother. When she was a child, her parents had separated. She remained with her mother, and the two lived in the most straitened circumstances, her mother taking in boarders, giving guitar lessons, and doing everything possible to keep her home together. Mrs. Cumming[1] centered her whole life around her only child and made great sacrifices for her education. The frail little girl was unusually bright and won a Phoebe Hearst scholarship to the University of California at Berkeley. Here she wrote poetry, excelled in phil-

[1]The family name was Cumming, but Marion spelled her name Cummings.

osophy, and because of her outstanding scholarship, attracted the attention of William Pepperrell Montague, who was then an Instructor at the University of California, and who later went on to Columbia University to become a distinguished name in American philosophy. Her college career was interrupted by ill health, but she received her degree in 1901 with Phi Beta Kappa membership.

Not long after graduation and her marriage to Bruce M. Stanley, she accepted a position on the faculty of the University of Arizona; her husband worked for the Southern Pacific Railroad in Tucson, and Mrs. Cumming made her home with them.

Though she was a lyric poet and was writing poetry at the time that Sara visited her, the scope of Marion's mind extended to more serious and comprehensive interests. She was greatly concerned with far-reaching philosophic matters, and, especially, a little later, with an enduring and idealistic concept of world peace that she called "Life-Idealism" as opposed to "Death-Idealism," which, in the form of war and patriotism, seemed to her to be dominating the western world around 1914. In later years, too, she wrote powerful poems in free verse, in which she showed her humanitarian outlook, such as "Eugene Debs in Cincinnati," for even in her poetry she could not wholly lose her genuine concern for mankind. Marion felt a depth of compassion for the bleeding heart of the world, and this was one of her most endearing qualities.

Already feeling very close to each other because of their letters and poetry, Marion and Sara became intimate and devoted friends in the days that followed Sara's arrival, though the two were different in many ways. For Sara, used to the care and freedom from hard work that material resources can bring, had learned to hoard her strength and had lived a far more secluded life than Marion had; she also possessed a valuable quality of organization and orderliness that enabled her to send her poems off over and over for submission to periodicals until they were accepted, and to get her books in order for publication in a systematic way, when the time came. On the other hand, Marion, who had been used to hard work and a struggle for existence, gave of her strength and vitality lavishly to all demands that were made upon her. The development of her philosophic ideas was more important to her than actual publication; very little of her precious time was spent on the routine task of getting work in order to submit it for publication.

But the two writers had much in common: frail health, the writing of poetry, a gentleness of spirit, an appreciation for intellectual interests, and a passion for beauty. A comparison of their early poetry will easily show why each one was attracted to and influenced by the work of the other. For in some of their poems there is a striking similarity of theme and style. Both spoke often of love, both used simple, unadorned language, and both wrote brief and delicately appealing lyrics.

The following poem by Marion illustrates this, for it could have been written by either of these friends:

APRIL TWILIGHT

How soft the shade is gathering
  Between the day and night;
A late lark cannot cease to sing,
  An early star is white.

One star still sweet along the land,
  One star in heaven above—
The Spring that cannot cease to sing,
  The star of love.

At the time of her stay in Arizona, Sara had published only one book of poetry; Marion had not published any book and did not publish one in her lifetime, but a number of her individual poems appeared from time to time in such periodicals as *The Forum, The Smart Set, Harper's, Lippincott's, The Commonweal, Poet Lore,* and *Everybody's.* Both of the poets were included in Ferdinand Earle's *The Lyric Year,* and both became members of the Poetry Society of America, which was founded in 1910. In the first bulletin issued by the Society in December of 1913, Marion's poem, "The Spirit and the Bride," was listed as one of those read by Dr. Merle St. Croix Wright at the November meeting:

When all my ravished senses sank
    Swooning to call her beauty mine,
When from her heart's red cup I drank
    Her kisses up like wine,

Oh, sad with riven robes of white
    I saw my lonely soul beside,
And sharp across the flaming night
    The wounded spirit cried.

When through realms of heavenly light
    My eager soul with joy doth run
Her eyes beneath the stars are bright,
    Her hair against the sun.

Oh God, and shall they never greet
    Who go so long unsatisfied,
The one with restless fevered feet,
    The one with wounded side?
Or past the world's rim shall they meet,
    The spirit and the bride?

During her Arizona visit, Sara was working on many of the lyrics and other poems that were to make up her second book, *Helen of Troy*. Because the two friends were both so deeply drawn to the Grecian age of glory, they were intrigued by the story of Helen. Sara's poem about her became the title poem in her second volume; Marion also wrote a long poem in blank verse about her, "Helen at Troy." Even in the blank verse of these two monologues, the style of these poets is very similar. Helen says through Sara's poem:

I will not give the grave my hands to hold,
My shining hair to light oblivion.

· 122 ·

And the Helen of Marion's poem speaks to the gods in the same lyric and tragic mood:

> For thou hast made of me a flaming brand
> Snatched from the hearth I warmed to fire the world;
> Mine eyes are stars to lead men down to death. . . .

About Sappho, another mutual interest of the two friends, each also wrote moving monologues in blank verse, and here again is a strong similarity of thought and presentation in their lines concerning the last hours of the Greek lyricist's life.

Sara and Marion had planned to have regular lessons in philosophy and psychology, and to read French together, but they never got around to much of this. There were too many things to talk about, and the hours went by on shining wings. Sara showed Marion some copies of *The Potter's Wheel* and told her in detail about her gifted friends.

These weeks in Sara's life bore a fruitful harvest of songs, for it was Sara's delight to write the ecstatic lyrics in which she excelled and to give them to her friend for her pleasure and criticism. Where before her lyrics had been mainly addressed to someone impersonal or unknown (with the exception of Bessie Brey), who strongly attracted her romantic and imaginative nature, like Eleonora Duse, now suddenly she possessed a rare friend, a spirit worthy indeed of devotion, whose very presence in the world served as a key that could unlock a treasure of lyric rapture. Given an ideal and an inspiration, Sara used her own particular kind of poetic genius to weave endless songs around it, and it was not hard for her to idealize Marion Cummings Stanley. It was important for her creative nature to have a "peg to hang Pegasus on," as Will Parrish used to say. "The Wanderer" was written to Marion; and in Marion's copy of Dante's *La Vita Nuova,* Sara inscribed the second "Triolet" that was also written to Marion and published in *Helen of Troy* with a note to this effect. "Primavera Mia," one of Sara's finest sonnets from this period, is another poem that was composed for Marion.

Of all of Sara's poems to Marion, perhaps the one that became the best known and best loved is the little lyric called "Song," also written in Arizona:

> You bound strong sandals on my feet,
>   You gave me bread and wine,
> And sent me under sun and stars,
>   For all the world was mine.
>
> Oh, take the sandals off my feet,
>   You know not what you do;
> For all my world is in your arms,
>   My sun and stars are you.

Sara loved Marion as deeply as she had loved anyone until that time in her life. It was a source of the greatest pleasure to her that a person so morally fine, so intellectually gifted, and so highly regarded by eminent persons in literary and philosophic fields should care deeply for her and be genuinely interested in her well-being and her literary career.

Not long before she left Tucson, she wrote in the copy of *Sonnets to Duse* that she had given her friend:

FOR MARION

> Before my golden sun arose
> The false dawn's fleeting light
> Allured these little birds of song
>   From sleep and night.
>
> And now they should be covered close,
> Their heralding is done,
> Save that for once I let them see
>   In you the sun.
>   S.T.T. Jan. 25, 1909

That Marion understood her friend wonderfully well, indeed, is revealed in an undated letter that she wrote her, probably

Marion Cummings

University of California
Berkeley
1901

soon after Sara returned to St. Louis from Tucson. Since each of them was always vitally concerned for the other's health, Marion wrote:

My heart fell—oh fathoms deep! when I saw the pencil address on my letter for I was afraid it meant you were sick. . . .

. . . I don't know what I should do if I felt that you were at all seriously ill. But oh, my precious baby, it is almost more than I can stand to know you are suffering even when I feel reassured about your safety. And yet sometimes I get to feeling worried through and through, not at all because of your present physical condition— but because of your temperament and environment combined. As to your physical condition when you left—my confidence in your curability and my assurance about the means of cure are increased at least threefold since the days I wrote such hopeful letters about your coming. . . .

Then Marion went on to mention that she felt that some of Sara's life habits, some of her greatest blessings, even, such as her family, her means, and "the consequent utter lack of any incentive" to force Sara "into the objective world" all stood in the way of her really getting well.

For Marion knew from experience the vast compensations of the creative artist's strong inner life, but she also knew the terrific drain that it makes upon the nervous system, and she had but one answer for it, the thing that she had known all of her life: work.

. . . You, the ideal life for you, is in many ways such a fundamental change. Nobody can understand how you live—what you use in living, I'm sure, but one who knows it from within as I do. So perhaps nobody else could tell you as I can the startling truth that it is probable that often you use in a single day with almost no purely intellectual or physical activity more units of force than the servant who puts ten solid hours on manual labor in your kitchen, or say, the antiquarian who puts in an eight hour day at his desk; you use more than even I, I am sure, in some of my most strenuous days—for often my most strenuous are least exhausting. . . .

... You see, the doctors realize in a general way that the drain on your system, whatever it is, should be stopped and they think it can be done by removing all incoming impressions of every sort possible—but they don't realize that people like us have a little factory inside where we can turn out enough excitement in a day's time to equal the ordinary cumulated stimulus that comes to the average person in a month. I'm thinking of myself, my blessed, when I was your age. You see, the great thing is to shut down the supply inside—and the best way to do that is to get a fair supply without—for you aren't going to be dead till you are, for all the doctors, and that's what it would amount to to have no feeling at all. It's like fighting fire with fire—it's the only way in the wood, you know; a small fire will keep back a great conflagration. Well, you see, dear—you have seen before, but I want you to understand so fully —why I feel that if I could choose for you one gift, the greatest, the best, that I could imagine in all the world,—it would be not even just now the love of a good man or fame, it would be—work. Because I think that perhaps, as it says in the Bible, that if you had this—after a while all these would be added to you; but that I think would mean most for your happiness. And it's just like being good—you can't be good because you want to be happy and then *be* happy—and you can't work altogether because you want to be happy—'tho in either case I think you will be happier in doing them even for that reason than in not doing them at all; but you must work because you want to accomplish something or because you feel a moral obligation to discharge to life (a little of both is, I think, the most satisfactory). You should assume that you have a long and fairly healthy life before you; you have genius and you should feel that you are responsible for making it most effective for yourself and the world; you should live a rather ordered life— almost a good part of the day laid out for various kinds of development that you need; and you would have the satisfaction of lying down at night in the consciousness that you were doing your heaven appointed part in the evolution of the universe though you were able to do only the tiniest bit each day; there is a genuine tonic in achievement, however small—and things are relative anyway—so it's in relation to one's power.

In spite of the wonderful qualities of character that Marion possessed, the tragedy of her life was that much of her work was not completed at the time of her death, and none of her philosophic studies was ever published. She compiled two anthologies of poetry and wrote *A Book of Life,* a text dealing with the evolution of life upon the earth, but these, too, remained unpublished, as did also her study of the Book of Job.

In 1913 a crisis was reached in Marion's life. At this time she and Mr. Stanley agreed to separate, and, later, they were divorced, although they remained friends for the rest of their lives. Always frail in body, Marion was worn out with long hours of teaching, lectures at various clubs in town, and other duties that drained her strength. She now decided to make a change, to strike out in a new direction and put some of her idealistic ideas into practice, and to try to interest some publisher in her work at the same time. Though her mother, who had centered her life around Marion, looked on askance, bitterly opposed, thinking that her daughter was scattering to the four winds all her opportunities and talents, Marion made up her mind to go to New York alone and seek a new life. Because she was honestly concerned with helping the world to find happiness, she evolved a plan for introducing certain selected men and women to each other— people who would never have met, but who would make ideal life partners. For this, she interviewed in New York churchmen, doctors, psychologists, teachers, and other prominent people.

But just as the hardest part of her work was done, just as success seemed imminent, word came from Tucson that her mother was critically ill; and though Marion left New York at once, Mrs. Cumming died on December 18 before Marion arrived home, and without a word from her daughter since the message telling of her arrival in New York, except a telegram after news of her illness came. Always the kindest of people, Marion was overcome with remorse. The only reason that she had not written to her mother was that she wanted to surprise her skeptical parent with word of success, and each day it seemed as if she could send this news in the next little while.

Mrs. Cumming's death was a stunning blow to Marion's plans and to her spirit. Her new project was completely abandoned, and, suffering intensely, she remained for a time in Tucson, blaming herself entirely for her mother's death. In her honorable and idealistic code of ethics, it seemed only fair for life to extract from her the suffering that she thought she had inflicted on her mother.

She never wholly threw off the terrible shock that the timing of her mother's death had given her, and when the first World War started in 1914, this only deepened her sense of despair. Because she was truly dedicated to wanting to make the world a better place in which to live, because there seemed little that she could do to stop the ominous guns of war, she became even more sick at heart. The world's illness became her own—a personal and deeply felt thing.

In the summer of 1915, Professor Montague introduced Marion to a protégé of his, then teaching at Columbia, Dr. Henry Slonimsky, who had been educated abroad, receiving his Ph.D. degree from Marburg University in 1912. The two had much in common, and in December of 1916 they were married. Soon afterwards, they moved to Baltimore, where Dr. Slonimsky was teaching at Johns Hopkins. Though Marion was continually ill during the next ten years, she expended much effort on her philosophic theories. She had developed an interest in the Far East and its future, and she foretold much of what has come to pass today in that region. A friend who visited her during those days recalls that she was working feverishly, feeling that the message she had for the world was far more important than even life itself. But the people with whom she discussed her ideas were not very much interested at that time. Her work was not organized, never finished; she went further and further into her subject matter; one idea gave birth to another and that to another, and at her death, only fragments of writing and nothing completed of her Far Eastern philosophic studies remained.

Marion Cummings Slonimsky died of cancer in 1926, in New York City. Dr. Slonimsky had her body cremated and the ashes placed in the Evergreen Cemetery, in Tucson, where her mother lies.

Some thirty-one years after her death, in 1957, a selection of her poems was privately printed in an edition of one hundred numbered volumes, which were given to libraries throughout the country. Called simply *Poems* by Marion Cummings (for some of her poetry was published under her maiden name), this book remains as a small memorial to a gifted, highly sensitive, and lovable human being, who, endowed with an exceptional mind, also suffered, like Cassandra, from the gift of prophecy without recognition. In the *Foreword* to this little book, Dr. Slonimsky wrote: "Her poetry was the smallest part of her. She was a tragic and saintly figure: tragic, in that all her efforts seemed to be doomed to frustration; saintly, because she had the supreme form of genius, namely moral genius, the love for all living things."

For a number of years after her stay in Tucson, Sara referred to Marion as her "best friend"; and though they did not see each other often, they kept in touch by frequent letters.

Many of the poems that appeared in *Helen of Troy* were written under Marion's influence and with her advice, and several poems of Sara's refer directly to the Arizona scene where she spent twelve happy weeks. One is called simply "Night in Arizona" and was published in *Rivers to the Sea*. Another, "Day's Ending (Tucson)," which is especially revealing for the new maturity of spirit that Sara found in Arizona, was not published in a book until 1926, in *Dark of the Moon*, after Marion had died. The last two verses of this poem are:

> It was not long I lived there
> But I became a woman
> Under those vehement stars,
> For it was there I heard

For the first time my spirit
Forging an iron rule for me,
As though with slow cold hammers
Beating out word by word:

"Only yourself can heal you,
Only yourself can lead you,
The road is heavy going
And ends where no man knows;
Take love when love is given,
But never think to find it
A sure escape from sorrow
Or a complete repose."

In 1924, many years after her Arizona stay, Sara sent Harriet
Monroe a poem for publication in *Poetry;* she told the editor
that the full title of this poem was "Epitaph for a Poet" or "Epitaph for M.C."; but they agreed, finally, to publish it with only
"Epitaph" for the title. This poem was also printed in *Dark of
the Moon,* and, significantly, it was included under the section
called "Portraits." Although Miss Monroe never did know to
whom M.C. referred, surely it must have been to Marion Cummings; and very probably the death of a poet of which Sara
Teasdale spoke was not a literal death, but the relinquishing of
the lyric medium of expression by a poet who was becoming more
and more involved, heart and soul, in the deep and far-reaching
philosophic problems of the twentieth century.

So be it; let the snow sift deep and cover
All that was drunken once with light and air....

Knowing its background, one cannot read this poem without
recalling Robert Frost's observation that poets die in many ways—
and one of these ways is that some poets die into philosophers.

Chapter 7

EXPANDING HORIZONS

•

WHEN Sara returned with her maid, Mary, to St. Louis from Tucson on the night of February 4, 1909, she carried with her a picture of Marion that she kept in her watch case, some of Marion's poems, and a copy of Sophocles's *Antigone* that Marion had given her to read on the train.

Soon after she arrived home, she went to see Grace and Will Parrish, who were planning to leave for New York in a few days to hear Mary Garden in *Salome*. The Parrish sisters had taken some interesting pictures while Sara had been away, and she asked them to give her one of Grace made up as Salome to send Marion. She showed them Marion's picture and read them her "Helen at Troy." They were very much impressed with what Sara told them of her new friend, and Will, characteristically, said she would like to "take her up." Knowing how much Marion already had on her shoulders, and feeling that she did not have the time or strength to add another correspondent to her list, even if it were Will, Sara did not encourage this idea. Eventually, when she came to St. Louis, Marion did meet some of Sara's friends.

Because the family expected to move to the new home around the first of June, and because Sara did not want to be involved in this ordeal, she returned to Connecticut again in May for a rest. When she changed trains in New York on the way, Will Parrish met her and took her for a drive around the city; this brief glimpse of New York intoxicated Sara, and she was eager to come back and stay longer.

In July she returned to St. Louis from Connecticut for a few days before joining her mother and father who had already gone on to Charlevoix. She was delighted with her attractive little suite, which consisted of a bedroom, bath, and library-study with four casement windows that opened upon a small porch. Her bedroom was decorated in green and white. The library-study, which was her special joy, had a bay window on the west side with three panels of glass over the window seat. The walls were green and the woodwork was brown; in the winter Sara intended to have a red Persian rug on the floor. Here she arranged her desk, bookcase, couch, and two comfortable chairs. Her goldfish were given a place of honor; and on the wall she hung a copy of Leonardo da Vinci's "The Last Supper." Over the bay window was a little decorated piece of vellum with these words on it from St. Francis of Assisi:

Blessed is the man to whom no created thing can bring evil, but more blessed is he who from everything he sees and hears receiveth good to the edifying of himself.

After she had arranged her rooms to her satisfaction, she went on to Charlevoix to spend the summer. In August Marion visited her there, and at Altasand the two friends spent many happy hours together, walking through the woods and on the beach, rowing on the lake, or sitting in the little summer house, poring over the poems that were to become Sara's second book. Marion gave her valuable advice and criticism about many of her lines, and Sara deeply appreciated her friend's interest and help.

When Sara returned home from Charlevoix in September of 1909, Marion came with her and left for Arizona from St. Louis. Because Marion had persuaded Sara to go back to regular studying again, she enrolled for two classes at Washington University. She had wanted to take astronomy very much, but as it seemed more sensible to arrange classes that came on the same day and near the same time, this was impossible. The trip out to the University from Sara's home necessitated quite a walk to the nearest car stop, then the taking of two different street cars, one of which ran only every half hour or so; after this there was a long walk to the University with many steps to climb when one got there. This tiring trip was, for Sara, something of an ordeal, especially in bad weather.

She finally compromised on a course called *History of Ancient Philosophy,* which included the Ionian Schools to the Neo-Platonists, and a course in French composition and conversation.

On September 25 she spent her first day in the two classes. There were five other girls in the philosophy class, and the textbook was Roger's *History of Philosophy.* Professor Charles Cory impressed Sara as a pleasant and interesting person, and since the class was to make a study of Greek philosophy, she decided to give her teacher a copy of "Helen of Troy," when *Scribner's,* which had accepted it, published this poem. She anticipated with delight his surprise when he discovered that one of his pupils was a poet. Professor Cory remembers his talented student of those far-away days as a "very gentle, sensitive woman, somewhat delicate in appearance. She had a quick intelligence and a pleasing manner."

The French class did not appeal to Sara so much. The work seemed hard, and the professor, somehow, did not stimulate her as Professor Cory did; she soon withdrew from this class.

She completed the philosophy course, but because she did not take the final examination, her course was marked *incomplete.* Undoubtedly, her reason for not taking the examination was that she had no desire to acquire college credits; she merely wanted to learn more about the subject matter.

During the latter part of 1909, Sara read Housman's *A Shropshire Lad* for the first time and was thrilled by it. For the rest of her life this little book remained very dear to her.

Sometimes, when she was busy reading or writing, the sound of Mr. Wheless's typewriter heard busily pounding away on the second floor would be too much for her, for Sara loved a quiet house; then she would take her things to the third floor and sleep up there in peace and solitude for a while. This location also had the advantage of being far away from the slamming of doors and the banging of pots and pans in the kitchen by the servants, who started their household chores early in the morning. For a time Sara considered moving all her possessions up to the third floor, but she could not bring herself to give up the little library-study that was filled with her precious books and pictures.

Having been ill so much with grippe during the winter, Sara went with her mother to St. Augustine in January of 1910. The Valencia, where they stayed, proved to be a pleasant hotel, and the climate was as warm as June. Under the tonic influence of the southern sun, Sara seemed to improve greatly, and Mrs. Teasdale left her in Florida when she went home in March. Someone in St. Augustine showed Sara how to write her first name in Greek, and this especially pleased her; it delighted her to be able to sign her letters to John Myers O'Hara in this fashion. In St. Augustine, too, she continued private French lessons, and, as always, spent much of her time reading.

In April she came home in much better health, and in May she went to Saxton's Farm for a few days; here, in the refreshing atmosphere of rural charm and peace, she wrote the little one-act play called "On the Tower," which appeared in the first edition of *Helen of Troy.*

The summer of 1910 found the family in Charlevoix, as usual, and during this time a very unpleasant affair happened that almost ruined their vacation. Their next-door neighbor brought a suit against Mr. Teasdale, on the grounds that it was unsanitary to have a stable where his was located, although this matter had previously been investigated fully and settled to the satisfaction of the town. As Mr. Teasdale was now over seventy, and since he was the very soul of honor, courtesy, and Christian kindness, this sort of public dispute almost killed him; the strain of long days in court was as hard on his spirit as on his body, and it was heightened by his devotion to his horses, the loss of which would have distressed him unbearably. However, the residents of the town, who had known and respected the Teasdales for many years, were on their side, and the case was decided in Mr. Teasdale's favor.

Marion came back to Charlevoix for another brief visit in September of 1910—and again the two friends enjoyed every minute of being together in the lovely surroundings.

In December of 1910, the Potters, who had continued their friendships, although they were now absorbed in their own careers and interests, held a Christmas reunion party at the home of Ned Wahlert, who had married Walter McCourt. Will and Grace were in Europe and could not be present. Petronelle, also, was not able to attend, but she had sent a check for what the Scribe called the "Potterpourri," and she soon received a long letter from Vine vividly describing the occasion:

I promised to tell you about our Potter party. It was as unique as any that preceded it, I assure you. *Everybody* came, although Nancy had a dying grandfather and Sara an imminent sore throat. It was a night of beastly rain, and we were all heavily laden with suitcases full of blankets, with umbrellas, and muffs—and we had to find Ned's house in wild Kirkwood, in the pitchy darkness. We sent ambassadors to the conductor so frequently that at last every soul on the car knew our destination, and a number of men called out, "Webster Avenue!" as we filed down the aisle. When we finally stacked our dripping umbrellas on Ned's porch, Caroline and I signalled the approach of the party by a vigorous "Hoo—aah!" The house had been converted into a spiderweb, by endless strings attached to the cards on the staircase. Our names, and a verse, were on the cards, and we followed the clues all over the house until we found their ends pinned with a holly sprig to our pillows. We nearly strangled each other with string. Then Ned and Nancy threw back the folding doors, and a scene of great splendor greeted our enraptured vision. A lighted tree [was] in the middle of the table and one of Nancy's cute baby cupids at each place. The color scheme of the supper did not dawn upon us until we discovered that what we took for shrimp or cheese was really pink butter. Nancy and Ned had produced a weird-looking feast by dyeing things pink or red. The water was bright pink, the butter was rose color, there were red-hots, tomato soup, ham, peppers, pink jellies, pink-iced cakes, red fruit-salad, and the greatest triumph, *cerise* mashed potatoes. You don't know how exciting it was to wait for the next course! We had been having great sport at the expense of Miss Halstead's book, *A Victorious Life,* whose heroine "pulsates with vitality" and sensuous appeal. So when these red topped macaroons appeared we called them "Halstead kisses." We began the banquet by drinking a toast to the absent Potters, in the pink water. After the dinner, we sat around Ned's open fire, and read William's letter aloud, amid peals of appreciation. After that, the watchword was "A certain amount of chastity is desirable." It was proposed that we get into our gowns and pajamas and sit around the fire late, but as Ned's husband was to return at half past eleven, we concluded that a certain amount of chastity was desirable. I slept between Celia and Caroline, and they sharpened their elbows on me all night. Caroline insists that what I called her elbow was really her back. At about 3 P.M. Gussie came and lay across our feet, and we tried hard to bore her so that she wouldn't stay, but our wit and charm proved irresistible, even though we were dead sleepy. Earlier in the evening Ned had told C.R. not to lie stretched out on the floor. "Remember this is a rented house." She meant the floor was full of cracks and drafts. After we were all in bed, a horrible door began to bang in the night wind. Every one was so sleepy she waited for someone else to get up and kill the door. Finally Celia, of the fair locks, arose in her pink pajamas, and saying, "O damn!" dashed into the hall. As she didn't come back, Caroline went after her, and got lost in the passages and went feeling pathetically along the walls. And then we began making ribald jests on the door. "Remember, it's only a rented door!" "Do they rent the bang with the house?" "I could make remarks on the situation, hinging on the door . . ." etc. Mr. McCourt didn't appear until breakfast time, which just shows what *can* be done with a husband. Poor chap— Nancy borrowed his raincoat and cap, Caroline his dressing-gown, and I his bed slippers, and he was turned out of his own house by a mob of Potters.

Besides the Potters and the Associate Members, there were in St. Louis a few other friends whom Sara saw now and then, who had the same cultural interests that she had. Zoë Akins, who was writing poetry and plays, had acted with the Odeon Stock Company while it was playing in St. Louis, and was now the secretary for her father, postmaster of that city; she saw Sara frequently. At that time Miss Akins was arranging her book of poetry, *Interpretations,* for an American publication in 1911, and Will Parrish and Sara went over the manuscript with her and offered their suggestions.

Hugh Ferriss, who was studying architecture at Washington University and trying his hand at creative writing in spare moments, saw Sara at her home now and then and sometimes went driving with her. One Sunday afternoon, Zoë Akins and Hugh Ferriss brought Orrick Johns along with them when they called on Sara. Occasionally, after this, these four gifted young people spent some time together, eagerly discussing the things that interested them or attending such a gathering as the Sunday night open house at Mr. George Blackman's home. One wonders what they would have said in those days if some prophet had told them that in the future one of them would win a Pulitzer Prize; one would win the Columbia-Poetry Society of America Prize; the third would win *The Lyric Year* first place award; and the fourth would become a distinguished name in American architecture.

Johns, who was shortly to become a member of the staff of *Reedy's Mirror,* writing criticism of the current dramatic offerings in St. Louis, as well as covering the art exhibitions and reviewing books, found that he had much in common with Sara and soon became a really close friend. In his autobiography, *Time of Our Lives,* he described Sara as he remembered her then:

... Visiting her in those quiet, handsomely furnished rooms, panelled in dark wood, one could not help but think of Elizabeth

Barrett of Wimpole Street, though the conditions were far different; certainly there was not the same parental severity. She was solitary, frail, and a devourer of books; modest about her own lyrics, yet confident and assured when the stanzas satisfied her. Her delight was contagious—it was childlike, extraordinary—when she read something of her own or of another's that pleased her.

. . . her appreciation was keen, and so was her criticism. She had very strong dislikes. Confused or decadent or too-clever work brought quick disapproval from her, but she would labor over a beginner's lines, offering suggestions rather than alterations. She was as firm of character as she was frail of body. The family had a surrey and I often drove with her through the park. One day going over a snowbank, the surrey tipped far over, its side scraped the side of a running trolley and the horse reared. I was at the reins and managed to ease down over the bump and stop the horse, but Sara was cooler than I was. We drove on without talking, and only after we got home did she say that her heart had been in her mouth.[1]

Now and then, Sara and Orrick Johns would send each other the poetry that they had written. An undated letter that Mr. Johns wrote to Sara some time later, probably about one of her poems concerning New York, shows further the spirit of their relationship:

Well, I've been wanting to write to you ever since the minute I got your poem. I like it so much I cannot express it. I mean that quite simply. I have read it I guess a dozen times—which proves much to myself. It is much better than anything cityesque that I have done. I mean that too. It is your destiny to get an exquisite success, with apparent ease and casualness. That is the gift that only poets have. All the rest is imitation. I shall be saying ten years from now, I think, as I have always been saying, that we are all imitations except you. The poem is different too—yet it has all of that inexplicable perfection of technique of yours—yet, I don't know how to say it—it seems to "reach out" more than the others— "take in" more. But you mustn't reach out too much—don't!

[1]Orrick Johns, *Time of Our Lives* (New York: Stackpole Sons, 1937), pp. 179-180.

Your success and value has been due to being satisfied with a corner of the world. Don't understand me to say this disparagingly. I feel that the artist must withdraw. For him, unlike Alexander, the question is how can I reconquer again and again this same world and make it new each time? The trouble with us all is that we don't sit anywhere and let the rest soak in from the same point of view enough. I believe in being level-eyed—the level-eyed prophet sitting on the same rock and seeing the sun go down in the same place—all of experience in that experience—why not? But this poem is *great*. Your repetitions are always effective, I think, and your choice of words so unconsciously perfect. But don't try too hard to conquer the greater areas—you may find you *have* to, which is different. . . .

And he added this postscript:

I have discovered a prayer for artists: "Thank God for our limitations."

In January of 1911, Sara made her first visit of any length to New York. Grace and Will Parrish were there for the winter, and Will made arrangements for Sara to stay at 53 Irving Place, which was a boarding house just down the street from where the Parrish sisters were living. Later, Sara arranged for Orrick Johns to live in this same boarding house when he first came to New York to edit a small paper. Will generously gave up much of her time to show Sara the many interesting things in New York that she wanted to see, and a number of her poems from this period allude to these places.

Here, for the first time, after a constant exchange of letters over a period of two years, she met John Myers O'Hara, who was now employed as a broker in New York. O'Hara, whose first book of poetry, *At Erato's Fane,* had appeared in 1908, and whose second book, *Pagan Sonnets,* was published in 1910, had gained by this time a reputation as a writer greatly influenced by Grecian art and literature. As he suffered from ill health, he did not go about socially very much, and even Sara saw very little of him. He was a devoted son to his parents and never married. Usually, his outlook on life tended to be of a melancholy nature; for Sara he had a genuine affection, and her letters must have been a vital part of his existence. Besides the love of Hellenic life that they shared, her sympathetic spirit understood him very well, and she had a very real admiration for his poems and a sincere interest in him as a friend.

Because Sara loved New York so much, and because John Myers O'Hara lived there, several months later the two poets planned a little volume of sonnets about the city, to be privately printed with merely their initials given as the authors. They intended to have only about thirty copies published, with six or eight to be sent to reviewers, and the others divided evenly between themselves. *Sixteen Sonnets to Manhattan* was to be the name of this book. Mr. O'Hara completed seven of his sonnets, and Sara completed three, "In a Restaurant" being one of these. But although they were enthusiastic about the idea, the work was never finished, and the plans for the book came to nothing. And after considering it more fully, Sara realized that it was almost impossible for her to write poetry without the element of love entering into the lines, and this, she knew, though entirely an innocent performance on her part, so far as Mr. O'Hara was concerned, might be misconstrued by the public.

Madison Cawein, who was then at his height in popularity, sponsored Sara's name for membership in the Poetry Society of America. Still young enough to have a child-like, openhearted joy in meeting the luminous personalities of the poetry world and in hearing her poetry praised by them, she attended her first meeting in February of 1911, when Witter Bynner read her "Helen of Troy" as one of the poems presented for criticism and discussion. Jessie Rittenhouse has spoken of this evening in her autobiography, when "Miss Teasdale, young and eager, tasting the first intoxication of contacts with older poets . . . listened to the beautiful rendering of her poem," while just behind her sat "Ezra Pound, on his one and only visit to the Society, as he was about to sail for England, being unable longer to 'bear the brunt of America.' "[2]

Sara had rented her room on Irving Place for only a month, and with two gentlemen waiting for it as soon as the month was up, she did not have long to stay in New York for this first visit. But it was long enough for her to attend a second meeting of the Poetry Society of America and to make many new friends. Jessie Rittenhouse, who was at that time Secretary of the Poetry Society of America, took Sara under her wing and introduced her to many contemporaries in the literary field. Miss Rittenhouse wanted her to remain longer and planned to give a party in her honor, but this was impossible, and Sara returned to St. Louis in March, her heart filled with beautiful memories of the city that was to become the symbol of joy and delight for her.

The summer was spent in reading the proof for her second book, *Helen of Troy.* It was brought out by Putnam's in the fall of 1911 and given a warm reception, since it showed a decided growth over the first little volume. Orrick Johns, reviewing the book for *Reedy's Mirror,* wrote in glowing terms: "Sara Teasdale as a maker of poignantly perfect songs of simplicity and love outranks all other American poets." The reviewer for the *New York Times* wrote of the book as having the "authentic accent of genius," and Edward J. Wheeler said in *Current Literature:* "Sara Teasdale embarrasses us with her riches." Edwin Markham wrote that "the long poems are lit with imagination and move with a fine and easy dignity," and H. L. Mencken commented in *The Smart Set* that the book contained "poetry reduced to its elementals, and yet who will miss the genuine feeling in it, and the genuine beauty? It is the very simplicity of the thing, indeed, that gives it its charm."

A shower of congratulatory notes and letters descended on Sara from admiring readers; some sent her their own books of poetry just because they liked hers so much. She felt strongly

---

[2]Jessie Rittenhouse, *My House of Life* (New York: Houghton Mifflin Company, 1934), pp. 228-229.

that courtesy demanded that she must answer all of these communications, and, finally, worn out with the excitement and the work, she escaped to Saxton's Farm with Will Parrish for a few days.

Among the letters of commendation was one that led Sara to a rich and satisfying friendship. For in the autumn of 1911 John Hall Wheelock happened to be browsing in a well-known New York book shop; by chance, he picked up *Helen of Troy,* and in his own words, "discovered that there was a new poet in the world." This was the first of her work that he had seen, and recalling this moment years later on a radio broadcast in honor of Sara, he said: ". . . out of the impulse of my excitement I wrote her one of the few letters of this kind that I have ever composed. Her answer was characteristic in its unaffected pleasure and appreciation. Some time later, she came to New York, from her home in St. Louis, on one of her annual visits. We met, and this was the beginning of an intellectual comradeship that was to last until the time of her death."

The dedication in *Helen of Troy* reads: *To Marion Cummings Stanley.* The Parrish family had rather expected that Sara's second volume would be dedicated to Will, but Sara felt so close to Marion at this time, and so many of her poems were intimately linked with her, that she wanted the volume to bear this inscription. Will herself was unconcerned about the matter. One poem, though, had Will's initials over it, and Will explained how this happened: "For New York she had a singing love, and many times has she woven its unique splendor in song. I was with her there in 1911 (her first visit to the Magical City, which afterwards became her home) and together we wandered from one beauty-spot to another, her poet's imagination kindling to its special charm, and the group of six lyrics in *Helen of Troy* was the fruit of our gay wanderings there. Of these songs, she said to me, 'You see, I have put my usual imaginary lover in. I cannot keep him out! I am like Mr. Dick in *David Copperfield* who could not keep the head of King Charles out of his writings. And who will ever imagine when reading these loverlike yearnings that it was just *you and I* who came to these places? It is cruel of S.T.T. to treat you so!' As a sort of recompense, she put 'For W.P.' on the 'Gramercy Park'—though I was never a Peg for Pegasus. Had I been, I could not have known this delightful phrase!"

In January of 1912, Sara went again to New York to attend the annual dinner of the Poetry Society of America. Jessie Rittenhouse had arranged for her to stay at a residence for young ladies on 85th Street, but Sara soon found the noise and confusion there too much for her. When some of the young ladies began practicing their vocal exercises in the middle of the night, she felt that it was time for her to leave. She moved to the Martha Washington Hotel, which advertised itself as the only hotel exclusively for women, and from that time on, until she married, she always made this her New York headquarters. Her parents were willing for her to stay in New York for long periods of time, because they realized that it was to her advantage to take part in the Poetry Society of America meetings and to associate with other writers.

During these days, probably through Jessie Rittenhouse, Sara met and became a friend of Dugald Walker, the artist and illustrator, and Stuart Walker, his brother, then on the stage in New York and later destined to become well known in the history of the American theater. Sara was deeply drawn to the exquisite imaginative quality that pervades Dugald Walker's art work, and she wrote a poem, "Pierrot's Song," to one of his pictures, which was published in *Collier's* and later in *Rivers to the Sea*.

Having told her once that he thought of her as an ideal playmate for fairyland, Dugald Walker sometimes signed his letters to Sara: "Robin." This reference was to one of the most popular poems that Sara ever wrote. Only eight lines long, it captured the public's fancy from its first appearance in *Harper's:*

THE LOOK

Strephon kissed me in the spring,
    Robin in the fall,
But Colin only looked at me
    And never kissed at all.

Strephon's kiss was lost in jest,
    Robin's lost in play,
But the kiss in Colin's eyes
    Haunts me night and day.

"The Look" was widely reprinted, and Sara was besieged with requests for permission to set it to music; this poem was also parodied over and over. With her delightful sense of humor, Sara must have thoroughly enjoyed such rhymes as the following, which appeared in *On the Square* by Tom Terry:

Colin only looked at me
    And never kissed at all
Because his wife was with him
    And he didn't have the gall.

And one can imagine how she must have laughed upon reading these lines in Franklin P. Adams's column, *The Conning Tower*, in the *New York Tribune:*

John invested in the spring,
Arthur in the fall;
But Joey only saved some eggs,
And never bought at all.

Johnny's shares were lost in jest,
Artie's lost in play;
But the eggs that Joey saved
Are going up every day.

These, too, from Wesley's column, *Facts and Fancy,* in the *Boston Transcript,* must have amused her greatly:

Not that Colin did not thirst
Honeyed kiss to sip,
Colin's plan was Safety First,
Colin feared the grip.

As her work and her name had become better known through
frequent periodical publication, Sara, always an excellent and
interesting correspondent, had become acquainted with some of
the most famous names in the literary world. A note compli-
menting a poem or a book would lead to a meeting in person,
and more often than not, this would lead to a friendship of loyalty
and devotion that continued throughout her life. Besides John
Hall Wheelock, John Myers O'Hara, and Jessie Rittenhouse,
such notable authors as Louis and Jean Starr Untermeyer, Amy
Lowell, Harriet Monroe, Thomas S. Jones, Jr., Eunice Tictjens,
Witter Bynner, William Stanley Braithwaite, Joyce and Aline
Kilmer, Edward J. Wheeler, and Marguerite Wilkinson were
among her friends.

The Poetry Society of America dinners in January of each
year, when the annual awards are presented, have always been
colorful occasions, attracting many distinguished, out-of-town
visitors. For years, before this dinner, Jessie Rittenhouse held an
informal gathering for some of the renowned personalities a night
or so before the meeting, in her apartment. Sara, always invited
after her first acquaintance with Miss Rittenhouse, mingled with
the other guests and was given a chance to know them better.
Speaking of those days, Miss Rittenhouse wrote:

St. Louis has contributed a poet to our group, a young and
delightful poet. She has Titian hair, a fair skin and wine-brown
eyes, and wears, as I recall her upon one of these evenings, a cream-
white satin gown with bands of dark fur, exactly the costume for
her type. There is nothing of the blasé about her. She is frankly
happy at being in New York and with the older and longer established members of her craft, though her own lyrics are rapidly mak-

ing for her a secure place. No one is more spontaneously unaffected both in her personality and her work than Sara Teasdale.[3]

The dress that Miss Rittenhouse mentioned was one that had been designed for Sara by Jean Starr Untermeyer, and when the family was at Charlevoix the following summer, burglars broke into the St. Louis home, as they did occasionally when the family was in Michigan, and among the articles stolen was the favorite satin dress, much to Sara's consternation.

Recalling this dress many years later, Jean Starr Untermeyer wrote:

It was a gray (not white) satin with bands of moleskin. This was wonderfully becoming to her fine skin and sandy hair. I remember the occasion when she first wore it. It was a party at our home when we were entertaining the Irish players (or some of them) along with a number of literary friends. Among the players was Sara Allgood, who recited the ballad, "La Glu," in her wonderful voice. Also "My Dark Rosaleen." Our little son, Richard, who early had an eye for such things, noticed Sara's appearance and said to her: "You look more like your name than the other Sara."

Sara often wore gray; this color seemed to have appealed especially to her, and one encounters it frequently in her poetry.

In March of 1912, Edwin Markham gave a reception for Sir William Watson at his Staten Island home, and it was here that Sara met William Stanley Braithwaite, the eminent critic who was then one of the Literary Editors of the *Boston Transcript,* and who was soon to start publishing his annual poetry anthologies, which continued from 1913 through 1929, and in which Sara was always included. Mr. Braithwaite recalled this meeting long afterwards:

I had stepped out from the crowded drawing-room for a bit of air, and standing just outside in the hall were three or four persons. A man stopped me and said, "Is this Mr. Braithwaite?" "Yes," I

[3]*Ibid.,* pp. 285-286.

answered. "I am Louis Untermeyer," he returned, "and I want to know you." Then the lady beside him said, "I want to know you, too. I am Sara Teasdale." She extended her hand for a clasp that was communicative and friendly. It began a friendship that was enriched with many hours of companionship and happy talk. The thing that impressed me first about her is what I call her "openness." Her voice seemed to come like a musical echo from hidden depths of her being. Her face was generally shimmering with a smile, and when it was not on the surface, the shadow of it was just beneath.

It was in April of this same year that Sara, John Myers O'Hara, Louis Untermeyer, Jessie Rittenhouse, and the latter's mother all made a pilgrimage to see Edwin Markham on his sixtieth birthday and to present him, according to Mr. Untermeyer, "with a (figurative) laurel wreath and an (actual) frosted cake." Mr. Untermeyer has described this occasion in his autobiography:

I remember little of our pilgrimage to the author of "The Man with the Hoe" except that a great deal of poetry was read and very little was said. We were all too polite to comment on each other's productions, and we were intimidated by our host, the one among us who had achieved fame (and some fortune) as an oracle. Besides, we were tired. There was a long preliminary ride on the 6th Avenue Elevated (Sara met us at the 28th Street Station), and the longer journey on the three o'clock boat at the South Ferry. Then there was the seemingly interminable trolley trip from St. George to Westerleigh Park, in West New Brighton. The bard welcomed us in vatic strophes—or so it seemed—and his silver-haired wife moved with charm and dignity among the teacups. Looking back from the disadvantage point of years, I see him as a deity dispossessed and declining on a suburban Olympus. But he did not seem that way then. Then it was the god who spoke, a god young at 60, and when we heard thunder in the air we knew whose power released the lightnings. The sonorous voice rose; the rain fell. We returned home in storm and silence.[4]

---

[4]Louis Untermeyer, *From Another World* (New York: Harcourt, Brace, and Company, 1939), p. 165.

Ever since Sara's trip abroad in 1905, she had longed to return. And in May of 1912, armed with an electric stove to combat the chill of Europe, she and Jessie Rittenhouse sailed to Europe to spend the spring and summer. Their destination was first Italy, whose colorful landscape and warm climate especially appealed to them, and then Switzerland and Germany. Miss Rittenhouse's own words give a memorable description of this trip:

...We had planned to spend a number of weeks about the bays of Naples and Salerno, before going on to Rome, and in the sunny afternoons on deck, during the long voyage of twelve or thirteen days lived the scenes in advance, making additions to our flexible itinerary.

I cannot recall a voyage, though I was in the habit of going to Italy in the spring, so warm and delightful as this particular one in which Miss Teasdale and I sat upon the deck without wraps and steeped ourselves in the beauty of the sea, while at intervals we talked of and wrote poetry.

Frequently, we carried our rugs to the upper deck and spread them in the sun while I read or wrote letters and Sara worked upon a long poem which she chanced to be doing at the time....

So the days slipped by until we arrived at Gibraltar, which by some retarding circumstance was reached in the evening. Most of the passengers went ashore, but Miss Teasdale and I elected to remain on board and enjoy the beauty of the lighted town from our favorite vantage-point of the upper deck. The harbor was filled with vessels anchored here and there, each bearing aloft a mast-light:

> A hundred ships in the harbor,
> When evening lit the stars,
> Were resting at their moorings
> With lamps upon their spars,

—began a poem improvised by Sara, of which I have forgotten the remainder. At any rate, the night with its tropic warmth, the gayly illumined town, the ships with their starry lamps, made an impression still vivid through the years.

When we reached Italy, with headquarters at Bertolini's in Naples, where from our balcony we could see all the islands and towns of that loveliest of bays, we set about making little excursions to the near-by points, returning at night to our delightful hostelry. On one of these drives along the bay, when the islands in the dazzling sun were like so many jewels, Sara, after a few minutes' silence, regaled me with the lines:

> Nisida and Prosida are laughing in the light,
> Capri is a dewy flower lifting into sight,
> Posilipo kneels and looks in the burnished sea,
> Naples crowds her million roofs as close as close can be;
> Round about the mountain's crest a flag of smoke is hung—
> Oh when God made Italy he was gay and young!

With this happy spontaneity she would toss off lyrics of the passing scene which, while often slight and casual, were never without their charm. Frequently, however, these "Vignettes Over-Seas," as Miss Teasdale named them when they appeared in her next volume, were among her most characteristic poems, particularly "Night Song at Amalfi," the memorial of an evening at the old Cappuccini Convento when we sat under the pegola roofed with roses, for it was early June, and lighted by the stars—the large, low-leaning southern stars whose rays pricked through the lattice of the leaves. On the beach far below we could see the fishermen spreading their nets, by the aid of lanterns hanging at the prows of the little vessels. It was a strangely poetic scene and not without its fruits, for soon Miss Teasdale said to me those beautiful lines:

> I asked the heaven of stars
>   What I should give my love—
> It answered me with silence,
>   Silence above.

> I asked the darkened sea
>   Down where the fishers go—
> It answered me with silence,
>   Silence below.

Oh, I could give him weeping,
Or I could give him song—
But how can I give silence
My whole life long?

Perhaps one more instance may be given of the spontaneous genesis of these over-sea vignettes. After several delightful weeks about the Naples region, Sorrento, Ravello, Capri, Anacapri, Paestum, and other points, we wandered on to Rome and thence to Florence, where our hotel was upon the Arno near the Ponte Trinità.

One night we stood upon our balcony, which looked across the river to the church of the Carmine, if my sense of Florentine location still serves me. It was very late, and the bells of the Carmine pealed out the warning hour. We spoke of Masaccio's frescoes and of Michael Angelo and others to whom this church had been both shrine and school. The antiquity of Florence, the pageant of her great who had passed, made human life seem but a moment of Time, and yet here was the Arno flowing on as before. It was a mood to give one pause, and soon Sara crystallized it into those brief lines which yet say so much:

The bells ring over the Arno,
Midnight, the long, long chime;
Here in the quivering darkness
I am afraid of time.

Oh, gray bells cease your tolling,
Time takes too much from me,
And yet to rock and river
He gives eternity.

Rivers to the Sea, Miss Teasdale's first volume to appear after our trip together, is full of poems whose origin is vivid in my mind, and I can still hear the very accent and intonation with which they were originally given. Particularly do such memories crowd about the region of the Italian lakes, and most of all about Villa Serbelloni at Bellagio, where Miss Teasdale and I spent several weeks, held always a little longer by the spell of this threefold lake—

Como, Lecco, Colico—whose waters, merging into one, were visible from various vantage-points of the terraced hill upon which the villa stands. Most romantic of all was the walk through the wood by paths lined with rhododendrons to the ruin of the ancient castle, the ancestral seat of the dukes of Serbelloni. Here, if beauty were the gauge, one might feel the kingdoms of the earth spread out below him.

After Italy we gave leisurely weeks to Switzerland and Germany, visiting the Black Forest, and later, on our way to Cologne, spent a night, for purely sentimental reasons, at Bingen-on-the-Rhine, being somewhat disappointed in the birthplace of the "soldier of the legion" who "lay dying in Algiers."

We sailed from Hamburg in the early autumn and returned to that ever-fascinating and unexpected New York a month or two in advance of the appearance of a book which was to introduce to the poetry world a new personality, that of Edna St. Vincent Millay.[5]

The fourth section of *Rivers to the Sea,* as Jessie Rittenhouse has pointed out, was made up of the poems that came from this trip abroad: the "Vignettes Overseas," a group of eleven lyrics, and a long and beautiful poem in blank verse called "From the Sea." As there was no typewriter available for her use on the ship going to Europe, Sara had the printer on board strike off the first draft of "From the Sea" in printer's type. Later, it was revised, and it was the revised version that appeared in her third book.

On the ship returning to America in August of 1912, Sara became acquainted with Stafford Hatfield, a brilliant Englishman who was a charming companion on shipboard and who helped to make her voyage back a delightful experience. With him she spent many happy evenings watching the starlight on the sea, the phosphorescent foam, the moon spilling its cup of gold on the water and leaving a liquid trail of pure enchantment in its path. This experience and the indelible imprint in memory of those late summer nights filled with water, wind, and stars formed

[5]Rittenhouse, *op. cit.,* pp. 245-249.

the background for some of her exquisite lyrics. In a poem called "Places," she spoke of these hours:

Places I love come back to me like music—
Mid-ocean, midnight, the waves buzz drowsily;
In the ship's deep churning the eerie phosphorescence
Is like the souls of people who were drowned at sea,
And I can hear a man's voice, speaking, hushed, insistent,
At midnight, in mid-ocean, hour on hour to me.

Stafford Hatfield, who was very much interested in all phases of fine arts, later set six of Sara's poems to music; and Paula Hegner, the accompanist for Elena Gerhardt, sang these at a gathering of Sara's friends.

Since her parents were in Charlevoix closing Altasand for the winter when she returned to America, Sara stayed in New York for a while. Marion Stanley came on to New York, too, at this time, for her first trip east. The Parrish sisters were there, as were John Myers O'Hara and the Untermeyers, and Sara thoroughly enjoyed seeing all of these good friends again. Stafford Hatfield remained in America until late September; although it was imperative for Sara to rest about twelve hours out of every twenty-four, she managed to spend some of her precious time with Dr. Hatfield, also, for she was greatly attracted to him. He recalls her as "the very rare Brontë type of woman, and as usual, physically very frail. She could not stay the pace of talk and mild sight-seeing for more than a few hours." Her brief lyric, "In a Railroad Station," was one of several written to Stafford Hatfield, who is today a physicist living in London.

Not long after her return to this country, the book to which Jessie Rittenhouse referred, *The Lyric Year,* was published by Mitchell Kennerley and served as a literary landmark of the year of 1912. Planned and financed by Ferdinand Earle, who at first wanted his name kept a secret, the book was to contain the one hundred best poems of the year as selected by Mr. Earle. In addition, three prizes, one of $500, and two each of $250, were to be given to the authors of the best poems as judged by Mr. Edward J. Wheeler, editor of *Current Opinion,* who was to serve as the President of the Poetry Society of America for ten years, Mr. William Stanley Braithwaite, and Mr. Earle. More than ten thousand poems were entered in the contest, submitted by nearly two thousand poets, and even the inclusion of an author in the book was considered a great honor. Orrick Johns was awarded first prize for his poem of social consciousness, "Second Avenue"; and the second prizes went to Thomas Augustine Daly for "To a Thrush" and George Sterling for "An Ode for the Centenary of the Birth of Robert Browning."

Writing many years later of "that momentous event in the inaugural of the new era of American poetry that witnessed the rise of new stars in the poetic firmament," William Stanley Braithwaite, who was so intimately concerned in the event, recalled:

Late in February I was in Kennerley's bookshop when a rather distinguished man came and was ushered into Kennerley's office, which was at the rear of the store. I had been talking to Laurence Gomme when he passed through. "Do you know who that man is, Stanley?" Laurence asked me. "No," I replied, "but he gives me the impression that he might be a poet." Which was no wise observation, for most of the people who came into that famous shop in those days were poets, though there were a goodly number of novelists, dramatists, and publicists such as Walter Lippmann, for instance.

Then Laurence told me the man's name. I knew him immediately as the famous character who had set the world a-tittering by a naïve statement. He was Ferdinand Phinny Earle, the scion of a well-to-do New York family, and whose father had at one time been Lieutenant Governor of the state. True enough, he was a poet, but one who had some years previously won a kind of satirical item of news in the press of England and America, with the appellation of "Affinity Earle." He had said at the time of a divorce trial, in sustaining his action, that what he sought in a mate was "Soul Affinity."

Shortly after this legal event he went to live in England at Oxford, remaining some years, finally returning to America, with the daughter of an Oxford Professor as his wife.

It was on this return, saturated with the English fervor of the Edwardian poets and the excitement of the symbolist moon magic, that he wanted to do something to stimulate the creative spirit of poetry in America, and so instituted and sponsored *The Lyric Year*. While at Oxford, he had published a volume of sonnets of significant technical achievement.

One day in early March of that year, he came into Kennerley's while I was there. I noticed a harried expression in his face as he came towards me. Scarcely had he made salutation when he said: "Mr. Braithwaite, what an interesting literary venture this poetry competition is, in which you are one of the judges. Do you know who might be the sponsor?" The moment he made the latter remark, some intuitive revelation convinced me he was the sponsor though I did not say so. But a moment later he confirmed my intuition by saying: "Oh, Mr. Braithwaite, I don't mind telling you, I am the sponsor of it and I want your help, for I am in an awful mess, really at my wit's end with the thousands of poems that come. I wonder if I can persuade you to come up (he had a big estate at Monroe, upstate New York) and help me straighten out and organize some system for grading the poems?"

When I finally arrived at Monroe, I ran into an extraordinary and interesting experience. He lived in a large stone house atop a high hill among the foothills of the Adirondacks, overlooking acres of farm, pasture land, and orchards. Except for his English wife, he lived there alone with his dogs, rugs, and books. He had been a great traveler in the East, and the vast house was adorned with fabulously rare Oriental rugs—they were on the floor, across divans and chairs, and hanging on the walls. Even in the dining-room from whose windows looking north and east one could see the smoky rims of the Adirondacks, they took the place of panel and paint, and drooping down to cover the mantel over the fireplace, kept one in suspense at the threat of fire. Around the second story of the house ran a balcony, buttressed with stone railings and arched every so many feet with groined roofs and openings such as I believe are seen in pictures of the Renaissance palaces; from this balcony one could see for miles over the landscape dotted with towns and villages, woods, and hills with gleaming ribbons of water threading the shadows, and all rolling in the sunlight off into the distance where the shadowy side of the mountains supported the sky with its panel of magic.

Indeed, he was in a mess with the thousands of manuscripts that had been submitted for the competition. We worked for days on them. Earle had folders and cabinets in which to classify the poems, but the system he had devised broke down. Eventually we established some order; I suggested, to avoid further confusion, that the poems obviously not up to standard be returned at once. You'd be surprised how much the quantity of these reduced both space and attention.

I read for the first time during those days Edna Millay's "Renascence," about which I was very enthusiastic; and T. A. Daly's "To a Thrush" about which I was equally enthusiastic. Torrence's "Ritual" was new to me, that is to say I had not read it, though I knew of it from Torrence, as the third in a trilogy of rituals he had conceived. With Sterling's "Ode to Browning" I was intimately familiar, because he had written it at my request for the *Transcript* page of original poems I edited in honor of the centenary of Browning's birth. I had persuaded Sterling to send it in to *The Lyric Year* competition.

But there was a living poem in the house muted by fate, and tragic in its bewilderment as a prisoner in a strange land and abandoned through broken ties. This was the lovely young English wife, who by one of those mysteries of telepathy had communicated to me a desire for sympathy and talk. She caught me on the pretext of showing me around the grounds, and on that walk unburdened her soul and its fears. She reminded me of the old English and Scottish ballads with their distraught women. Out of her spirit escaped, but with a delicate indirectness, the agony of folk heroines, tragically deceived, and caught in the web of dark machinations. Her mood and intuition were premonitory, for the poor girl was badly abused, even to physical violence. Eventually, I heard her Professor-father came and took her back to England.

As the lily with all its gorgeous beauty of petal and ecstatic perfume flourishes in the muddy soil of the pond, so *The Lyric Year* flourished in the turbid atmosphere of the manor house at Monroe!

The final awards were decided at a private gathering at Mitchell Kennerley's home at Mamaroneck, New York, at which neither Edward J. Wheeler nor myself was present; I was at Winthrop, on the Massachusetts sea-coast, at the time; but Willard Huntington Wright (the famous S. S. Van Dine of the popular mystery stories and one of my dearest friends since his Harvard days) was, and he told me of the proceedings. Kennerley was a man of arbitrary and unpredictable moods; he had a deep and sympathetic feeling for Orrick Johns, a young poet from St. Louis, who as a boy met with a frightful accident which necessitated the amputation of a leg. Kennerley had printed his verses in *The Forum,* and since he was leading a precarious literary life in New York, decided the first prize money would be a boon to him, and insisted it be given for his poem, "Second Avenue."

The judges were somewhat displeased at the maneuver, but revealed no dissent for fear the public confidence of any internal controversy based on such a violation of trust might hurt literary competitions.

Orrick Johns, whose winning poem was inspired by the depressing slum scenes that he had witnessed in New York on Eldridge Street and lower Second Avenue, was unaware of what lay behind the judges' decision, and he has left his own interpretation of this event:

... Impressed by the contrast between dire suffering and great wealth, I wrote a poem called "Second Avenue." Sara read it and introduced me to Jessie Rittenhouse and Louis Untermeyer, then the leading New York critic of poetry. These friends spoke well of the poem and urged me to send it to Mitchell Kennerley, the keen Englishman who had come over and started *The Forum,* the literary hope of younger people. Kennerley accepted "Second Avenue" and suggested that I submit it to *The Lyric Year* contest....

Sara and Miss Rittenhouse took me to the Poetry Society in the National Arts Club on Gramercy Park, where I heard white-haired

Sara Teasdale, Easter, 1912

Photograph by
Williamina and Grace Parrish

Edwin Markham read his poems, and declare: "There are no poor people and no rich people for me; there are just people." There I met and heard Ella Wheeler Wilcox, Arthur Guiterman, Percy Stickney Grant, Joyce Kilmer, and Shaemus O'Sheel....

... In the fall of 1912 came the news that "Second Avenue" had won *The Lyric Year* first prize of $500. Nothing had been further from my expectations, and when the book arrived I realized that it was an unmerited award. The outstanding poem in that book was "Renascence" by Edna St. Vincent Millay, immediately acknowledged by every authoritative critic as such. The award was as much of an embarrassment to me as a triumph. A heated controversy ensued over it in New York, and I received critical letters, and clippings from correspondence columns. T. A. Daly, of Philadelphia, the remarkable poet-interpreter of the Irish and Italian immigrants, had won second prize. He warned me, through Reedy, not to take part in the newspaper scrimmage. I refrained and I also declined to attend the banquet that was given in New York in honor of the book. I did not want to be the center of a literary dog fight.

The choice of "Second Avenue" had been largely due to one man, the late Edward J. Wheeler, editor of *Current Opinion*. It appealed to him for the same reason that it delighted father; it had a "social content." It was the cry of the *plebs urbana* of my youthful environment, the expression of the "little" middle class of the previous century. Its theme was: economic equality, more leisure, high-thinking—all very romantic and confused, of course, but something that found an echo in the political feeling of the older liberals of that day.

The money went for debts incurred on my small pay at the *Mirror* and for clothes. I loved well-tailored clothes and bright colored neckties, and now I got me them in abundance. I also found that a brief bit of national ballyhoo makes it easier to accomplish things.[6]

Reading through this rare volume today, one is struck with the large amount of poetry in it that now, after nearly half a century,

---

[6]Johns, *op. cit.*, pp. 202-204.

naturally seems old-fashioned and dated. Much of it was written in a hortatory style, and exclamation points greet the reader almost everywhere he turns. The editor announced in his *Foreword* that he had "endeavored to give preference to poems fired with the Time-Spirit," and that explains much of the subject matter. For at this period, Walt Whitman's ideas concerning democracy and the powerful influence of Edwin Markham's "The Man with the Hoe" were stirring minds and spirits. Consequently, the voice of the social conscience that America was just finding and the influence of the city upon the life of the individual are in great evidence, not only in Orrick Johns's contribution, but also in poems such as "Pittsburgh" by James Oppenheim, "The Steel Age" by Florence Brooks, "From a City Street" by Armond Carroll, "Morning" by Anne Cleveland Cheney, and "The Cities" by Mildred McNeal Sweeney.

The effect of the city upon the poet was such a matter of concern in those days, in fact, that at the very meeting of the Poetry Society of America to which Orrick Johns referred, in February of 1912, a spirited discussion was held on the subject: "Is Modern City Life Favorable to the Production of Poetry?"

Arthur Guiterman, as reported by the *Boston Transcript,* rose to say that "as long as a man has experience and absorbs material, it does not matter whether he is in the country or the city. The great thing is contact of mind with mind, and that cannot be had in the country. In looking at the lives of the great poets of the past, you find that Shakespeare left the country for the town, Herrick detested Devonshire, Milton spent his life principally in the city, and Keats was spoken of as a cockney.

"Solitude, absolute stillness, you find in the city, not in the country. The country has nothing so quiet to offer as the silence of the office building."

Jessie Rittenhouse declared: "The great drawback for the writer to living in the city is that city life eats up time and energy. I think the question should be: 'Is modern life unfavorable to the production of poetry' instead of 'Is city life unfavorable to it.'

The trouble is that modern life is negative in its attitude toward modern poetry. Many of our ultra modern writers are giving us new aspects of city life, are striking an unconventional note; but they are themselves impressed with the hardness and horror of the conditions they are depicting, with the result that their work is frequently revolting.

"The ideal is for the poet, after contact with the city, to get away from it in order to assimilate and reach its mystical side."

At this meeting it was announced that James Whitcomb Riley had accepted the Society's invitation to membership, and that other new members included Ellen Glasgow, Mary Austin, Fannie Stearns Davis, Mrs. Edward MacDowell, and Mrs. Richard Mansfield.

It was also at this meeting that Sara's poem, "I Shall Not Care," which appeared in *The Lyric Year,* was read in public for the first time, anonymously, according to the Society's rule for poems submitted by members for discussion. This poem was so well liked that it was read twice and then commented upon at length. Mr. Guiterman referred to it as charming. At this, Joyce Kilmer rose to say that he considered it a pity to call such a tragic and great poem charming. Mr. Guiterman defended himself by saying: "The poem has a humorous effect upon me, because the writer is evidently playing with serious emotions. He's trying to be tragic, and he knows he's trying to be tragic."

Miss Rittenhouse commented: "I think the poem is tragedy in a small compass, like the poems of Christina Rossetti."

Mr. Guiterman once more defended his remarks by saying: "I think the charm of this poem is enhanced by the fact that the writer does not take himself too seriously."

And to this, Edwin Markham diplomatically replied: "Every man's opinions are governed by his craft; and we all know that Mr. Guiterman is a humorist, so it is natural that he should find humor in everything."

Among the names that are today well known, which were included in *The Lyric Year,* are Zoë Akins, William Rose Benét,

Witter Bynner, John Erskine, Arthur Davison Ficke, Hermann Hagedorn, Julian Hawthorne, Thomas S. Jones, Jr., Joyce Kilmer, Richard Le Gallienne, Vachel Lindsay, Percy MacKaye, Edwin Markham and his wife, Catherine, Edna St. Vincent Millay, Edwin J. O'Brien, Shaemus O'Sheel, Ridgely Torrence, Charles Hanson Towne, Louis Untermeyer, John Hall Wheelock, and Margaret Widdemer. Very few of Sara's close friends were omitted; one of these was John Myers O'Hara, and he did not submit anything. Sara told him that he should not have been so haughty, and intimated that perhaps he was in the book, in her poem, after all.

Perhaps the greatest significance of this volume is that it shows the essential difference in the language and manner of writing between an older, established generation of poets and the younger authors, who were already lifting their voices in a more simple, more direct flow of words. The contrast is very striking, and the perceptive reader can feel the drift of this changing tide as the poetic renaissance of the early twentieth century in America began to get under way.

For hidden in the generally outmoded pages of this book, among the *thee's* and *thou's* and the welter of social comment, there are still a number of poems that are essentially modern in their outlook and presentation. Witter Bynner's tribute to Browning, Joyce Kilmer's "Martin," Louis Untermeyer's "Caliban in the Coal Mines" are all such poems; and the little lyrics by Louise Ayres Garnett, Margaret Root Garvin, and Charles Hanson Towne sing today with an undeniable charm. But the majority of the poems have not proved to be of lasting importance. Foremost among those that have—that are as fresh, clear, and timeless in their appeal as they were in 1912—is certainly Sara Teasdale's "I Shall Not Care":

> When I am dead and over me bright April
>   Shakes out her rain-drenched hair,
> Though you should lean above me broken-hearted,
>   I shall not care.

I shall have peace, as leafy trees are peaceful
When rain bends down the bough,
And I shall be more silent and cold-hearted
Than you are now.

Marion Cummings Stanley's brief lyric is also simple in expression and modern in its approach to a universal question:

Yet in this little brain is wrought
The glittering web of time and space,
And in the compass of a thought
The rolling worlds have place.

In vain I seek the sages all,
In vain I question earth and sky.
I am so great, I am so small,
O God, what thing am I?

And finding John Hall Wheelock's musical and moving lyric, "Confession," in these pages is like hearing the sudden silver song of a bird, unexpectedly, in the darkness of a forest:

Look in my songs and you shall find her,
Though by my lips a name so dear
Be uttered never, lost forever—
Lean with your heart and listen here!
For words too sweet, for speech too holy,
Lean to my song and listen well,
Here as the heart's blood in the heart-beat,
Here as the sea's voice in the shell:
Though from my loving vanished, vanished,
Still in my song it slumbers deep,
Like the one thought all day close-guarded,
Betrayed by passionate lips in sleep.[7]

Edna St. Vincent Millay's "Renascence," an interpretation of the spiritual death, burial, and resurrection of the author, who

---

[7]John Hall Wheelock, *Love and Liberation* (Boston: Sherman, French and Company, 1913), p. 161.

wakes to a new awareness of the brotherhood of man, still rises from these pages like a clear flame of poetic utterance, as great in stature today as it was in 1912, when it introduced the nineteen-year-old girl to the American literary scene.

Such poems as these, all of which deal with eternal qualities of the spirit and the emotions deeply felt in the heart of man, which do not change much from century to century, are proof indeed that poems with universal and timeless appeal are the ones that live on through the dust of the years. Though the current scene is important and arresting at any given moment of time, it is temporary and soon passes from the conscious memory of the individual; but the emotions experienced in his innermost heart, his age-old love, longing, joy, and despair, are part of his awareness forever; the poems that sing of these are the poems that will endure. Nothing could prove this more conclusively to the reader than an examination of *The Lyric Year* of 1912.

Chapter 8

CRISIS

•

SARA returned to St. Louis for a few months after her trip abroad with Jessie Rittenhouse, but it was not long before she was back again in her beloved New York to attend the January, 1913, dinner of the Poetry Society of America. It was at this time that Sara met John Hall Wheelock, for whom she retained a life-long affection and admiration. He represented to her all that was finest in a poet and a man. For his poetry she had only the highest praise; she considered him one of the most promising younger poets writing in America. The years have justified her faith in his character and his work, for today his reputation is firmly established as one of the most distinguished and beloved of American poets, and the recipient of many honors.

Mr. Wheelock's unfailing kindness, his reserve, the spiritual quality of his poetry, his integrity, his sense of humor, and his unusual mind all endeared him to Sara. Though she married and loved her husband wholehcartedly, Mr. Wheelock's friendship remained very precious to her. For he was a part of her life even before she met the man whom she married, and together they spent many enjoyable evenings at a time when New York appeared particularly glamorous to her. With him, her beloved city seemed to hold a quality of endless enchantment; they fed the swans in the park or walked through the streets in the deepening shadows of dusk, watching the lights appear like luminous blossoms. A number of her poems written from these days, such as "Swans," cannot fail to recall some of these memorable hours.

For Sara loved this handsome and gifted young man, and her thoughts found their way into her poems.

She was also devoted to Mr. Wheelock's mother, and it was for her that she wrote "The Mother of a Poet," which begins:

> She is too kind, I think, for mortal things. . . .

At various times throughout her life, Sara was the guest of Mr. Wheelock's parents at their home near the southeastern tip of Long Island—a beautiful place that has been the family's residence during the summer time for three generations. Here, surrounded by the loveliness of the open country—the sea, the sky, and the woods—the poet spent some of the happiest days of her life.

Before Sara had met Mr. Wheelock, she had been intensely drawn to his poetry. She told Orrick Johns that she was "simply mad" about Mr. Wheelock's first book, *The Human Fantasy,* which appeared in 1911: "It is the finest book of poetry published in America in years. I can think of nothing else and am telling everybody in a radius of 2,000 miles to read it."

When Mr. Wheelock's second volume, *The Beloved Adventure,* was published in 1912, she was ecstatic with praise. She urged Orrick Johns, who was writing for *Reedy's Mirror,* to give the book an excellent and well-deserved review, for she said:

> . . . Some of the lyrics are as fine as any in the language and the spiritual vision is as splendid and even more all-embracing than in the other book. . . . I was amazed to find a line in the book almost exactly like a line in my Sappho.[1] His line is:

> "The wind of morning has blown out the stars."

I shan't cut out my line, tho', because it was written before I had laid eyes upon W.'s book. Orrick, we've found a master—the biggest thing America has given to the world. More than with almost any other poet, his work has to be read in its entirety. . . . His work is

---

[1]Sara's line reads: "The breath of dawn blows the stars out like lamps."

like sea-water—if you get only a little of it and look at it in the hollow of your hand, all its color is gone. You have to take him in his own way—which is true of all great creators.

Not long after she arrived in New York, Sara sent a note to Edna St. Vincent Millay, whom she knew only through her poetry, asking if the two of them could not arrange to meet.

She had an eager and swift reply:

135 E. 52nd St.
Monday

My dear Miss Teasdale

"Cup of tea together"? By all means,—and soon, please! You are an old friend of mine, tho I am one of your newest acquaintances.

It is always fine to meet old friends, and it is nothing less than thrilling to meet old friends for the first time!

So I shall await eagerly a second note from you suggesting a date.

Most sincerely,
Edna St. Vincent Millay

P.S. In justice, but with considerable reluctance, I confess that there is no real necessity for haste, as I expect to be here till June.

E.St.V.M.

A few days later, these two young poets met and liked each other immensely; they dined together and took a ride on a bus-top up Riverside Drive, enthusiastically discussing the people and things that interested them.

In the summer, after both of them had left New York, Miss Millay wrote Sara:

Camden, Maine
July 14, 1913

Dear Sara,—

I don't feel so very bad about not seeing Dugle,[2] but I did want to see your new suit. And did you get a dress like mine?—Very likely not, or you would have told me, but you should have; it was a good investment. It washes. Yes, my dear; Ivory Soap; it floats.

---

[2]Dugald Walker.

Against your advice I am going to Vassar in the fall. Provided I pass my examinations in algebra and American history, that is.

Sara, if you know anything about algebra, for cat's sake write and tell me. I don't. I couldn't tell a radical from a radish. And if I can't vote what do I care about American history? There's a flaw in the curriculum, that's all. (And please don't scan that word too closely or you may find it!)

Tell me, why, instead of spending all your winters in New York, don't you spend some of your summers in Camden.—Most everybody does. And it would be sort of fun to have you around. You have such nice brown eyes. You really have, you know. Alfred Noyes is going to be here this summer, or very near here, and I'm here, and if only you'd come we'd all be here.

I have been visiting the Kennerleys and having a wonderful time. Also, I'm in love at this minute with three different men. However, none of them knows it, because I'm being good. (And, by the way, it really isn't so bad, you know, being good. Try it sometime.)—

Sincerely

Vincent Millay

Years later, after Edna St. Vincent Millay's *Fatal Interview* had been published, Sara sent her this message:

April 18, 1931

Dear Edna Millay: I can't accept the happiness I have had from Fatal Interview without sending you a word of thanks. To find you with the power and the glory still burning is a matter for gratitude, not to you only but to life. And I like to think that when I first read you, long ago, I knew you and named a star.

Sincerely,

Sara Teasdale Filsinger

Another friend whom Sara met in New York, some time later, was Marguerite Wilkinson, a poet only a year older than Sara, who wrote strongly religious verse. She and her husband, Jim, then principal of Roosevelt High School in New Rochelle, New York, were devoted to Sara. More than as a poet, Marguerite

Wilkinson is remembered today as a respected critic of poetry, for she reviewed books for the *New York Times* and other periodicals, lectured all over the country, and brought out her own volume of criticism, *New Voices,* which contained a fair and balanced commentary on contemporary poetry. At Mrs. Wilkinson's request, Sara contributed a discussion of her theory of how poetry is written, as well as some of her poems, to this book.

After Sara became acquainted with Harriet Monroe, first through correspondence, and then in person, she began to visit Chicago now and then. Because of the poetic excitement and the new interest stimulated by *Poetry: A Magazine of Verse,* founded by Miss Monroe in 1912, Chicago became somewhat of a literary mecca. Poets from all parts of the country visited the little office on Cass Street to meet the editor, leave their manuscripts, ask for criticism, or simply to discuss poetry. Carl Sandburg, Vachel Lindsay, Arthur Davison Ficke, Alfred Kreymborg, Maxwell Bodenheim, and Edgar Lee Masters were some of the writers who turned up from time to time at the desk of the editor.

Though a feeling of rivalry sprang up between the eastern poets living near New York City and the western poets, championed by Miss Monroe, Sara was not involved in this issue at all; for she had friends equally dear to her among both groups, and she was not in the least concerned as to whether New York City or Chicago was the more vital center of the poetic revival that America was beginning to witness.

Harriet Monroe was impressed with the quality of Sara's work and respected her highly as a poet; she also loved her as a friend, was always glad to see her, and retained an active interest in her affairs. Sara met Miss Monroe in 1913 on her first visit to Chicago; at this time Sara was graciously entertained and introduced to a number of literary personalities. But she was appalled to find that many of her Chicago acquaintances seemed to have little moral or romantic restraint. Her Puritan spirit recoiled from the atmosphere of bohemian living, which she saw so vividly in evidence all around her.

Eunice Tietjens was also living in Chicago at this time and was to join the staff of *Poetry* in the fall of 1913. Through Zoë Akins, Eunice had first become acquainted with Sara by correspondence, and soon they met in person at the Blackstone Hotel, where Miss Monroe introduced them. Later, during the summer, when Eunice was in Charlevoix, Michigan, conducting a private kindergarten for the grandchildren of Mrs. Daniel Burnham, they became the closest of friends. Recalling those happy days at Charlevoix, Eunice Tietjens wrote:

We spent nearly every afternoon walking together in the woods or by the lake; more often still we rowed or punted in a rowboat on the shallow stream. We would sit for hours talking of the wellsprings of poetry, or of the people we knew, or of the varying moods of nature. I have never known anyone so sensitive to certain aspects of nature as Sara, or more influenced by them. It is visible in her poetry everywhere. But she always talked concretely, of the wild plants by the stream bank which she knew by name every one, of the lake and its various personalities, "the unchanging, everchanging sea," or of the stars, which were all individual friends of hers. Indeed she used to keep a big chart of the heavens on her bedroom wall on which she had always pricked the positions of the planets. She seemed never to talk in the abstract, never to trouble herself about the difficulties of formal thinking. She had a touchstone of her own and she seldom varied from it.

In the evenings, when it was warm enough, we often sat in a little summer-house built over the bluff beside her father's home, looking over the lake where the small moon went down into the waters and the breeze sang past us. I could scarcely see Sara then, but her voice came from the shadow, warm and clear, speaking with a depth of human understanding and a beautiful spiritual honesty that lifted me into another world. She was passionately devoted to the poetry of Sappho, though she chose not to believe the stories of her sexual aberrations and held it a great pity that the memory of the greatest woman poet of antiquity should be so smudged in the popular mind. But she knew every scrap that remains to us of Sappho's writings and used to recite them lovingly in the darkness and to speak of evenings ... now become cloudy with legend, when Sappho would recite her poems and the other poets answer, and the clear light of pure beauty shone from the spirit as well as the stars.

Sara was always frail in body, needing a quiet life, needing to rest long hours of every day.... But much of the beauty of her spirit came from this very fact, and in the long quiet hours of solitude her very self grew and took root.

She was capable too of sudden moments of exaltation when she seemed to give off a palpable light of some inner ecstasy. On these moments she fed later in her solitude. Unexpected things often produced them, sudden beauty most often, or an unexpected meeting with a friend, or even at times a quick intellectual stab of understanding. . . .[3]

After those happy summer days, Sara and Eunice Tietjens remained intimate friends for the rest of their lives.

During the summer of 1913, though they had not yet met each other, Sara and Vachel Lindsay began corresponding regularly. In 1912, at the suggestion of Witter Bynner, Sara had written to Lindsay for a copy of his publication, *The Village Magazine*. But it was Harriet Monroe who was responsible for their really becoming acquainted. Lindsay was in Chicago in the early summer of 1913, and Miss Monroe urged him to stay a little longer and meet Sara, who was soon to arrive. Unfortunately, he had to return to Springfield and so missed seeing her. On August 7, 1913, however, he wrote to Harriet from his Illinois home:

Our little friend you thought I might stay over in Chicago for:— Sara Teasdale has written me two letters and I have written her two. What do you think of the correspondence? Does it contain great and unfathomable things for each of us?

Near the end of September Sara went to New York City to stay for a few months, and Lindsay's letters followed her there. A few weeks later Lindsay reported to Harriet Monroe:

---

[3]Eunice Tietjens, *The World At My Shoulder* (New York: The Macmillan Company, 1938), pp. 26-28.

You have woven quite a web in giving me a spiritual introduction to Sara Teasdale. Our correspondence has become almost intimate —but a bit humorous still—yes, still a bit humorous.

Since both these poets were blessed with a delightful gaiety and wit, their letters at this time, as Lindsay indicated, were full of a certain light-heartedness, as this one written by him on November 8 will show:

Excellent Rascal—Sara Teasdale: I hope you get better soon. I wish you well in all things. . . .

Yes—I am rumored to be engaged. But my first love is the good God—the second the Devil—the third my ink bottle—the fourth mine own people—(Papa, Mama and little sister,) and the fifth the road. Yes—Woman is number six. I can't help it. That's just the way it is. Nobody ever believes it, often I do not believe it, but in my inner soul I *know* it.

And as for New York—get away from there. Go back home and write poems about St. Louis. If all the prodigal sons and daughters who were gathered there would return to their native hearths, America would be remade in a generation. Temperament set atremble in that exotic air has nothing to do with cornfed America.

Come back through Springfield and visit Mama and Papa and little sister. Can't you scrape up a girl friend in Springfield to visit? We will go out and write poetry in red chalk on the State House walk, where he who runs may read. That will be a conjunction of planets, and a fine thing for the populace.

Well—I wrote you a long silly letter and tore it up. You shouldn't —you shouldn't—well you know what you shouldn't.

All that I have to say about you is that you are either a very *young*, or a very *frivolous* young woman. Take *that*.

Very distantly yours,
Sara Teasdale's correspondent
Nicholas Vachel Lindsay

Sara sponsored Vachel's name for membership in the Poetry Society of America, and she urged him to come to New York for the annual January dinner. When Jessie Rittenhouse also extended her invitation to him to recite for the Society, Lindsay seriously considered going. But his acceptance depended on a payment from his publisher, Mitchell Kennerley, and this was not forthcoming.

It amused Vachel (and he wrote Sara of it) that Joyce Kilmer, reviewing William Stanley Braithwaite's first *Anthology of Magazine Verse* in the *New York Times Book Review*, in January, 1914, mentioned their poetry as being the antithesis of each other's. Kilmer wrote: "There are many beautiful poems in Mr. Braithwaite's collection. Indeed, he includes few poems that are not excellent. And he is wise enough to include poems widely different from each other in theme and spirit; to include, for instance, so classical and stately a composition as Sara Teasdale's 'Sappho,' and so buoyant or rather boisterous a bit of enthusiasm as Nicholas Vachel Lindsay's 'The Kallyope Yell.' "

Since they could not yet meet in person, Sara, in response to Vachel's pleas, sent him a lock of her hair; though it was auburn, Vachel always referred to it as "golden," probably because of its beautiful sheen.

"Letters mingle souls," John Donne once wrote, and as this friendship by correspondence progressed, the Springfield poet showed Sara that he had a profoundly serious side to his nature, too. Early in February of 1914, he wrote her a revealing and compelling letter:

My dear Lady:

They say that the Trappist monks are allowed one word. When they meet in the morning they say to one another "Remember death."

Now I think on death tonight, and it is not that I think on decay or sorrow or skulls. Nor yet on something sublime. It might be called the middle wood.

I think on death as the apparent end of the illusions that encompass us. They all have a sudden and unexpected end, that challenges any faith we have pinned to their worth. Therefore if one would be above the vexations, above the passionate whirl, above the hunger and thirst of the body, that he may think and judge, in the mood of the stars, let him remember death. The mood of the stars is really the mood most worth while. To be cold and gentle and in a sense fixed, and beholding all that transpires—that is the conquering mood. I look at and dearly love this little circle of gold hair, this hint of a sensitive human creature, and then I say in my heart in all gentleness, *remember death*. Would I be strong as the stars I cannot lean upon any passing thing. The joy must blow upon my face if it will like a perfumed wind, but God help me to remember death and be fixed and gentle as the stars though friendship come or go.

The free spirit is indeed pitiful and weak, but he may *somehow possess himself sometimes*, but he who surrenders to the whirl of life is drowned drowned drowned.

When a flattering notice comes of my work, when some new editor sends a little intoxicating praise, when my overardent friends here, my too kind partisans overpraise me, let me think then of death and the stars and be not drunk with the wine of my own flattered blood.

When I feel the people shrinking from me as a curio, an alien, an Ishmaelite, let me think upon death and the stars and be content.

When they speak of money as the one thing worth while, and when I see that all the chief sweets of life for which I grow almost frantic are to be purchased with money, for which I am to sell my soul, let me think upon death and the joy that glitters in the eyes of the stars, and be content.

When the pleasure lovers tell me that it is not worth while to worry about humanity, that all men are greedy and marauding thieves, that corruption is inevitable and reform a delusion, and Utopia the last folly, let me think upon death—hoping that some day the old order will die, laboring to bring about its death, in some small way giving my sword stroke. Let me think upon death, and let me watch and hope, as the stars watch for sunrise.

The most beautiful friendship may end in bitterness, or a sort of grey dimness, or a parting that is a slow and painless death. I pray God to keep all my friendships strong and honest and vital as possible, as for the women friends, neither denying passion's existence, nor putting too much faith in it. And even if I cannot put all faith into friendship God keep me brave enough to fill every

Vachel Lindsay
1913

friendship with tender hope. Let us still hope great things of every friendship, but, lest we be doomed to some day stand alone in the cool strange night, let us prepare our hearts for that loneliness and think on death—and the stars.

I have much delight in the thought of you, my child, and though I had three times the delight, still I would say in my soul, let both of us make the eternal God our lonely and certain goal, and though I kiss your hand again, let us think on death and the stars.

With love
Nicholas Vachel Lindsay

Sara, who loved New York more each time she stayed there, was having such a good time that she delayed ending her visit as long as possible. Meanwhile, Lindsay, intrigued by her interesting letters, was becoming eager to meet her; he began urging her to come home. But she wanted to hear Yeats speak at the luncheon in his honor on February 10. Two days before this event Vachel wrote to her:

Now being a letter-answerer is not a great moral virtue in a lady, but to find a person with the same weakness for ink that I have is indeed a delight. To find the conversation coming back like a well-served tennis ball as it were, back and forth over the net of distance and mystery that separates us—so far, so strangely—is one of life's glories. But I have reached the point where I am so very hungry indeed to see you, that letters are more like marking time than playing tennis. . . .

If you are staying over for that Yeats dinner, I weep great weeps. . . .

* * *

. . . There is a whole lot in the fraternity of a common craft and a certain similarity of fortune and future. And I am awfully sensitive to your words. They are like words spoken. And never did I have within me so many untied tangled strands of expectation and curiosity and damned up, pent up good humor in regard to a person I have never seen. . . .

Soon after the Yeats dinner, Sara returned to St. Louis, and about a week later Lindsay accepted the invitation of her parents to spend the night at their home. Before he left Springfield, he wrote her:

Never did I know a poet lady romantic—unattached—and me own age and period and stage of ambish. I peep down in the St. Louis direction filled with speculations, thoughts and esteems and cautions. I lift up me torch and look south-west.
> Believe me—
> > I am devastated with anticipation
> > and remain
> > > Nicholas Vachel Lindsay

Meeting Sara was fully as rich and exciting an experience as Vachel had expected it to be. He was not disappointed, and he wrote her immediately after returning to Springfield from his visit:

> Springfield, Ill.
> Feb. 19, 1914

My dear Sara:

Being now in the bosom of my family: I sit down to address you with sentiments and observations.

Sing till you shake the city!

So much went into our little visit. It is a new starting point for both of us. We can think it over now, and see what it all amounted to.

I should say that coming home on the train my feeling about you was that you were a bearer of the atmosphere of the old New York Bohemia around 56 and 57th St. where I used to live.

The Art-Student atmosphere and the Poetry Society atmosphere is something the same I believe, now, though the theme of conversation is different. I have been through so many other strata of society since, you jerk me back to my youth—when I was writing the Queen of Bubbles, and all that. It needs such as you to remind me there ever was such a world. I feel infinitely *old* when I think of it. I have to look back through such a vista.

You are much more accomplished than I ever was in such an environment—such a medium,—and quite wise I am sure. But dear me—it is so alien from my habit now—and I cannot help but think what I have been through since—what different *stripes* and terraces of society I have crossed. Everywhere but in jail almost—and in a way hardened to it all—or at least looking it all in the face, and getting some sweetness out of it—enough.

You have the most remarkable eyes child—the velvet of the Gods —the eyes of your genius. All the rest of your face shows your talent and blood and your culture—but I certainly have to get back to those eyes—watching watching me—to get you.

Your face is so much *longer* and more sensitive than in your pictures that they are an utter disappointment to me now. I have to look and look into the dark and see your jewel eyes. I do not want to live in your alleged heart. Everyone does (!) But in your eyes. They are more exclusive. You are certainly an intense egotist, and have a most sharp tang and savor to your egotism, and a great delicacy and charm to it as well. You are a sharp arrow and I want you shot straight into the heart of America.

This world is *such* a wilderness—we go groping for each other through it—we mortals—it will be a long time before you and I, separated by so many things of time and sense and custom, and experience—will achieve the complete story of our friendship. Even living in the same town and seeing each other once a week—it would be hard to completely learn each other in a little while. We are going to be like a serial story in a magazine—we will get each other on the installment plan. Once a month installments take a whole year to cover a little silly story—and *our* installments sepa-rated by God knows what intervals—will not soon complete the novel of friendship that our knowing each other should be. In the half light I saw the glory of your eyes and in the morning I read your force and ambition in your eyes—and I am with you in it. I want the noblest song ever woman sung to be uncoiled from your soul. I want the noblest noblest art and glory and dream from you.—Of all the high hearted women you celebrate I want you to be the empress.

You are one of those anointed and set apart. I never knew a woman who impressed me with it so surely—and I want you to be

true to the Holy Ghost within you. Sing till you shake the city.
With love,

Nicholas Vachel Lindsay

The very next day he wrote a still longer letter, addressing her as "My dear Velvet-Eyes":

Our first evening in your study was such a pent-up thing—*so* much unsaid—and I was getting the sense of you, the notion of you clearer every minute, and your particular quality of personal dignity, which means everything, and your pride's anchorage, and all that. I felt the sure pride of the artist in you—deep deep down in you—established like granite. It did not escape me. . . .

* * *

Sara, I want a place to live, in your virginal and untouched night-dreaming eyes. . . . The kind of mutual fire and friendship I want to weave and achieve with you, burns in your eyes. Though your songs be exquisitely beautiful they do not equal your eyes. It is your eyes that justify all the blind faith of my letters to you, and the spiritual dependence I have sent in your direction. It is your eyes that hold my "diary that talks back." The lines of your lashes sweeping back with such marked and strange drawing toward your temples, speak the language of genius and personality—the untouched personality that no sentimental adventure has the least invaded, a fire that burns perpetually without ashes.

And in your night-dreaming eyes I see far more of fantasy—Tree of Laughing Bells fantasy—than blood-beating human imagination. *That* is in your speech and your ways, but I see in your eyes something cooler, safer and more permanent and yet more tender—the velvet of the gods, the blackness behind the stars, and the eternal dream-garden of Mab.

As a singer-of-love, I have little to say to you. The kind of love you sing about, realized or desperately attempted love between man and woman has never brought me anything but desperate sorrow, a house burnt down as it were. . . . As a fellow warrior and untamed spirit I greet you. I want to be a permanent part of what is permanent in you, the unsubdued, fighting soul.

· 176 ·

...I hope that which I see in your eyes outlives these loves that come and go you speak of so lightly and beautifully. If the Holy Ghost has laid hold on you to make you a singer, of passion, very well. You are the veritable nightingale at your best. Let them all, all the rest drink of it, since it is their wine. But some day you will go back to the good God that made you and these fires will have passed with the world that holds them. I would think of Him with you—and of the eternal stars. . . .

Vachel's younger sister, Joy, who was in a romantic mood in these days with her wedding only a few weeks away, suggested that he call his new friend "Sarafimm." This sounded exactly right to Vachel, and soon Sara was "Sarafimm" or "Saraphim" to him. On February 24 he sent her a little poem explaining this term of endearment:

> Who are these creatures, red of hair
> A chanting with the cherubims?
> Just what are they, grey traveller, say?
> The traveller answers right away:—
> "They're Sara, Sara Saraphims.
>
> "They flit above the shining trees,
> They perch upon the upper limbs—
> Half-bird, half-angel—chirp and chant—
> They fill the streets with ardent hymns.
> Their silliest song is yet so sweet
> The tear of joy my eyesight dims.
> In short—they're what I said they were:
> They're Sara Sara Saraphims."

Sara left her first impression of Lindsay in a letter that she wrote on February 28 to Louis Untermeyer, commending him for his review of Lindsay's *General William Booth Enters Into Heaven.*

The review of Lindsay is great! I've this second finished it, and I've got to tell you that I'm wild about it. You have put down the *man* as well as the poet. I've not written since he came to see me, have I? He is a real man—full of eccentricities—aggressively himself. He is about middle height, blond, with eager, keen blue-gray eyes full of humor; a good talker—almost a monologist if he gets on a familiar and favorite train of thought. His voice is good, but too loud much of the time and *very* Middle West. When he reads his own poetry (recites it, rather) in this tiny study of mine, it is like being compelled to listen to a pipe-organ in an hermetically sealed safe-deposit vault. Your ears ache, and so do your nerves. The "Kallyope" *is* a *YELL!* He leaves no doubt of it.

Yet the fresh humanity of the man—his beautiful exuberance—fills you with delight. He is a real lover of mankind, with a humorous tenderness for its weaknesses. . . .

You will like him. He has, quite literally, clean hands and a pure heart. He is coming back again in a week or so, and I'm looking forward to it. In his conversation there is the same racy fluency that there is in his prose, and here in St. Louis, where everybody is in New York (Irish bull) it is a joy to have him come.[4]

At this time most of the people whom Sara had known best in St. Louis were either out of town, or married and absorbed in their own families and careers. Orrick Johns had moved to New York and married an artist. Zoë Akins was also living in New York; the Parrish sisters were abroad. Few of the Potters were still in St. Louis. Sara's parents, now in their seventies, were in failing health. Mamie and her husband, Joseph Wheless, were no longer living at the family home. The prospect before Sara of being chained to St. Louis, where almost none of her friends of kindred spirit remained, and where she had to watch the heart-breaking picture of two once vigorous and energetic parents slowly becoming more and more feeble, saddened her immeasurably. Her correspondence, however, brightened her life. Now and then she had a word from Stafford Hatfield; frequently, letters came from John Hall Wheelock and John Myers O'Hara. She

---

[4]Louis Untermeyer, *From Another World* (New York: Harcourt, Brace and Company, 1939), pp. 175-176.

also heard from Louis and Jean Starr Untermeyer, Eunice Tietjens, Jessie Rittenhouse, Harriet Monroe, and other friends; and soon she was having an overwhelming avalanche of letters from Vachel Lindsay.

For in Sara, Vachel had found an interested and sympathetic spirit who made an ideal audience for him. When one contrasts Sara's physical frailness and need of long hours of rest and solitude with Lindsay's inexhaustible energy and restlessness, or her need of the things that financial resources could provide with his complete indifference to money, it is clear that these poets were different in many ways.

But Vachel looked beyond the obvious realities and found that they were also alike in many ways. He told Sara soon after he met her that he knew that she "valued her kingdom" even as he he did his; he also realized at once that she was a serious artist and craftsman, even as he was, and that she was willing to dedicate much of her life to the development of her lyric genius. Both of them had sprung from a religious ancestry; each had a grandfather who had been a minister. Furthermore, he saw in their home situations a certain similarity; each of them was the last single child living with elderly parents, and coping with the same general problems that inevitably arise when adult members of two generations live under one roof. Of greatest significance of all to him, perhaps, was that he felt that the life of the spirit was of major importance to both of them, and that beauty was a supreme influence in their lives. It is true that their approach to beauty differed, for Sara's was an aesthetic response, while Vachel's was rooted in a love for the soil and a humanitarian desire to make his country aware of its magnificence.

Though Swedenborg, Jefferson, Ruskin, Governor Altgeld of Illinois, the legendary Johnny Appleseed, and others had left their imprint upon Lindsay's character, three essential gods had molded the poet whom Sara knew at this time. From the great heart of Lincoln, whose memory was still very much alive in Springfield, he had absorbed an undying love of the common people and a concept of an idealistic democracy. From Buddha he had learned the strength of peace and silence, and the riches to be gained when one forsook the multitude and communed with the infinite; Buddha had also taught him the wisdom of going among the people and preaching his personal gospel—in Lindsay's case, the Gospel of Beauty. And from St. Francis, who had embraced poverty and lived a life of austere purity of the soul, he had learned to turn aside from the commercialism and materialism of the world.

Money and its power had no appeal for him, and one of his basic ideas was that poverty itself could well be a blessing. He was never concerned with temporal possessions. His kingdom was one of ideas, dreams, and visions; his deepest purposes in life centered around making Springfield the most spiritually perfect place in the world, writing poems of startling rhythms and power that would make America aware of its heritage, and carrying his evangelistic message across the country and into the hearts of its people. For Lindsay was truly dedicated to his self-appointed mission in life: the making of drab lives more radiant by the alchemy of beauty.

It was this clear and pure dedication of spirit that appealed to Sara in the youthful Lindsay, as well as the flow of thoughts generated by his restless mind that was always seeking more ideal universes for the heart to inhabit. Sara was never fooled or attracted by the insincere, and there was nothing of pretense, nothing artificial about this poet. His deep seriousness of purpose, his concern for mankind, his lofty thinking, and the sweep of his vision, no matter how impractical, aroused her interest. She recognized instinctively that Lindsay was a rare individual—a person of complete honesty. Though they came from two entirely different worlds, he stimulated her intellectually. One might become weary of the overpowering vitality of this poet, but one could not become bored with him.

There was more than a little of Thoreau's philosophy in Lindsay's beliefs; but Thoreau was no reformer, no crusader. And though he took some walking trips, the New England philosopher was largely content to spend his hours quietly observing the strange and wonderful world of nature on his native soil. Vachel Lindsay, however, wanted to know every inch of ground in America.

Several times in the past, Lindsay had taken strenuous tramping trips through various parts of the nation. And only two years before Sara met him, he had set forth on a typical pilgrimage from Springfield with his pockets empty of change. About the only possessions he carried with him were the clothes on his back, some copies of a pamphlet of his own poems called *Rhymes To Be Traded For Bread,* a number of leaflets stating his *Gospel of Beauty,* and a scrapbook filled with pictures and clippings that he thought might be of interest to his scattered audiences. He intended to walk across the country to California, exchanging his poems for food and lodging along the way. As he once wrote about this experience, he was "knocking at the door of the world with a dream in my hand."

This trip took him into farm houses, huts, hotels, Mexican shacks, log cabins, churches, country stores, strange post offices, railway stations, and libraries. He worked as a farm hand for a Mennonite family; he slept in haymows, in livery stables, in an open shed, on the cement floor of a garage, and in a roofless barn wrapped in canvas. All along the way he preached his Gospel of Beauty and chanted his poems for daily sustenance wherever he found a willing ear. When this failed, he cut weeds and cleaned up gardens, mixed concrete, split kindling, and harvested wheat. Together with the hunger, thirst, and discomforts of which there were many, he had some fascinating adventures. He stored his mind and heart full of the wonders of his country, its varying landscapes, its promise, history, and legends; he came to know intimately the very heart of the people in America in all their generosity, understanding, coldness, kindness, ignorance, courtesy, and indifference.

During these days he found the inspiration for some of his most memorable poems. A friendly Negro told him that the meadow lark that sang to him was called the "Rachel Jane," an identification that found an echo in his "Santa Fé Trail." "The Bronco That Would Not Be Broken" came from a haunting and cruel incident that he witnessed, and the first seed that later flowered into "General William Booth Enters into Heaven" was planted when Lindsay lustily sang the refrain, "Are you washed in the blood of the Lamb?" high in the hills of Colorado.

The familiar words, "I hear America singing," could, in Lindsay's case, become, "I *am* America singing."

"The people of America walk through me, all the people walk through my veins, as though they were in the streets of a city, and clamor for voice," Lindsay once told Sara. "I want to find the core of the heart of God, and man, *and America* and make them into song. . . . I can almost hear the beating of God's heart sometimes and I only wish the United States was as easy to conquer—I wish I could hear *that* great heart."

Like Walt Whitman, he wanted to sing of America to America, and he took for his starting point his own town of Springfield, for which he had a very warm affection. In discussing his life's ambition, he wrote to Sara:

It is to give as complete a voice as possible in song, to the America I came from, and to put my whole life-strength to the task. . . .

* * *

. . . Sangamon County is in a way more American than the total of all the counties of the land, and I want to make American song through Sangamon County.

And I want to get way way under the world, and look up, and understand it from underneath, and not be corrupted by the ease of the world or the praise of sophisticated friends. . . .

* * *

Saraphim, my only possible excuse for living is to sing my song well. I am not worth the mud that made me otherwise, and I must make every sacrifice to this end, and renew my vows, and forget all flatteries and set my soul to the task. I must keep singing more and more clearly the voice of my little dumb county in dumb laboring America, till I am 70 years old, in the year 1950. . . .

Whether I do this work well or ill, it is all I am fit for—my only chance at the Judgment throne. I must put my all in it.

But Springfield never wholly understood her poet son and never fully accepted him. As the world at large has rarely been able to understand the drives and needs of a creative artist, so the conventional minds of Springfield were mystified as to why an able-bodied man, after years of studying art, would be content to live at home with his parents and spend his hours writing poetry; the citizens of Springfield thought, as the citizens of almost any other twentieth-century American city would think in similar circumstances, that there was something a little odd about a man who did not care about earning money and "respectability" by holding a nine-to-five job. They did not understand, nor were they much interested in, the *War Bulletins* that this poet issued in Springfield, telling of his battles against commercialism, shallowness, and stupidity. And only a few of them were impressed by the poem distributed free by Vachel called "The Soul of the City Receives the Gift of the Holy Spirit," which spoke of censers swinging over the town as this miraculous event took place. Even in the later years of Lindsay's life, when he brought fame and honor to his native city, though the bars were lowered to some extent, he was never taken comfortably and wholeheartedly into the inner circle of Springfield. And he once confessed to Sara:

My Achilles heel—is found in my old neighbors that passed me for thirty years on the street with curt nods, who now want to make me just like one of themselves, or torture me for *not* being such.

His mode of life was an old source of friction, an old battle that the poet had fought out with his family over and over again; it was especially hard for his father, a doctor, who drove himself relentlessly in his profession, and who had hoped to train his only son in the same field, to understand the chosen direction of Vachel's life; and his mother, from whom he had inherited his strong missionary zeal, was also disappointed that he had not become a distinguished artist or a substantial citizen in some other profession. It was equally difficult for Vachel to explain to his parents that he had to follow the "north star" of his destiny, and that the only way he could do this was to let his talent develop along the natural lines that he knew were right for him.

By the time that Sara became acquainted with Lindsay, this situation was more or less unhappily accepted by his father and mother. Though Dr. Lindsay did not approve of the way his son spent his time, when some literary honor came his son's way, he was pleased and spoke of it to his friends. Still, as Vachel explained to Sara:

... there is not one laurel-crown I could ever win that would be worth as much as my working as a life-insurance agent we will say—with ten dollars a week sure income. Every time I ask him for a cent—it means to him I am *deliberately* postponing the day when I am a real grown up man. . . .

But Vachel had come to terms with himself on this matter, and it did not hurt his pride so much any more.

It used to just break my heart to ask the family for one cent— it just about drove me raving crazy. But gradually I have come to the place where I feel I am just as much a credit to the combination as any of the rest, with all their fidget and hustle—and I go serenely about my business. And as long as what I do is in the accepted routine—there is no family objection. . . .

In one of the first letters that he wrote to her after they met, Vachel referred to "golden Sara," probably because her gleaming auburn hair was touched with golden high-lights; but the word came to have a far greater significance to him, and in the years to come, when he spoke of "golden Sara," the adjective meant her shining nobility of spirit. Not long after his first visit to St. Louis, he told her that her new name was Gloriana. And a number of his poems refer to "Gloriana."

When Vachel first met Sara, he was just getting over an unhappy affair of the heart with a girl who lived in Springfield. He still saw her occasionally, and she still had the power to cause him moments of exhilaration or despair. Late in February he wrote to Sara:

I don't want to be your sweetheart. I don't want to ever love anyone again in the Romeo sense, for years. It's too deadly. But I want you for the dearest kind of a faithful friend.... Your one act of service and faithfulness to me is to keep a mind willing to receive and gently welcome my letters—and give me live enough answers to show me friendship has not grown weary.

Early in March, upon Harriet Monroe's invitation, Lindsay went to Chicago to attend a dinner given there for Yeats. Harriet Monroe, who was very fond of Vachel, thoughtfully placed on the night table in her guest bedroom by Yeats's bed the issue of *Poetry* that contained Lindsay's "General William Booth Enters Into Heaven." This diplomatic gesture had the desired effect; when Yeats spoke to the distinguished audience assembled in his honor, one of the first things he did was to mention with high praise this poem and its author. The audience was deeply impressed by the homage paid to one in their midst by such a notable visitor. And when Lindsay was called upon to recite some of his new poems, the response to "The Congo" was overwhelming. His Chicago visit was a genuine triumph, not only for himself, but for Miss Monroe, and he left the city, where he was royally entertained, in a cloud of glory. Yet he was glad to escape the attention and praise and return to his study in Springfield where he could pick up his pen and write:

Dearest Saraphim: Here I am back in my quiet room again, and *so* glad to welcome myself home again. All is quiet. I can hear my watch tick.

Now I have that peace where I can call in your soul—you, or the imaginary creature that I *call* you.

I had to break away from Chicago by main force. Engagements looked like they would pile up mountain high, and I strutted and hooted around in a way to shame the gods. I am *glad* it all happened. Everyone was superlatively *grand* to me, but another week would have utterly spoiled me.

You have no idea how baffled I felt each midnight when I sat down to write to you and realized I must be in my own room beneath that big picture of Altgeld—before I *could* write to you in spirit and in truth. Those people except, of course, the closest just loved the *shell*—and the *noise* of me, and it is my quiet self that writes to you, and finds such comfort in you.

* * *

People are crowding me with invitations. I must just refuse them all and pray to the good God to restore to me the Holy Ghost, and help me to write with only the Divine Spirit in mind.

Yes, I want to come to see you—but I have only fifteen cents. And I cannot come till I have done a *little work* and satisfied my self-respect. Unless I can read you at least *one* new piece I have no right to come. . . .

* * *

We are strangely separated—strangely united—and I am deeply grateful to you for your fairy listening ear.

With all respect I kiss your hand—and bid you goodnight.

Nightingale—nightingale
nightingale—goodnight.
With love
N.V.L.

On the next day, with the spell of Chicago still exerting its influence over him, he wrote again:

. . . I must be free from this smothering world. I want to do my work, and nothing else, and be an honest beggar, loaded down with no contraptions.

You have no idea how the hunger for the good God and the desire to escape the snare of the world—lays hold on me. Yet I am perpetually half ensnared, always hungry for kisses I do not take, and always drunk on praises I should ignore.

Yet through it all my heart cries to the infinite God and I desire to be cold as the stars, and live only for what my pen shall create. I want to set the world dreaming, to heal its imagination with dreams, and never be myself wounded with arrows.

* * *

Write to me Saraphim. Do not ignore my letters. It is your womanly duty to walk in the ways of the spirit with me and help me back to the land of song.

We must resolve to be celestial nightingales together. Celestial nightingales—together or apart.

* * *

Let us think upon the stars and save our hearts from every desire, but the desire of song.

Though they had seen each other only once at this time, Sara and Vachel had come to know each other intimately through their correspondence. He knew the problems of her home life, her longing to return to New York, the seriousness with which she worked at her poetry, and how much her friendships meant to her. And she, in turn, knew the ambitions, conflicts, and ideals that shaped his life. On March 11, he wrote to her:

This old-folks question seems suddenly to infest my world. Every single soul I know and love, almost, is suddenly vexed by it. The best souls in the whole world are vexed in the same way as the most frivolous. Old age and youth live in two universes. I feel for you child, in your struggle. Yet it is a battle I myself have somehow strangely won these latter years, and my home now is such that I have entered into a second boyhood almost—and am as naturally in place as though only twelve years old. But many special circumstances may have brought this about. Few others work it as well.

I wrote to your friend Untermeyer today. I didn't write to Wheelock. I am just a bit jealous of his place with you—and am not going to pretend. I don't want it—but am just mean enough to be a bit envious, and as I say, I am not going to go through any insincere motions. ...

Sometimes I feel that after finishing one more piece of writing I ought to take to the road for awhile, and not have any mail forwarded, or anything. The welfare of the spirit is above all, and everything seems to smother me and keep me from the Eternal Presence. I have not yet completely shaken off the flatteries of Chicago. And your sweetness binds me, and the sweetness of other women, and sets my heart to bleeding. You are all my darling friends, the enemy. Try as I will, I cannot always remain cool with you Sara. Yet I *must* be cold as the stars.

By the end of March, Vachel was very eager to see Sara again, although he made it clear that his interest was not, at this stage, romantic:

... I don't pretend to be making desperate love to you, but I am certainly very hungry to see you.

* * *

... I send you my love, and say I hope to meet you, as soon as it is right—and that meeting or not, we will never take one step forward we will have to retrace, but continue gravely and steadily to the end—loyal in fine friendship whether there be the fevers of spring between us or no. I want my life to be full of elements as eternal as the stars.

Getting to St. Louis, however, presented quite a problem to a poet with no income. Only as a last resort did he wish to approach his father about the money for such a trip. But the urgency of his desire to see Sara again made his mind whirl with plans, and on April 4 he appealed to Harriet Monroe:

Now I want you to do me a very great favor, if it can be arranged with no great trouble to yourself. I want to be asked to St. Louis by some one you know, to entertain their friends. If I could for instance have such a hostess as your sister Mrs. Monroe it would be ideal—though that would be a deal to ask. I would like to spend about three days in the town, between Easter and May the first—enough to call on our mutual Sara about three afternoons. Now don't explain to my hostess my motive. I will tell her, if she is a real leddy—when the time comes. I want to be asked down on my merits—and my car-fare sent me by my hostess and five dollars pocket-money. $10 altogether. In return for this I will recite for any number of people (10 to 1000) if my hostess desires—any number of evenings. I will include the Santa Fé Trail in my performance. I hate a hotel. I am dead broke. I want to see Sara and I don't want to ask the folks—Springfield home—to pay for my picnic. Sara lives in a lovely home—and her old folks are very sweet and kind—but they are *so* old—and they are not likely to be the sort to collect my crowd anyway, or get much fun out of the show. They are eminently dignified Baptists as I understand them. ... Mr. K[ennerley] owes me $250 to $300, and will not answer my letters. And my letters to him have been respectful—and not particularly frequent. I mention this not to be telling on him—but just to show there is a reason why I am reduced to makeshifts. He is my principal publisher at present, though another looms on the horizon, and I don't want to wait till I make some money before I call on my St. Louis lady friend. Mama says I *ought* to wait. Maybe I *ought*, but I ain't. Now my dear Harriet—unless there is somebody who would want me—in a perfectly natural way—I don't want the thing to happen. Maybe some of my other Chicago hostesses can suggest some one. Just tell them I am brash and vain, and want to spread myself in St. Louis.

And now—curiosity box—of course you want to know what is *in* all this? A purely PLATONIC admiration. But since I have written about 'steen thousand letters to Sara—*and* have only seen her 24 hours of me life—one long rather strained day—we were so dammed up with things to say—well—I want to correct the lop-sidedness of our acquaintance, and be able to chat at leisure.

No—I do not *belong* to anyone in the world. Never will.

On the whole I hope it's a neighbor of Sara's—somebody in walking distance. But I am getting too full of specifications.[5]

---

[5]Scattered sentences from this letter appear in Harriet Monroe, *A Poet's Life* (New York: The Macmillan Company, 1938), p. 281.

A letter from the editor of *Poetry* with a check of $5 enclosed for a book review crossed his plea for help with his problem, and soon afterwards, he wrote again to Miss Monroe:

First let me thank you for the $5, for the criticism on Ficke. If it had arrived a day or so sooner (by some divine accident) I would not have written you my letter. As it was I wrote to St. Louis I was coming in a minute and went—and it is surprising the number of things that can be done with one five dollar bill in the company of some one who makes a chirping noise in your ear as you do it. And I read the lady the Santa Fé Trail and was properly chastened and will make it a bit less like an unmitigated noise before I forward it to you. It is a Kallyope yell with *few* flute-notes at present. It needs a few *more* flute-notes from the Rachel-Jane (meadow lark) to mellow the middle. Then you shall have it.

My present financial crisis having passed, you do not need to *rack* your comradely brains to get me to Saint Looy. *And* Sara's sister having taken a hand in the matter, *may* get me an address before some Woman's Club down there next fall.

And then Reedy talks about having me down to hoot for his crowd as soon as he recovers from what he calls "gout and delirium tremens." I met him and had a talk with him for a few minutes. A most amazing man.

* * *

Sara was all commendation, but I could just see the harshness of the auto-horns jarred her. I must put in a bird and surprise her.

Vachel was keenly sensitive to Sara's feeling for beauty; and because of her influence, certain of his lines and phrases are endowed with a quality of grace that they probably would not otherwise have had. Not long after reading her "The Santa Fé Trail," he confessed that he would do his best to

. . . bring in dozens of refinements and overtones and tiny flutes and fairy whispers and Yeatsy quietnesses and twilights, and they shall all be done with the thought of you, if *you* only *care enough.* To put it very realistically I am in love with your kind of a literary nervous-system. I want to please it and ensnare it. I would not jar or discomfort it for the world.

After his second visit to St. Louis, Vachel felt closer than ever to Sara. His letters became even more frequent, and in one he said:

I know it looks self indulgent to write you two letters a day, but I just *must* write of an evening or I go to sleep feeling I have missed something.

* * *

...I not only like Sara, but I like her a heap, and turn toward her more and more with an unharnessed and unbridled heart.

By the end of April, the thought of her stayed with him so constantly that he was seriously pondering their relationship:

I tell you dearest of Saraphims—I have been so desperately whirl-windy in love *sometimes* I *know* I am not *in love* with *you*. I am not spinning around in that desperate distressing cyclone manner, not in the least. This by way of preliminary and vindication! BUT I think of you and toward you as a fellow spinner of dreams, most every minute, and the thought of you is good society. It is companionship and happiness and calm and smiles. It is so good to have a playmate that plays the same game—and understands the same world of words.

There is one very very great objection to you. You are *not* a daughter of the soil. My mother has more culture than any woman I ever knew—and more talent—and essential civilization. Yet she is still a farmer's daughter. She has spoiled me in a way—for none of the Darling Saraphims have any of the Kansas Harvester in them.

My only real fear in loving you—(if I should ever come to such a fire!)—is that I would be so far from that embrace with the green earth which is my natural goal. I have been thinking of it a lot lately. If I have a destiny it is to give voice to the six feet of black earth beneath us—yet the more I know of you the more I want to do the usual man's part to keep you from treading it.

I want to keep your feets out of the mud. Yet the only place I would have a legitimate right to kiss you would be on the edge of a wheat-field—the thermometer at 108 degrees—but I fear me you will never wear the necessary sunbonnet. Or in a pouring rain forty miles from anywhere. But you would be scart—that far away.

I do not know whether you like the rude truth or not—but these are things I have been thinking. And a hundred like them, but worse.

Life itself is always as curiously complex as our little fraternity of two—delicacy at war with desire—and the simplicity of the soil at war with sophistication—in both of us, but in me the most at war.

To have been a farmer's daughter would probably have kept *you* forever from those final delicate influences that make your song such honey in my fancy, yet the lack of being one is what I fear in you most. Suppose I take a two-years' tramp, and then come and put you in a hut?

And yet I would not want to drag you through one of the rough things I have been through—I do not want one harsh breeze to ruffle one hair of your head. And you would hate to be a peasant in a hut—really.

Frequently, these poets sent their new poems to each other for criticism. Vachel, especially, grew to rely on Sara's judgment, and he once told her: "You are a darling friend, and when it comes to English we drive almost like your own team of black horses, I believe." Almost every poem that he wrote from the time that they met through the rest of his life was submitted to her for her critical reactions. During the spring and summer of 1914 he was preparing his new book, *The Congo and Other Poems,* for fall publication, and he told Harriet Monroe:

With the help of Sara I winnowed down 108 poems to 68 and took most of her corrections which confirmed most of my misgivings. She has given very liberally of her time in the matter and her best attention and I am ever so pleased and grateful.

To Sara, after she had gone over the manuscript for this book, he wrote:

Thank you for your most industrious and delectable criticisms. You voiced almost every misgiving of mine. Yours might be a carbon copy of mine—on the same typewriter—with one or two exceptions where you were too lenient. You have helped me to be firm on the very matters in which I was uncertain—but darkly suspicious.

Because their interests naturally ran in the same channels, they often discussed other poets and their works. Sara lent Vachel *The Human Fantasy* by John Hall Wheelock, and she was eager to hear his verdict of it. On April 28 he wrote to her:

. . . I honor you for liking the author just as I honor him. . . . I'll have to admit a person with a soul such as this book shows is a credit to any young woman. If he isn't a thoroughbred—I am much deceived.

In the spring of 1914, Dr. and Mrs. Lindsay went to China for a much deserved vacation, to visit their elder daughter who was married to Dr. Paul Wakefield, a medical missionary. It may be that this visit focused Vachel's attention upon China at this particular moment in his life; for in May of 1914, he wrote Sara of a new poem that he had started to compose, which was to become his finest work. Possibly, many influences contributed to its evolution, for the Lindsays had a Chinese laundryman, and since Dr. Wakefield and his wife had been in China for several years, the country and its legends had a close family interest for the poet. Too, Sara's lyricism was responsible for the idea of a nightingale being very much in his thoughts in these days, and he told her:

I have been altogether absorbed in The Chinese Nightingale. I am afraid I will be talking it now in my letters till you are completely sick of it.

You must grant me absolution. I walked round and round the Square yesterday with the most wonderful unworded music going through my head—hunting for words that would even *hint* at it. . . .

During this time Sara's father had a stroke, and the doctors warned the family that he must have no excitement whatever.

Her mother, who also had gone steadily downhill in health, was far from well, and Sara felt the responsibility of her parents' care more each day. She confided her worries to Vachel. He sympathized with her, but at that moment he was so full of the thrilling experience that his new poem was giving him, he had to speak of it to her.

While you have been so unhappy—to tell you the truth, child, I have been *very* happy. The Chinese Nightingale has been singing in my heart till it was like to burst, all the long days. Only a few broken phrases on paper to show for it.—I haven't had quite such an experience since I wrote The Last Song of Lucifer (!) perhaps. (Well—I *will* omit it!)[6] So—as I say—the nightingale has almost drowned out the universe. If I get the poem within a thousand miles of the enchantment that holds me I will have a good one.

I will venture the refrain.

A ghost-nightingale—thousands of years old—sings in a Chinese laundry for the night-shift—about 4 o'clock in the morning, sings of the most ancient possible days of China.

> "I remember I remember
> That spring came on forever
> That spring came on forever"
> said the Chinese nightingale.

His memories get dimmer and dimmer as he goes back through the ages—verse by verse—but always from the beginning—spring after the snows of winter.

It may sound strange—but I said to myself yesterday—this happiness has made my whole life worth while. It was as though there was a bough in my breast—and there the bird sang as though his throat were a river or a fountain.

It is something utterly beyond me. I hardly know what to do with myself. Certainly the poem may turn out to be a third rate thing. But I will never forget that ghost of a bird.

Much of Sara's time in the early spring of 1914 was occupied with the poet from Springfield. She was drawn to the unaffected

---

6Evidently, Sara had suggested that Vachel omit this poem from his book.

simplicity of the man and the fresh vitality of the poet; she was flattered by his attention, coming so suddenly upon the unexciting landscape of her life and increasing in intensity daily. She could not help but be intrigued by the little ink sketches that illustrated his voluminous letters, or the stars that he drew, each one of which stood for "a kiss for thy hand" or "a kiss for thy brow." But her store of nervous energy was drained by his visits; his exuberance wore her out; she was sensible enough to realize, after a time, when she was left exhausted, that perhaps their temperaments and ways of life were not ideally congenial.

In the midst of this strenuous friendship with Lindsay, Sara met, in April of 1914, through Eunice Tietjens, another unusual and interesting person—a man destined to play an important part in her life. For in spite of Vachel's overwhelming attention, Sara was hungry for the companionship of some of her other friends who were out of town or far away. When *Harper's Magazine* sent her a check for ten dollars for a poem, she sent the check to Eunice in Chicago and told her that she could think of no better way to spend this money than on Eunice's train fare for a visit to St. Louis. Eunice, who was living on a limited budget, used the check as it was intended, and she has left in her own words the way Sara and Ernst Filsinger met:

Now Paul Tietjens came from St. Louis and I had often visited there, making many acquaintances. But on this occasion there was only one whom I wished to see, Ernst Filsinger, at that time in the shoe business, later to become the well-known international trade expert. I phoned Ernst, and the last day I was there I lunched with him. When I told him I was visiting Sara Teasdale something extraordinary happened to his face. It seemed to melt completely. I had never seen the real man in him before, but now it shone out like a light. Without answering directly he began to recite:

> When I am dead and over me bright April
> Shakes out her rain-drenched hair . . .

and he continued through most of the poems Sara had then published. I was amazed and touched.

Then Ernst told me that he had loved Sara for years through her poems, but that he had never met her. She lived very quietly with her family and almost never went out in society. He had joined a literary group to which she belonged with the hope of meeting her; but she seldom came, and he had always missed her. Would I now introduce him?

It was too late to do so in person; but I felt that so much devotion should be rewarded, and I arranged the matter with Sara. He called the next evening and many evenings thereafter, and the friendship between them ripened fast. Ernst was tall and very distinguished-looking and bore even then the hall-marks of his later success. I could not blame Sara for her interest.[7]

Reserved in manner, sympathetic by nature, and very much interested in the worlds of art, music, and literature, although he was a businessman, Ernst Filsinger was six feet, two inches tall, and most attractive in appearance. He was born in St. Louis on June 10, 1880, the son of Henry J. and Katherine Ernst Filsinger. Though he was a very good student, he attended high school only two or three years and was not able to go to college; law was the field that he had expected to enter. But the devastating tornado that struck St. Louis with sudden fury, killing hundreds of people, in 1896, wrecked the Filsinger home and seriously injured his mother, and he thought that the family needed what aid he could offer. He applied for work at a wholesale shoe company and was the one boy selected for the position out of one hundred applicants. However, he continued studying at night, concentrating on foreign languages; he spoke Spanish, French, and German, and had studied Portuguese, Italian, and Russian. His business ability eventually brought him wide recognition as an expert on international trade, and inclusion in *Who's Who*. He contributed a number of articles to technical journals, gave a series of lectures at the Harvard Graduate School of Business Administration, and was the author of

---

[7]Tietjens, *op. cit.*, pp. 53-54.

two books: *Exporting to Latin America* (1916) and *Commercial Traveller's Guide to Latin America* (1920).

When Sara first met Ernst Filsinger, she was attracted to him because he reminded her of John Hall Wheelock; both men were tall, reserved, and had what she called "the same philosophical temper." After that first delightful evening spent with Sara discussing all manner of things, Ernst took her to the Contemporary Club for dinner and to an Ethical Society lecture during the same week. Soon she was seeing more and more of him.

Meanwhile, Vachel wanted to return to St. Louis for another visit; it was impossible for Sara to ask him to stay at the Teasdale home with her father so ill and her mother unwell. Feeling the strain of family cares more every day, early in May Sara went to Saxton's Farm for a week, where the soft air, the fragrant fields, and the glorious spring moonlight revived her body and spirit. Here both Vachel and Ernst came to see her.

For the first time, Vachel realized that Sara was more than just a very dear friend to him. He began to look at his home town through her eyes, and he wrote her after his visit:

I do not know where we are going, lady, but I have gotten this far. I want to know if you *like* Springfield and Springfield people— or if it appears a hopeless place to you. I want to know if such a set would wear you to the bone or if you could enjoy them.

Maybe I owe my town only a nominal allegiance—maybe I owe *more* to you—*wherever* you happen to be.

These things cannot be arrived at in a hurry. At present the town is *very much* a part of me, foolish little place that it is. In a sense, you do not know me till you have seen it. And yet—the road calls so loud—I sometimes think my destiny may weave me in as a sort of thin silk fiber all through the warp and woof of the dreamers of the United States. I feel myself as it were—a shuttle going back and forth to make a strong cloth of dreams. Whichever I am: (1.) a man of the road, (2.) a man of Springfield or (3.) Sara's man renouncing all other allegiances, I love you dearly, and I must henceforth keep thinking thinking on your real place and mission in my destiny, and my real place and mission in your destiny.

Slowly, Sara, his good friend, had become to Vachel the girl he loved. He told her that "one more golden hair is wound round my heart every day." To his own surprise, the poet now began to think of marriage, but he knew that there was an almost impossible barrier so far as he was concerned, and he shared his thoughts with Sara:

... If I stick to my ideals, I will never have the coin. ...

... I admit it would take scads of money, and scads of money is the last thing I will ever turn my hand over to get. So there you are.

And yet you make me so happy I beat my wings against the cage and peep out at you every minute and try the bars, and wonder and wonder, and wonder. If we *can't* have a *courtship*-and-marriage, we must have *some* kind of a lovely adventure, like bringing out a book together or co-laborating on a play or something. Or we must get lost in a snowstorm together or I must rescue you from drowning, or you must nurse me through a great sickness on the edge of the desert or something. We must have *some* kind of a mutual-living-and-breathing—before we part—before the book of friendship "softly closes."

Harriet Monroe had not forgotten the poet's urgent request; and at her suggestion, Mrs. Charles Parsons Pettus of St. Louis invited Lindsay to her home early in June to read his work for a group of friends. This gave Vachel another much-desired opportunity to see his Gloriana; and when he left St. Louis he sent her some flowers with this note:

Tuesday morning.

Gold flowers—
    to the Golden Lady—
    with moon-gold and sun-gold and
    flower-gold thoughts of her. N.V.L.

By now Sara's parents had recovered sufficiently to consider spending the summer in Charlevoix; and Sara decided that she would go to New York before she joined them at Altasand. She planned to stop on the way in Chicago and visit her friends there. It had been a number of years since Vachel had been in New York; his memories of it were not especially happy ones, as he had had a desperate struggle, financially, when he was attending art school and working at various occupations to support himself. But Sara urged him to come to the city while she was there, see his publisher, and meet some of the literary people whom he should know. However, he was not inclined to want to leave Springfield; his roots were firmly planted in Illinois soil, and he felt that he should spend every bit of his time in his study, writing. Furthermore, he told Sara, half in fun and half seriously:

If you want to go to New York just to study your spiritual barometer in regard to Wheelock weather, I do not see what business I have around disturbing the *observation* station.

But he was beginning to realize the value of literary contacts in regard to his future speaking tours. And it was hard for him to ignore Sara's request. She had grown to mean so much to him that he wrote her on June 5, 1914:

... I have come to the point where I am willing to make a considerable sacrifice of my plans to be with you a little while. It looks like a little to you but it is an enormous step for me. Please take it as seriously as possible.

And if, through this,[8] my only possible source of real income that shows at present on the horizon, I can come anywhere *near* the income that can keep you safe and happy and living your life as life has been for you, I shall certainly ask for your heart forever. ...

* * *

You see, I *cannot* go on writing forever, like a machine, especially poetry. But I *can* go on speaking forever once I am carefully established. And one should not marry till he is doing something that he can do every day the year round. And I am perfectly willing

[8]Reciting.

and able to work at this for you—the year round, if it can be made to pay.

* * *

...I am quite sure that you are going to New York to see Wheelock. I love you well enough to almost forget that.

Remember, some day you may have to choose, and choose forever. But we will not cross that bridge till we must.[9]

Harriet Monroe, who always had Vachel's interests at heart, invited him to Chicago, too, when she learned of Sara's impending visit. She even offered him financial aid, if he needed it, but he replied:

Everyone is so good to me it makes me ashamed. No—I don't need an advance to get to Chicago. But while there, there is a present I *hope* to buy for Sara—if—you owe me enough!

Just before he left for Chicago, Lindsay suggested to Sara that they meet by the statue of Lincoln in Lincoln Park and talk things over.

You have completely disarmed my heart. I am bare and open for any hurt or cruelty you may do to me. So deal gently.

Well, I hope Father Abraham stands me in good stead. I hope you are his daughter. You are the one person on earth for whom I could cheerfully and even joyfully betray him. I hope that by being true to you I can be even more true to him. I shall see half the world through your eyes henceforth, if I continue in this gentle slavery.

Good night—pillar of gold, and ivory and moonlight.

In Chicago, though Sara had not committed herself in any way, Vachel bought the ring that he had in mind, and he told Sara to send for it just as soon as she was ready to accept it. After she left for New York, Vachel remained in Chicago for a few

---

[9]Vachel Lindsay apparently assumed that John Hall Wheelock also was a suitor under consideration by Sara, a very natural assumption under the circumstances, but, of course, a mistaken one.

days. His mind was constantly turning over any possible financial arrangements that would make marriage possible. It was an entirely new experience for him to be concentrating so strongly upon the best way for him to earn a steady income. Once, long ago, it had been necessary for him to break an engagement for this very reason. Now his love for Sara had completely changed his outlook; and thinking of these things he wrote to her from Chicago.

... I *must* start the bank account. My zeal in this matter is my real sacrifice for your sake—certainly well worth making, and I am willing to stand or fall on this test. It is the hardest possible test to which I can be put. As a general rule I certainly hate money. But you make the attempt a happy enterprise. I want to alter the course and motives and point of view of my life enough to *get you and keep you safe and happy.* I am by no means certain I will ever get there, *but* I am dearly loving the attempt. I *want* you, and that is all there is of it. I want you for keeps. I gave you my *soul* with my kisses.

As for an *establishment.* Papa and Mama in their way are truly *generous* in an *emergency,* far more than day by day, which is natural. They would certainly do their best to set us up in housekeeping *right*—and they are very anxious for me to get *married,* as Mama has written of late, and she has said over and over. So, *practically* speaking, what I need to provide for us is not so much an *establishment,* as a *sure income* for the day by day expenditure. I see that plainly. Creative work will never get it—it is too exhausting. Reciting is about my only chance—for I can recite the same piece day after day, till new ones come. I can approximately recite for every meal I eat. *Whatever* one's *business,* he generally has to do something like that—some routine.

I think when once we see an *income* that has a reasonable appearance of steadiness we can go ahead. Even a fairly large windfall or temporary success, as success of *one book* will not do.

There is a great peace in my heart when I think of you dear, and whether you decide for me or the other man—I shall dearly dearly love you and never be angry. I cannot but wish him good fortune in general—a fair field. I do not think anyone but a thoroughbred could have written The Human Fantasy. It *is* the wise thing for you to marry . . . and I have no right to ask you to wait very *long* on my uncertain fortunes. But certainly if you are undecided you ought to wait till Christmas to see how my next book goes—and if you truly care—you darling Sara—you *ought* to wait till I get at least one reciting tour going in the East—Jan., Feb. and March—to see if there is a *reasonable* hope of me having an income. If there is no hope by this time next year—you certainly ought to give me up. I shall love you dearly till I die, whatever you do.

I love you very tenderly and devoutly—and want you very very much. Please send for the ring—the minute you can honestly put it on.

With love
N.V.L.

A few days later he wrote:

I cannot pretend to be certain about our future. I only know that you fill my heart—that the very thought of you is like a breath of high mountain air.

* * *

I suppose that about half the time I am in a trance of desire for you—and the rest of the time or even all the time there is a great peace in my heart in the thought that I love you—a strange trance of gentle happiness—that comes above the fire I may say—and is such a very very different thing from the fire your beauty makes.

There is one thing of which I am so sure that nothing will ever change it—that you will always be exquisitely lovable—whether I win you or not—I have given my heart to one of God's finest creatures—that every thought and memory of you will be sweet and gentle—if we keep together or part. You are so exquisitely fine—such a thoroughbred, such a tender heart—such a gentle lady. I have done myself the highest possible honor in giving you my heart.

Vachel Lindsay was royally entertained in Chicago, but it was not long before he yearned to escape this adulation and step back into the simplicity of his Springfield life. He explained to Sara:

But I believe now I ought to go home, clear up my mail, and walk over Sangamon County. I will cut my boarding house for a week or so, walking all day in some direction every day and getting in by dark each night, turning around at noon. I want to learn every road in the County. I laid out the plan long ago. Now I must go *to* it, to get the sugar of all these flatteries out of my system. I want out of doors and dogs barking—yet a little different task than before. A spiritual map of Sangamon County appeals to me at this juncture. I want to approach my home from a new angle. And I want to develop a method of road-work that will not make you anxious if we are married, and I want to get away from the beautiful flatteries of Chicago, and the mixed flatteries and spites of Springfield. And I want to stick to my dreams in a fashion.

Sara darling, I love you with my whole heart and I want you, and I am full of happy happy allegiance. I want our lives to be one roof, one pillow, one kiss, one life-work-of-song for America, one glory, one sadness, one mutual loving and praying....

All through the month of June, Vachel was exploring every possible solution to the financial problem, and he always reached the same conclusion: that he must establish himself as a public speaker, and when his reputation had become firmly fixed, he could support Sara in this manner the rest of his life. While still in Chicago on June 19, he sent her this message:

Our fate—is more or less in the hands of the American people. I keep thinking about it....

I want you very much, but I must not put you under a strain by courting you very hard or dragging you into a marriage that will put you on the rack. I have got to keep on being myself—and submit to that fate—for when I try *too* hard to change I only bounce back again. I went through such a horrible nightmare when I was younger, trying to make money, and not making it, that I do not want to exhibit myself again before you in *that* character. Never do I appear to less advantage. I must just let my work unfold itself to a certain extent, or else I will just go crazy. I want you to be happy and quiet and serene all along, spared from a flabbergasted courtship and a flabbergasted marriage.

But somehow I am *very* hopeful. It is hard to say—"move slowly," when one's heart is afire. . . .

Though Vachel's heart was certainly "afire," he confessed to Sara late in June:

I am always haunted by the 90 million Americans. They are your deadly rivals—more than any one woman—is, and their mighty chaos, compared with your golden star-like unity is a strange antithesis. Half my ambition and love given to a mystic chaos and half to a girl-jewel that I could hide under a shawl. It is a strange rivalry. It is no literary affectation with me. The 90 million haunt me day and night. I wonder if I ever could make you feel as I do about them.

* * *

. . . The 90 million are your rival, just as Wheelock is mine.

When Vachel arrived home from his Chicago trip, Sara was still suggesting that he come to New York while she was there; she knew that they would enjoy being together, and she also knew that he could accomplish a great deal to further his own career. He finally decided that she was right and confessed:

. . . I have been struggling with myself ever since I reached home, and your letter has decided me. My heart fought my head every minute. Now my head is quite convinced.

And since their future financial affairs were still weighing heavily upon his mind, he went on to explain:

I used to be terribly touchy about money, when my work which never paid was received only with contempt or coldness. Now that it reflects a certain amount of publicity and alleged credit upon my people, they and I have both greatly relaxed on the question, and it has been less a matter of conscience on either side. For a long time they thought it a matter of duty to whip or torture me by any possible psychological thumbscrew into earning my living at ANYTHING honest, and quit what I was doing. I grew to hate the very name of money as I would hate the face of the devil.

Ernst Filsinger

But now they no longer grudge me what I really need. They take a sort of pride in giving it and I have no more heartaches about taking it. But though this attitude may be all very well for a single man and a poet, the only child still left at home, it's no frame of mind for Sara's lover, who should be grown up. To marry you without an income of my own would be torture. Yet torture will never make me a business man, or it would have done so long ago. I cannot *hustle* my fortunes. They move slowly like a little deliberate inevitable glacier. Not an avalanche! ...

Vachel planned to spend most of the month of July in New York; his parents were still in China, and the Springfield home was in the hands of a family who was renting part of the house. His last letter to Sara on June 27, before he started for the East, left her in no doubt as to how completely and deeply he was in love with her.

Child, I want to unravel all the skein of love this side of marriage. I say it most solemnly. I do not think it right to put it in words here. I must write my thoughts on your shoulders. I want to be bound hand and foot and I want to bind you hand and foot. So I beg you prepare your chains.

... Never for a moment pretend with me. I want to kiss your hand when that is your mood, and your heart when that is your mood, and be sober and a brother when that is your mood, and follow the music of your mood. Yet I want you to have mercy upon mine. There is so much of you that is unplowed prairie soil, that I would sow with kisses and make my own.

We must be dignified before folks—*be stern with me there*—for I am half-mad with hunger for your young Botticelli self. I think of you everlastingly in your white shawl with the cherub border. There are times when the breathless vision of your earthly physical self seems the very incarnation of your *whole self,* so very white is the whiteness, so brave with love the eyes. Yet I KNOW behind it all is not Eve or Aphrodite, but my sober master and comrade Sara, whom I desire to obey and respect always, to whom all this is but one wave of the dark strange tide of life.

I must be dignified in company and when we are alone together. If I am not perfectly worshipful, please tell me so every minute, for we are these hours weaving our mutual soul, and in a sense beginning the weaving of our mutual bodily self. And God knows I want to weave both—finely, intimately, strongly—in the fear of Heaven, so they can never be untangled, yet as much character and harmony and pride in our mutual self, as in our best selves separately. We must walk through the fire—not blindly—but with a certain snowiness and dew in the midst of our hearts, as though we were gray sweet philosophers after all, and patriarchs to be, in 1950.

For if we are doing anything worthy of the respect of the angels, we are building our mutual spiritual house, that must come before the real house, and last as long or longer. . . .

* * *

When we plan marriage, we must expect as many ups and downs, quarrels, jolts, sorrows and spiritual *successes* as our parents have had. And in all our loving let us *not* dream this *weaving* is the goal or exact it of each other literally forever. If we do as well at the age of sober old folks, as our sober old folks, we will do as well as mortal clay can expect. We must see the grey hairs through. It is all *a part* of the game, and we must not refuse the game because it will not be all the first day of spring. We must be true to *Love* and also to *Life,* which is another, subtler name. I know not how to say it, except that the thought haunts me, and I *must* say it.

I am trying to say that a true and not a false eternity must be in our dreams, the eternity of being actually together in 1950. . . .

And we must be so happy and sober in the fiery furnace that when it is gone, there will be left fine fighting steel—the mutual Sara and Vachel blade—*not* ashes or cinders.

Sometimes it seems to me the only difference in all the world in people and work and worth—are the differences between silk and hemp. They can be made into the same sized rope, but for the same size, a silk rope would be infinitely stronger. And so dear golden-hair, I pray the dear God in every sense—I may love you *well.*

In this letter, Vachel enclosed the first draft of "The Spice Tree," which he had just written to her and to the memory of their being together.

With Vachel in New York, Sara enjoyed many happy moments; among other things planned for her pleasure was a party given by Mr. Edward J. Wheeler, which was attended by Vachel, John Hall Wheelock, Louis Untermeyer, and other of her friends. But though Sara respected Vachel's vigorous ability as a poet and the idealistic concepts of which he dreamed, and though she remained until the end of her life deeply devoted to him as a friend, she realized more and more that she was not equal to living with his tremendous vitality, nor was she romantically in love with him. Her experience in New York, where for the first time they had the opportunity to be together for long periods of time, convinced her as nothing else had done that her physical need for many hours of rest and solitude could never be adjusted to the rhythm of Vachel's life.

Yet the tenderness in Vachel's spirit that Sara came to know moved her immeasurably; and the fact that he loved her so deeply, and needed her so desperately, caused her to weigh seriously the possibility of marriage with him. She realized, too, that because of their literary interests, they had much in common. Because she loved *love* so much, she hoped she could persuade her heart to respond to Vachel's pleas, but it was impossible.

Her practical vision made her foresee that if they married, very probably they would have to live on an allowance from her family, and she did not wish to place their relationship in such a situation, for she knew it would only bring ultimate conflict and unhappiness to both of them.

She never deceived Lindsay about her uncertainty, and he, though earnestly hoping that she would decide in his favor, understood her position and sympathized with her. On July 27, at the end of his stay in New York, he reported to Harriet Monroe:

Poor dear Sara is a monument of indecision so far as the *future* goes. As for the *present* there is no indecision about her. She is worth coming to New York to visit. Yes indeedy, and yes—again

And I am so happy with her I can't worry about losing her till I am dead sure I will. This has been a great month for yours truly. . . .

Lindsay did, indeed, have a "great month," for he managed to accomplish some other things of importance besides spending precious time with Sara. Mrs. William Vaughan Moody lent him her apartment for his stay in New York, which was a great help and convenience for him. With a lawyer he visited his reluctant publisher and came away with part of the money due him. Having written to a number of people in New York over the years, he now had a chance to meet them personally and thoroughly enjoyed doing so. And he made an engagement to return to New York in the fall for a recitation of his own work.

Near the end of Vachel's stay in New York, he and Sara went out one evening in bad weather, and, unfortunately, Sara got wet and developed a severe cold. When Vachel left for home, Sara was still quite ill and confined to her hotel room. For the first time, Vachel realized how physically frail Sara was and how necessary it was for her to guard her health constantly. Much concerned about her, he wrote as soon as he arrived in Springfield on July 29:

And if you only get well I will even admit it was good fortune for me that you caught cold. The very sight of your struggle made me understand the whole vista of your noble, exquisite and struggling life, and understand the rare triumph of your concentrated personality against such odds. . . .

And I am loving you so dearly, and in such reality, your struggle has brought you home to me as nothing else could—the real you that has triumphed over these things in times past, and will triumph again. You are as real and near to me as this bracelet round my neck.

* * *

To court you is like courting a snowflake, you fade so easily. That is from one standpoint. Yet from another, you are nearer to an indestructible personality, a walking immortal soul than anything else I have met on this planet. . . .

Vachel arrived home in the mood of a man who had drunk of a strange and wonderful elixir. After the enchanted horizons of New York, his native city appeared in a slightly different aspect to him. He told Sara: "I have been in Fairyland, and it makes Springfield a strange place, except my study, where I feel more at home with myself than ever." Filled with renewed strength and inspiration, he was ready now to plunge into hard work for several months, since he had arranged a speaking tour in the fall, and he wanted to have some new poems to give his audiences. His desk was covered with many, many half-finished manuscripts, among them "The Chinese Nightingale" and "The Ghosts of the Buffaloes." The spell that Sara and New York had cast stayed with him, and on July 31, he wrote her:

All my little world has so changed and little Springfield has so changed in my eyes, and you have grown so much more wonderful and real, I look at my life in a dazed way and am lost in wonder. To tell you just the change is hard at midnight, in a short letter. I feel the call of the Middle West *much stronger,* yet I have a much keener sense of just why New York is worth much to you. I see your whole noble civilized little self in its setting much plainer.... And I am drowned in the wonder of my own thoughts about your destiny and mine.

Not long after Vachel left New York, Ernst Filsinger arrived to spend a few days. Just as Harriet Monroe had helped Vachel's cause along, so Eunice Tietjens was looking out for Ernst's interests. When Sara had been in Chicago on her way to New York, she had discussed her problem with her two good friends, one day in the little office of *Poetry* on Cass Street. Eunice Tietjens has left a detailed account of what happened:

...Harriet and I were there. Sara, with her lovely grace, sat down on the floor between us and asked for our advice. Both Vachel Lindsay and Ernst Filsinger loved her, she said, though Ernst had not yet formally asked her to marry him. She was half in love with each of them, but she could not yet make up her mind which it should be. What did we advise?

Harriet spoke first and said that, though she did not know Filsinger, she thought that when one had a chance to marry a great poet like Vachel Lindsay, one should accept it gratefully.

I thought otherwise, and said so. "But one does not marry the great poet! One marries the man, which is a very different thing!" I protested.[10] Sara and Vachel were so divergent in their every angle on life that I was sure it would be bad for the work of both of them. Moreover Vachel was always penniless, and Sara, who was never well and who had been raised in luxury, needed the things which money could buy. Then too Vachel was a dynamo of energy and exhausted Sara. (Once when he had been courting her strenuously for a week she was obliged to take to her bed for three to recuperate.) Ernst on the other hand would always take care of her. She would be to him the moon and the stars. And besides, in spite of the Brownings, I thought that any two great poets were ill adapted for marriage. So I argued.

Sara arose, still undecided, and went to New York. A few weeks later I had a letter from her telling me that Vachel was there, courting her in his usual strenuous way. I could read between the lines that she was fast veering towards his side of the case.

So I wrote a letter to Ernst and told him what was happening and that if he was really interested in Sara it was time he acted. He proved to be a man quite capable of taking a tip. I had a telegram the day he received the letter asking me to be near the phone at six o'clock that evening. He wished to talk to me over long distance. When the time came, he did little but burble disconnectedly in dismay and confusion to the tune of, "She should never be allowed to do this! It will be bad for her, bad!"

But he acted at once. Sara told me afterwards that her room in the New York Hotel was filled to overflowing for the next few weeks with letters, special delivery letters, telegrams, and all the orchids and other flowers and candy to be had in the city. It stopped her

---

10At this time Eunice Tietjens was in the process of obtaining a divorce from the composer and conductor, Paul Tietjens, who wrote, among other well-known compositions, the score for *The Wizard of Oz*.

from slipping into matrimony with Vachel, and presently she sent for Ernst. He came through Chicago riding a crest of hope, like a man beside himself. . . .[11]

The more Sara saw of Ernst, after he arrived in New York, the more harmonious their natures and interests seemed. As she was soon to leave New York for Altasand, she invited him to visit her family there where they could have more time together. But she was still undecided as to what her ultimate decision would be. When Eunice Tietjens inquired about the state of her heart, Sara could only answer that she had suddenly grown beyond her own forecasting.

Her family sympathized with her and sent her words of loving encouragement. Mr. Teasdale wrote her on August 3: "Try to take matters as calmly as possible, and be assured you have our prayers." Mamie, speaking of Ernst's good habits, added a postscript to her father's letter: "Good luck to you little girl. That a man be good is the most important thing in getting married."

And on the next day, her mother sent this message from Altasand:

Now Sadie, my child, I think you will be happier if you are married to *suit yourself* and if you do that we will be glad and we will always make the best of it. I think both are good men and you may never have as good a chance again. However you must decide, you may like Mr. F. very much if you see much of him and you must have time to make up your own mind and don't get upset. . . . We are sorry not to be with you on your birthday but don't come till you are able and you are welcome to bring Mr. Filsinger here for a week if you want.

Try to get well, and then you can see your way more clearly about everything. Let us know when you are coming and when he is coming or if he is not coming. Be sure to take good care of yourself and be thankful 2 *good men* want you. (Remember some ain't got none) and we want you too. Love from Mama and Papa.

---

[11]Tietjens, *op. cit.*, pp. 54-56.

As soon as Sara was well enough, Ernst went with her to Altasand. And it was not long before Sara realized that Ernst was the man who had won her heart and who was going to be her husband.

However, before giving Ernst her definite answer, Sara consulted Mr. Wheelock. She had come to place great confidence in the judgment of this very good friend, who seemed, also, so natural and appropriate a person to turn to. Mr. Wheelock, who was fiercely intent on making poetry the main purpose of his life, had never contemplated marriage and would not, at that time, have contemplated it, even if he had been so placed, financially, as to be able to consider it at all. He was, therefore, while a devoted friend, an impartial outsider, in a sense, where a question of this sort was involved. Certainly he was not, and had never been considered by Sara to be, a suitor. He approved of her decision to marry Ernst and told her so.

Vachel, working hard on "The Ghosts of the Buffaloes" in the family home at Springfield, could not help but feel that Sara was falling deeply in love with Ernst; and with mixed emotions he wrote to her early in August:

I have lived a hundred lives since we parted. Every minute I was not writing the Red Gods I have been with you, happy or unhappy, going over every possible argument, conversation, plan, hope, scheme to meet again soon, and I have been amid it all, for the most part happy, and I think it is because of your whiteness. For the whiteness of your truth speaking soul moves my desire as the whiteness of the rose-garden moves my desire. So how can I be angry or restless? I do not want to fret you. And if you will send me just the tiny notes, or just an envelope with a daily card with a star on it, on the days when you think of me, and are not forgetting me, that will be all I will *beg* for. Just a sign is enough. I was so glad to get your card today—I have had nothing for a week—. Finally last night I took down all your letters since before I started to New York and read and read—and looked at the bracelet till I was as in love with the color of gold as a miser.—And the spice-tree flower that is always in an envelope on or near my pillow I took out and its perfume always brings me your whiteness and your glory, and then the golden hair you sent me just before I went to New York—if I shut my eyes and hold it against my cheek it is almost like you when there is a masque—and it has the same perfume and then I look at the color of it in the lamplight and read all your last letters but one I tore up where you called me your fine friend. I am your *lover*. You quit being Saraphim somewhere in Chicago—you are my dear lover and I am your dear lover—and that is all there is to it. You were trying to get sober and polite.

I know you are trying to turn away from me, but I honor you dear, whatever you do. I shall not be angry; I shall thank the God that made you a thoroughbred, whatever you do. It is *not* easy for my heart to feel that some one is taking you away from me, an inch at a time, every day, aided and abetted by all around him, even your own judgment aiding and abetting him. But on the other hand I am at least glad you are with your folks for your health's sake, even if they do fuss over you too much. I *want* you to be fussed over too much, and abundantly taken care of. Your cold is on my conscience and my heart....

* * *

I would rather have the tiniest star of love from you than all the friendship that was ever brewed.

A few days later he sent her another fervent appeal:

... You are in a sense my saint, even now.

* * *

... I know I can be just as true to you as I am to Poetry itself. I have not wavered since first I kissed you and found the home of my spirit. Why should you turn me out of your spirit's nest? You yourself are Poetry, and I must be true to you as I can.

* * *

Poets are so few—life is not planned for them—they must make such plans as they can with honor. And they have to pay the price of being different.... I see how even your physical beauty as well as your soul's wonderfulness is all bound up in your fragility, and I want to keep it all intact, a singing harp on my heart.

· *213* ·

... You are nearer my natural partner though the marriage is incomplete—than any other woman could be—married or single. We live the same life—we have the same friends, we read the same books—we have the same selfish ambitions for our own work, and the same unselfish ambitions each for the other's work. We cannot avoid each other if we live our lives out to their natural literary goals.

* * *

Sara—I will stake my life on this bargain with you. I will give you all my years—gladly, gladly, gladly. You have no idea how happy I will be in the hope. And you can ask no more than *all* my years, can you? What more can I the artist offer that I am *sure* I can give completely, if I offer you my faithfulness?

If it is your will to cross the Rubican you are now contemplating —and perhaps shut me out forever in a little month, we are indeed parted forever—beginning then. Why? For the simple reason I cannot look you in the eye or write to you honestly, without calling you my darling—and I will never covet or appear to covet what is another man's. It just isn't in me to endure the thought or the hope of taking what is not mine completely. . . .

I claim you against the world—child—to the last hour of your fragility. . . .

By August 11, it became clear to Vachel that Sara was going to decide in Ernst's favor, and he sent her a final plea:

... I have very little to say—except that the one desire of my heart is—do not turn away from me. Just as we are and just as we stand is *infinitely better than goodbye.*

* * *

Sara, do not get one inch farther from me in spirit till you absolutely must. . . .

Having to tell Lindsay of her decision must have been one of the hardest tasks of Sara's life. Not long after his return from New York, he had told her that her lines:

> I found more joy in sorrow
> Than you could find in joy . . .

had stayed with him and impressed him deeply. Now life was teaching him the truth of that first line through his own suffering. But the thought of giving her up forever made him write:

I not only know I will always love you, but I want to always love you finely. Please think of some honorable way to keep me always loving you and happy, for I know I will then be noble—at least my life will be keyed in the region of dignity and worth where I always want it to be. Plan some way I am to always be in touch with you, even if we cannot nightly meet. If you cannot send anything else, not even a word in time to come, mail me one blade of grass every day.

I keep re-opening this letter while I write the Ghosts of the Buffaloes. If there is anything I have said that I shouldn't, or hurts your heart—please consider it unsaid.

You give me far more happiness than anything else, this minute.

And this message soon followed:

If you cannot take me as your husband—and if you make such a distinction between the life of the one and the life of the other—take me at least as your love-consecrated poet forever and ever—and never let the arms of your poet's spirit leave me—and never drive me from you, or turn me from the door of your house invisible, in fairyland, where there is neither marrying nor giving in marriage. Keep me so close that our songs shall be our children, I care not how, so it is done in honor. God give me the essence of your spirit forever. Amen.

From Vachel.

Vachel Lindsay's basic integrity never deserted him even in this, his most trying crisis; a deep sense of honor had been bred into him and was bone of his bone and flesh of his flesh. And on August 19 he was able to write: ". . . in this letter I can send my congratulations to the winner—my respect and friendship to the members of your family, and so I do."

He burned all the letters that Sara had written him and noticed that the aroma of the spice tree, from the leaf she had sent him, mingled with the smell of the smoke; but he could not burn the lock of her hair that he had treasured so long. And he could not endure the thought of his life without Sara; she had lifted his poetry and his spirit up to starry heights, and he could not bear to descend from them. But by August 20, he had come to an understanding with himself:

But now I am resolved, if it be possible, so far as human strength lies, you shall be my Beatrice. Why should I leave your fine ladyhood and exquisite sense of honor, all for one more inevitable turn on the breaking wheel of passion. If I drive you out of my life, another spirit will come in. Young faces move me more with desire every day. Yet I know they are an illusion and a snare. God knows I want to be true to your fine and immortal part, and keep your new vow in letter and spirit as well as you will keep it. I may fail and have to forget you. My blood grows redder every year. But on the other hand I cannot give up my saints. If I was only as cold as at 25 I could live with them alone, but in these last few years my heart has turned red. St. Francis means all the world to me, if I could only serve him. God knows that was what I wanted yesterday, that old coldness of the saints. But I know my own absurdities. I know that I would keep cold three months and no longer. From plain dog-loneliness; from sheer heart-chill and shiver, I would make a sweetheart of the nearest. Yet I do not like this. I will even then in the midst of the new dream know of my fate, and my north star, and the passion for ink that kills all other hope in the end. And that new sweetheart will be but folly too.

And so, my lady, I shall be true to you, rather than to any other as long as strength lies in me to be resolute, and in my strange life, one Beatrice is worth a score of sweethearts, if I can achieve it. *Certainly the attempt is better than the old eternal wheel....*

During his period of deep anguish, there was no one in Springfield to whom Vachel Lindsay could turn. His parents were still in China, and he had no close friends in his home town who knew Sara well or had any idea how deeply he felt about her. The one person who understood the whole situation was Harriet Monroe, and on August 24, he poured out his heart to her:

I have wanted to see you very very much the past weeks since Sara told me of her sudden engagement to the other man. I suppose it would have been sudden to me, if she had waited several years. I have one thing above all else to be thankful for, that is that she has kept my deep respect and so I am all mixed up trying to forget and *not* to forget her and to think of her as one should. It is easier to harden the heart and forget her entirely than to remember as my best spirit demands, and walk with her among the stars.

Well, there is no use writing. The only person who knows me well enough and I know well enough to fight this out with, is my brother-in-law in China, and China is a long way off. We were friends for years and years and years. I would like to talk to him.

Certainly the God that made Sara sent me an authentic message about ladyhood through her, I cannot forget. She has been the living truth from first to last.

I have thought over a hundred expedients that I shall not write you, one most of all, to beg her to change, but she is a woman of her word, and it would not be her, if she broke it. I have every reason to suppose she has the right man. She is a shrewd and keen judge, and I do not think she could be deceived by a crooked person. And it isn't proper for me to want him to prove a disappointment in any way—and so—there you are.

Really, I am so afraid for my soul. I do not want to lose any of the spirit she gave me because I have to give her up for a sweetheart.

The idea of a woman being a staff and a prop is pretty largely an intoxication and a fiction, though intoxication has its place. But Sara *was* a staff and a prop to the spirit, and I do not want her replaced by any mild intoxication. I want to be true to that fine self she gave me, that fine "myself" that I find in me when I look at her picture, and I am so afraid the picture will dim.—I *cannot* think of her as being mine and another man's.

The next day, probably in a calmer mood after writing to Harriet Monroe, Vachel sent this note to Sara:

Dear Fellow-human—
You have many endearing frailties and vanities:

But—

I pray to the good God-maker of all things lovely, that I may be worthy of the memory of your truth, your clarity, your fine grain, your pride, your honor, your beauty and your gentle goodness. That I may always be trying to be worthy of these things—and trying for nothing less.

Still wrestling with his problem, the next night he felt impelled to write to her again, and he said:

... I cannot bear to come down from that high plane where I moved with your spirit, and to begin a letter takes me back there again. I cannot bear to give you up—and to give you up—that is to *try* to give you up in *one* way and to keep you in another is utterly beyond me. Sometimes, it seems to me I am turning away from my very best self in turning away from you, and in turning toward you I know I cannot be moderate. And then I know I ought to forget you and so it is all a terribly sad-humorous mix. And just because your picture brings happiness I would not be unhappy if it were not for this restlessness—this something that tells me I dare not give you up—for my soul's good I dare not—that my life will go back to something shabby—half-fulfilled, satisfied with half-measures. I cannot bear to be anything but reaching toward my best self and keyed to my highest—and my spiritual best and highest is you. And I am *not* deceiving myself by the glories of remembered fire and youth's adventure. Your little picture here that I cannot help but kiss twenty times a day is the picture of a lady, an exquisite keen spirit, a sober, worthy, dignified, friend of the holy angels.—I cannot be deceived—that is what you are essentially—amid all the accidents and beauties and ups and downs of life as it is lived by Sara—her essential self is clear divinity, crystal clear and darling and flawless.

* * *

I only wish we could be as the angels of God—. Every day your most celestial self puts me into a whirlwind of most earthly love—and I do not deceive myself.

Beatrice turns to Juliet in one moment—in the twinkling of an eye. And I want with all my heart to keep Beatrice—and I am honor bound to give up Juliet. I only wish we were as the angels of God and I could walk with you forever upon the winds and rainbows in the sky.

The very minute I can turn away I will—but you must not ask it tonight of

Vachel.

Chapter 9

MARRIAGE AND FAME

•

LATE in August the engagement of Sara and Ernst was announced from the Michigan summer home. Eunice Tietjens, in Chicago, received a wire from them that read:

Thanks to you we are the happiest people in the world![1]

Sara sent a letter to Irma, Ernst's sister, whom she had met only once, in which she said:

... My own parents are so devoted to Ernst and have already such an admiration and fondness for him that I can only hope his father and mother will feel the same affection for me.

I will not try to tell you, Irma, of the glorious happiness of such a love as ours. It has surpassed my highest hopes. The most sacred and the greatest desire of my life is to make him happy always. You who know so well his nobility, his intellect, and his tenderness, understand how deep a devotion he could inspire.

Sara's family was, indeed, well pleased. Her parents liked Ernst personally, and since he was embarked on a promising career and also had an interest in cultural affairs, his life appeared to hold a combination of qualities that seemed ideal for their daughter's happiness.

Because her time was so filled now with her plans, and, possibly, also, because she thought it might cause Vachel further suffering

---

[1]Eunice Tietjens, *The World At My Shoulder* (New York: The Macmillan Company, 1938), p. 56.

Sara Teasdale in her wedding gown
1914

to continue to write her of his innermost feelings, Sara asked him to wait a month before sending another letter. And he agreed that this was a wise plan.

Since Ernst loved her poetry so dearly, after they were home again in St. Louis, Sara gave him her first two volumes. In *Sonnets to Duse* she wrote:

September 1914

Here is the "thin first book," my love,
Of songs I used to sing,
Less than the winter-beaten leaves
Beneath the feet of spring.

Yet from the leaf strewn April earth
The violets grow blue
And from the songs of long ago
I learned to sing for you.

And in *Helen of Troy* she wrote:

For my beloved Ernst
This, my last copy of the first edition from Sara.
September 18, 1914
"Not one of all my songs
But unto thee belongs."

As her parents were not well and could not stand any undue strain or excitement, Sara decided to have a small family wedding. While she was busy with the preparations for it, Vachel sent her his two new books, *The Congo and Other Poems* and *Adventures While Preaching the Gospel of Beauty,* the latter being dedicated to her. The month of silence that she had requested had now passed, and a letter from him soon followed:

You are really the lady, in the Chinese Nightingale, though much covered up with costume, I admit. When you read that poem, find yourself.

...I am a very very restless creature. I am perfectly willing to admit I am spending a heap of time with the ladies of Springfield.

And I suppose, without really thinking about it, I am groping around for my Filsinger, so to speak, but while I honor and deeply respect my friends the hunting is largely to keep from looking back, and it will be a long hunt, I fear.

I only know I must not look back too much.

I have so many vague inexpressible thoughts about it all, but the substance of it all is—that you still have the highest place among all the powers of the earth or sky, and to think of your gentleness and kindness gives me peace and happiness—happiness and peace. It is such a good gift—to look back upon—this memory of you— when I know from bitter experience the memory of a lost love *may* be a perfect nightmare.

It is a kind of a precious legacy you have left me, and truly child, there is more peace in it—than I ever thought there could be. . . .

In the middle of October, Lindsay left on his speaking tour, which was to start with engagements in Chicago and New York and end in Kansas in a month. Just before he left Springfield, he sent Sara the manuscript of "The Chinese Nightingale," which he recited on the tour for the first time and polished as he went along.

A month later, with the very successful trip over, and with the applause of his enthusiastic audiences ringing in his ears, he was beginning to know an end of suffering; the passage of time had eased his burning heart. He confided to Sara:

As it is you are a blessing to me, a source of serenity and dignity and peace. And for that reason a marvel, and amaze, and for *that* reason—a happiness. Someone is waiting for me, I suppose, around the bend in the road, but I am in no hurry. There it is, in as plain hard phrase as it can be stated. The peace of memory is beautiful, and peace is a rare thing, these days, anywhere, and should not be quickly given up.

Just before Sara's marriage, Vachel sent her a gift and this message:

Darling Sara: I send you your wedding present by express.

They are two phoenixes, those embroidered birds. They are the symbols of the Empress of China. They are rising from the sea. Yet we can call them nightingales, if we want to, now—can't we?

The picture by Edmund Dulac is just from Harper's Bazaar so do not show it where the Philistines can mock. But the Princess was so much like you looked in my poem, I wanted you to look well at her.

Put her on your shelf where you can see her once in a while. The bird I s'pose is a heron, but we can call it a nightingale if we want to, or not, as we please.

Mama and Papa gave me the old Chinese embroidery. You can make a spread of it on your present-table unabashed. They, Mama & Papa brought it from China for me.

Sara was married on December 19, 1914, at her home in St. Louis. Wearing a long, lovely, white satin wedding gown, she came down the stairs and walked the length of the living room to the rear where there was an altar arrangement banked with flowers. Though only the immediate families were present, the occasion was a full dress affair, and nothing marred its perfection. After a buffet supper, the bride and groom left on a train for an eastern trip. The *Globe-Democrat* of December 20 carried the following description of the wedding:

The marriage of Miss Sara Teasdale and Ernst B. Filsinger took place Saturday at 6 o'clock at the residence of the bride's parents, Mr. and Mrs. J. W. Teasdale, 38 Kingsbury Place. Only immediate relatives were present. There were no attendants except a flower boy and flower girl—Master Rudolph Schulenburg Teasdale, nephew of the bride, and Miss Catherine Filsinger, niece of the bridegroom.

The ceremony was performed by Dr. W. J. Williamson, pastor of the Third Baptist Church, of which the bride is a member, assisted by Percival Chubb, leader of the Ethical Society, to which the bridegroom belongs.

The bride was gowned in white satin, draped in tulle and trimmed with rare old duchess lace. The court train was held at the shoulders by loops of pearl. She wore a veil crowned with orange blossoms and carried a shower bouquet of lilies of the valley.

The house was artistically decorated, the living room, where the ceremony was performed, being in white bride's roses and ferns. The couple stood under a canopy of roses and smilax. The dining room was decorated with white butterfly sweet peas.

During the ceremony Arthur Lieber played the "Love Song" from *Die Walküre* and the "Prize Song" from *Die Meistersinger* on the organ.

After the wedding Mr. and Mrs. Filsinger departed for an Eastern honeymoon. They will make their home in St. Louis.

The bride is a frequent contributor of verse to the magazines. She is the author of *Sonnets to Duse, Helen of Troy,* and other poems. Her third volume, *Rivers to the Sea,* will be published next year.

She is an officer of the Poetry Society of America.[2] During the past few years she has passed most of her time in travel or in New York.

Mr. Filsinger is the consul of Costa Rica and Ecuador in St. Louis, and has long been identified with Latin-American trade development. He twice served as president of the Latin-American and Foreign Trade Association, for which organization he acted as commissioner to Mexico, West Indies, and Central and South America. He has traveled extensively in the Latin-American republics. He is active in the City Club and various civic, business, and social organizations.

The newly married Filsingers went to Boston on their honeymoon, where they stayed at the Essex Hotel. On December 23 Sara sent a note to Ernst's parents, in which she said:

Ernst and I want to send you our Christmas greetings and our love. We are so happy that the days go by like a dream. Neither of us can realize that all of this happiness for which we have longed is really ours. . . .

An affectionate message came back to Sara:

Our dear daughter Sara

---

[2]Sara was a member of the Advisory Committee of the Poetry Society of America at this time.

Yours of 23 inst. with greetings and love came today, the same to you and Ernst. May the New Year and future years be to both of you what the past four months have been, only in larger measure and may your love for each other never grow less.

With love from
Ernst's Father and Mother

On Christmas Eve they had their own private little celebration with a delicious dinner served in their room. Then they lit three tiny candles on a miniature five-inch tree, dimmed the lights, and watched the candles burn down slowly, their hearts full of happiness.

Christmas Day in Boston of that year was white and cold, and Sara and Ernst went over to Concord to spend the afternoon and evening with their friend, William Stanley Braithwaite, whose second anthology of magazine poetry had been published in the fall.

On the day after Christmas, Sara's joy spilled over into a letter which she sent to Ernst's sisters, for she said:

... We walk about in a sort of glory and everything seems to have a holy enchantment. Often and often we say to each other that love has never been expressed by any poet or any musician—the peace of it, and the ecstasy—and the sheer fun of being together. We both feel about sixteen years old and Ernst is looking so well and handsome that it is splendid. I too have never felt better....

... We are alternately full of the wildest and most whimsical high spirits, and then touched with sadness at the thought of how short life is at the best and how many years of our lives passed without each other. If only all the people that we love could find such utter happiness! May it come to you both, my dearest Wanda and Irma!

In a few days they returned to New York where they attended the December meeting of the Poetry Society of America. At this gathering they were honored guests, and several of Sara's poems to Ernst were read and much admired.

Because it seemed wise not to burden Sara with housekeeping problems, on returning to St. Louis, they moved into the Arthur Hotel, which overlooked Washington University and Forest Park. Here they had two rooms and a bath, which their wedding gifts helped to make charming. Eunice Tietjens had sent them a lovely magazine cover, which occupied the place of honor on their living room table. At this time Ernst had established his own wholesale shoe business with a partner; they knew many of the same people in St. Louis, and life seemed to stretch ahead into a vista of happy years.

In June Sara's parents went to Charlevoix, and she and Ernst lived in the Kingsbury Place home for a while before they joined Mr. and Mrs. Teasdale for a summer vacation. October of 1915 found Sara in St. John's Hospital in St. Louis, and soon after this, she and Ernst moved to the Usona Hotel.

Ernst's family, with whom Sara got along most harmoniously from the very first, were especially thoughtful during her stay in the hospital, and she never forgot their kindness at this time. Besides his mother and father, he had two sisters, Wanda and Irma, and two brothers, Adolph and Harry. Irma Filsinger, who was closer to Sara than the others, being nearer her age, sensed from the beginning that Sara was too delicate to be visited for long periods of time, and that she did not have the strength to devote to both her poetry and outside demands. Because of this complete understanding, they were the friendliest of sisters-in-law, and a happy relationship was established between them immediately. Sara's poem, "Child, Child," was written to her. Later, after Irma Filsinger had married, and when her daughter, Miriam Lisette, was born, Sara lovingly sent the baby this message:

I wish I had a fairy pen to write with, so that my writing would be small and dainty and fit for your dainty self. ... As soon as your hands are large enough to hold anything except your mother's finger, I think you will like a pearl and silver rattle that was mine too long ago for me to enjoy recalling just *how* long. I am sending the rattle to you and a tiny gold bracelet for your smooth fat little wrist. You will be as gay as any four-weeks-old fairy needs to be without any gifts at all, but I want you to have these things because I had them when I was as small as you.

During the early years of their married life, Ernst and Sara seemed ideally happy. Vine Colby, who visited the couple at their hotel soon after their marriage, remembers: "She was half-reclining on her bed, wearing a negligee of pale green, with her auburn hair spread out on her shoulders. Before I left, Ernst came in. Her whole face lighted up with joy, her sherry-brown eyes sparkled, she opened her arms wide, and he stooped to embrace her closely. I was a trifle embarrassed to be the witness of such a passionate love-scene, but Sara's gesture was perfectly spontaneous and natural."

Ernst, who was immensely proud of his wife's poetic talent, encouraged her to continue to write. He did not want the responsibilities of married life to stand in the way of her great gift. While she herself never liked to read her poetry in public, sometimes he was prevailed upon to read his wife's work for friends or at literary gatherings; and the high regard in which he held both poet and poetry was easily discernible to the audience by the awe and reverence with which he read.

A favorite pastime in their early married life was to make up poems in free verse together. One of these, "The Lighted Window," was published in *The Century,* and though it was brought out under her name, she always gave her husband credit for the idea, since she said that she had set the poem down almost as he told it to her.

In the fall of 1915, Sara's third book, *Rivers to the Sea,* was published by Macmillan. John Hall Wheelock had suggested the name for this book, which was taken from a poem that he had written in 1909, while he was a student at the University of Berlin, Germany, engaged in graduate work:

As rivers rush in tumult
   And crumble in the sea,
I am lost, I am slain in you,
   I am drowned eternally.

Yet back in a cloud of joy,
   In a shower of living rain,
To his heights among the hills
   You pour love back again.

Oh, to the being belovèd,
   To perish and be reborn—
The strange and luring presence,
   Refreshing as the morn,

Love runs on forever
   As rivers to the sea;
From myself you set me free!
From myself you set me free![3]

Mr. Wheelock's words had echoes in two of Sara's passages
that linked the book revealingly with its title. One is in the
poem, "From the Sea":

Yet when I heard your name the first far time
It seemed like other names to me, and I
Was all unconscious, as a dreaming river
That nears at last its long predestined sea....

The other is from the first section of "Sappho," which originally
appeared in *Helen of Troy:*

The little street lies meek beneath the moon,
Running, as rivers run, to meet the sea.
I too go seaward and shall not return.

Rivers to the Sea was dedicated to Ernst, and in his personal
copy, Sara wrote:

---

[3]John Hall Wheelock, *Love and Liberation* (Boston: Sherman, French
and Company, 1913), pp. 115-116.

For Ernst with the eternal devotion of his Sara.
October 7, 1915.

The critics were high in their praise of this book. The *Review of Reviews* reported: "There is hardly another American woman-poet whose poetry is generally known and loved like that of Sara Teasdale. *Rivers to the Sea,* her latest volume of lyrics, possesses the delicacy of imagery, the inward illumination, the high vision that characterize the poetry that will endure the test of time."

Louis Untermeyer, writing in the *Chicago Evening Post,* said: "Sara Teasdale has a genius for the song, for the perfect lyric, in which the words seem to have fallen into place without art or effort."

And William Marion Reedy wrote of this book: "It is poetry of limpid, liquid quality, the expression of blended thought and feeling in the last reduction of simplicity. The words are those of the most unornate speech, falling into place with inevitableness, as if they owned no synonyms. The poems have joy of life with a certain wistfulness. They do what poetry supremely should do, they sing."

The poems in this book were compared to those of Christina Rossetti, to Blake's, to Housman's. Harriet Monroe, Edwin Markham, Jessie Rittenhouse, Arthur Symons, and William Stanley Braithwaite all gave the book a warm welcome. Rudolf Rieder, who taught at the University of Wisconsin, translated many of the poems into German for publication in Munich at the close of World War I. With this book Sara's place as a poet of distinction, as well as one of popularity and promise, was assured.

Fortunately for Sara, the editor who worked with her at the Macmillan Company was Harold Strong Latham. Mr. Latham was associated with this company for his entire business life, and when he retired in 1952, he had been editor-in-chief and vice-president for many years and was regarded both here and abroad as an outstanding leader in the field of publishing. Because of his warm human sympathy, perception, and personal magnetism, Mr.

Latham was beloved by his associates at the Macmillan Company, as well as by his authors. He was the very good friend of some of the rarest personalities in American literature, among them Edwin Arlington Robinson. In the publishing world, he is especially remembered as the discoverer of Margaret Mitchell, for he was the first person outside of her family to read *Gone with the Wind,* and he was, in fact, various rumors to the contrary, the only editor who saw the manuscript before it was accepted for publication.

Mr. Latham also worked with Vachel Lindsay, and both Vachel and Sara were very fond of him and had the deepest respect for his judgment as an editor. Frequently, in later years, Vachel, with a cry of genuine anguish, would employ Sara to "get hold of Latham for me" and give him last-minute instructions about printing problems that distressed Lindsay greatly, for he felt that only Mr. Latham would give him (and Sara, as his intercessor) the kind of personal attention he desired so deeply in regard to matters concerning his books.

Vachel Lindsay had not seen Sara since her marriage. He had been absorbed in his speaking tours and in his writing since they had last met. But a trip to her native city and the publication of *Rivers to the Sea* inspired him to send her a letter early in October of 1915.

My dear Sara:

I passed through St. Louis yesterday and took dinner with Reedy and formed a very high opinion of him personally and enjoyed him exceedingly. Practically my first real session with him, and quite rewarding it was.

But I would not do myself justice if I did not write to you tonight, and tell you just going to St. Louis is a kind of a visit to you.

I am mighty glad about your book and it is fun to see it advertised alongside of mine in the *Dial* fall announcement. I was in Chicago two days last week visiting the Hendersons and straightening out my immortal soul, and I had the pleasure of looking over the foundry proof of your book and tracing the footprints of the fairies upon the sands of time all to myself. I do not think anything escaped me.

* * *

When it snows this winter, catch some perfect snowflakes on the back of your glove. You will note that every one that is complete is shaped like a star, six pointed.

I find a six pointed snowflake very hard to draw. A five pointed star is easier.

With this October sentiment—I will close.

Very sincerely
Vachel

A few months after *Rivers to the Sea* was published, Sara was invited to be one of the guests of honor at the January, 1916, annual dinner of the Poetry Society of America, which was held at the National Arts Club in New York. The guests of honor at this meeting also included Edgar Lee Masters, whose *Spoon River Anthology* had been published in 1915, Robert Frost, whose *North of Boston* had appeared in 1914, and Gutzon Borglum, the sculptor, who in later years was to carve the famed Mt. Rushmore faces.

After the excellent reception of *Rivers to the Sea*, it was not long before Macmillan informed Sara that the company would be happy to publish another volume of poetry just as soon as she had it ready. But she did not want to be rushed with her work; and besides, she had another project in mind. She had decided to gather together a number of the best love poems written by women and make them into an anthology. Sara had discussed her idea with John Hall Wheelock, and he suggested that she use the title, *The Answering Voice*, for this volume; gratefully, she accepted his suggestion.

When Sara asked Edna St. Vincent Millay for permission to use one of her poems in this anthology, she received this letter from Vassar:

· 231 ·

Sara,—you sweet old thing!

—I would so like to see you!

Whadda you mean by having husbands & anthologys at the same time like that *Vile Inseck the Emancipated Woman?*

You may do anything you like with my *Ashes.*—('Scuse the Elizabethan wit—I come from an exam on the drama of that period.)

Seriously (but not sadly) you may do anything you like with the poem,—even translate it into German.

So you have the nicest husband in the world? You always were a lucky baggage.—Does he like your eyes?

I am sure that your book will be a very nice book & I hope that everybody will think so.—Though I don't particularly care what the post-office inspectors think of it. I am glad you wanted me to be in it.

If you ever have time to write to me again, I should be very happy.—If you don't have time,—why not let your husband do it?— If he's as nice as you say, I wouldn't mind at all.

Dear Sara, goodbye,—

It was so pleasant to hear from you.

Vincent

Ernst was just as enthusiastic about the idea of the anthology as Sara was, and he helped her all he could by bringing home an armload of books from the library almost every day. For advice in selecting the poems, she turned to a number of her friends who rose nobly to the occasion and went to much trouble, procuring lists of suitable poems and even sending her books. For their generous response to her requests, she wrote in her introduction:

I want to acknowledge very gratefully my indebtedness for counsel and suggestions to Harriet Monroe, Jessie B. Rittenhouse, Louis Untermeyer, Henry L. Mencken, William Stanley Braithwaite, Thomas S. Jones, Jr., John Hall Wheelock, and Thomas B. Mosher. From my husband, Ernst B. Filsinger, I have received unfailing aid and encouragement.

Sara's plan was to select the poems and prepare her anthology, and then submit it to a publisher before she wrote to the various authors for their permissions and cleared all the copyrights. In the midst of assembling this material, she was called upon to write an ode for the Shakespearean Tercentenary Celebration of the Drama League of America, which was to be held in St. Louis. She accepted this honor with misgiving, as she did not think that odes were much in her line of endeavor. In this she was instinctively right, for her lyric talent was not particularly given to creating commemorative poetry. The lines that she wrote for this occasion were adequate, but they can in no way approach the high level of the best of her lyric poetry. And perhaps because of this trying experience—working under pressure to meet a deadline—she never again agreed to write a poem on order.

On April 28, 1916, several thousand people gathered around the statue of Shakespeare in Tower Grove Park in St. Louis for the ceremony. A mulberry tree, mentioned by Sara in her long poem, was set out near the statue in memory of the day, not far from two other trees that had been planted by Adelaide Nielson and Olga Nethersole. Elizabethan songs and dances took place, and garlands of flowers were placed upon the statue. William Faversham, the actor, read Sara's "Ode to Shakespeare," and he also read a short poem by her to Mary Arden, the mother of Shakespeare, which had been written at the request of Mr. Braithwaite for a page in the *Boston Transcript*, honoring the playwright. Percival Chubb, who had participated in Sara's wedding, was President of the Drama League of America at that time, and Richard Burton, Archibald Henderson, and Mrs. Otis Skinner were elected Vice Presidents. Both Sara and William Faversham were charter members of this organization, whose Shakespearean celebration received wide publicity.

Because she had worked so hard on her anthology of love poems while trying to complete the ode, Sara was exhausted; and after she sent the book to a publisher for a decision on its publication, she went to one of her favorite places in Connecticut for a short rest and vacation. Williamina Parrish and Ernst agreed to see the book through the press and go into the extensive correspondence concerning the permissions, upon its acceptance. While she was in Connecticut, word came that the Houghton Mifflin Company would bring the book out in the fall of 1917.

Meanwhile, in 1916, Ernst became the Foreign Sales Manager of Lawrence and Company, a textile house of Boston and New York. This new position necessitated their moving to New York City, and they established their residence first at Hotel Bonta, at Broadway and 94th Street, and then moved to the Beresford at 1 West 81st Street in September of 1917.

Sara's lack of strength and endurance made it advisable for them to continue living in a hotel rather than attempt to keep house, and Ernst was in complete agreement with this arrangement.

Their New York residence made it possible for Sara to keep in closer touch with a number of her friends, for though she was not equal to going out much, she and Ernst were always glad to have their friends visit them quietly at home. John Hall Wheelock, a valued friend of both the Filsingers, saw them often, and he and Sara frequently showed each other the new poetry they had written. William Stanley Braithwaite dined with them occasionally when he was in town. Sometimes they prevailed upon Witter Bynner, whose voice was a joy to listen to, to spend an evening reading aloud to them. Mr. Bynner wrote this well-known poem to Sara:

VOICES

Oh, there were lights and laughter
  And the motions to and fro
Of people as they enter
  And people as they go
And there were many voices
  Vying at the feast,

> But mostly I remember
> Yours who spoke the least.[4]

During her life and after it, many poems were written to or about Sara; besides this one by Mr. Bynner and many by Vachel Lindsay, other notable authors who wrote one or more poems concerning her or inscribed to her included Jean Starr Untermeyer, John Myers O'Hara, Orrick Johns, Louis Untermeyer, John Hall Wheelock, Eunice Tietjens, Edward J. Wheeler, Joyce Kilmer, and Dr. Merle St. Croix Wright.

Sometimes, Sara also wrote lyrics designated for certain people, such as the memorial poem to Frederick Oakes Sylvester, a painter of St. Louis, whom she considered a friend. In *Rivers to the Sea* are two poems written for children whom Sara loved: one for the little son of the Untermeyers, and one for the daughter of the Kilmers. When Jennie L. Wheeler, the wife of Mr. Edward J. Wheeler, died, Sara wrote the lines that may be seen today on a bronze tablet at the head of her grave in Woodlawn Cemetery in New York City.

Edgar Lee Masters and his wife, Ellen, Mr. and Mrs. Edwin Markham, Louis and Jean Starr Untermeyer, Marguerite and Jim Wilkinson, Harriet Monroe, Joyce and Aline Kilmer, and other writers and critics visited the Filsingers from time to time.

Early in February of 1917, Vachel Lindsay came to New York. Ernst was delighted to have a chance to know him, and he and Sara entertained the poet on Thursday evening, February 8; the next day Lindsay sent them an appreciative note:

My dear Ernst and Sara Filsinger:

Thank you indeed for the party. I give you my two hands in blessing and fellowship. My dear friends, you do not know yet how much pleased I was at the atmosphere of the little assembly. I felt the delicacy and sensitiveness of their welcome most keenly, after

---

[4]Witter Bynner, *Book of Lyrics* (New York: Alfred A. Knopf, 1955), p. 50. Copyright 1955 by Witter Bynner. Reprinted by permission of Alfred A. Knopf, Inc.

several very fine moments already in New York this year. They were like a group of dear cousins to me.

* * *

It is one of the rewards of life to meet Edward J. [Wheeler] again, and Bynner and Jessie Belle [Rittenhouse] and the Kilmers and all the rest. I do not like to feel that I am being jerked from my moorings in this world, or that any interest of the day has wiped out my chance of a homecoming, and seeing these people last night was a sort of homecoming, and it reverberated in my mind all the time. I felt in harbor, among them.

From that time on, whenever Vachel Lindsay came to New York, he always called upon the Filsingers, and he and Ernst became close friends.

His work being deeply demanding, Ernst had to be out of the city and even out of the country for long periods of time. This was distressing to both Sara and him, for they dearly loved each other, and nothing could have been more disastrous for their marriage. Unfortunately, it was impossible for Sara, who was never well or strong, to accompany Ernst on the majority of his trips. Though she loved to travel at an easy-going and leisurely pace, Ernst's trips were necessarily of a swift tempo, for he had to be rushing from one city to another, and even from one country to another, as he kept business appointments all over the world. Throughout her married life, when he was away, or when she would be recovering from one of her frequent attacks of grippe or simply from nervous exhaustion, Sara would stay in some lovely or secluded spot where the peace and quiet would help her to get well. Besides the Connecticut towns that she loved, Colonial Inn at Concord, Massachusetts; Pudding Stone Inn at Boonton, New Jersey; El Elcanto in Santa Barbara, California; Brook Bend Tavern in Monterey, Massachusetts; the St. Aspinquid Hotel in Ogunquit, Maine; and Buck Hill Falls in Pennsylvania were all visited at various times by the poet. Sometimes she spoke of these places in her poems.

In the fall of 1917, Sara's anthology, *The Answering Voice,* was published and was well received. Though the collection did not contain any of her own love lyrics—and how great a pity!— within its covers the voices of three of her Potter friends were heard: for Edna Wahlert's "To Him," Vine Colby's "The Rainbow," and Williamina Parrish's "The Name" were included. Zoë Akins was represented by three poems, and other personal friends who were included were Jessie Rittenhouse, Marguerite Wilkinson, Harriet Monroe, Amy Lowell, Jean Starr Untermeyer, and Margaret Widdemer. Elizabeth Barrett Browning was the author of five of the poems; and five were by Christina Rossetti and four by A. Mary F. Robinson, two poets, who, with Sappho, exerted a major influence over Sara's own work. Both Moira O'Neill and Nora Chesson, writers of the Irish Renaissance and beloved by the Potters in those days of long ago and far away, were represented. The book was dedicated to Sara's sister, Mamie Teasdale Wheless.

In compiling this volume, Sara's intention had not been to present the most famous love songs by well-known women authors, but rather to gather together those that she thought especially charming and appealing, regardless of the status of the author. In this she seems to have succeeded. A review in *The Bookman* said of the anthology: "Miss Teasdale has not taken away the joy of discovery by giving us only poems already belonging to us. We are the richer by many lovely things unknown before. One wanders through the book with few disappointments and with an almost constant sense of charm and beauty."

In 1928 a revised edition of *The Answering Voice* was issued, and Sara added fifty more poems to the original one hundred; she also added a *Foreword* in which she traced the changes of attitude of women toward love in the eleven years that elapsed between the publication of the two editions.

In October of 1917, also, Sara's new book of lyrics, *Love Songs,* was published and met with an overwhelming acclaim and success. A collection of the best love poems from her three previous books plus some new verses, it captured the reader's heart from the beginning with lines such as these from "Barter":[5]

> Life has loveliness to sell,
>   All beautiful and splendid things,
> Blue waves whitened on a cliff,
>   Soaring fire that sways and sings,
> And children's faces looking up
> Holding wonder like a cup.

Seldom has any book of poetry published in this country been accorded the honor and popularity that this one received. Louis Untermeyer, writing in the *New York Evening Mail,* declared: "No woman in America (and only one in England) has voiced more plangently the delicate halflights and luminous backgrounds of passion. Sara Teasdale's words will always suffer by being set to music. They are already music set to words."

Edward J. Wheeler stated in *Current Opinion:* "Sara Teasdale's *Love Songs* gleam and glow like a collection of opals. They sing like a field full of meadow larks. They are pure lyrics that might have been written a hundred years ago, and may be read with delight a hundred years hence."

And William Stanley Braithwaite in the *Boston Transcript* said: "Love is illuminated in *Love Songs* as it has not been illuminated before by a single poet in American poetry. The gift of song among the poets of today is possessed by no one in a measure equal to Sara Teasdale's."

Love Songs was dedicated to Ernst, and Sara used a particularly lovely dedicatory poem to precede the volume, of which this is the second verse:

> *But all remembered beauty is no more*
>   *Than a vague prelude to the thought of you—*

---

[5]When "Barter" was first published, in *Poetry,* June, 1917, by a strange typographical error, which Harriet Monroe never understood and was at a loss to explain, one line was replaced by a line of John Hall Wheelock's, which had the same rhyme and rhythm pattern. However, it made no sense whatever in this poem. Miss Monroe apologized for this in *Poetry* and reprinted the poem correctly later.

You are the rarest soul I ever knew,
Lover of beauty, knightliest and best;
My thoughts seek you as waves that seek the shore,
And when I think of you, I am at rest.

Ernst's personal copy was inscribed:

For my beloved Ernst from Sara. October 1917.

Sara sent copies of her two new books to Vachel Lindsay. He had also just had a new book published, and soon he sent her *The Chinese Nightingale and Other Poems,* dedicated to Sara Teasdale, Poet. In the back of her personal copy he wrote a poem, "Dancing for a Prize" (later included in his *Collected Poems*), and illustrated it. And in the front he inscribed an acrostic poem, "To Sara Teasdale the Unforgotten":

This book is yours, the faults and all,
O Lady of the golden shawl:
Shawl that gleams in incense yet,
And though its power I half forget,
Renewing fancies fade and glow
And white dream-roses come and go.
The days of music-weaving when
Each watched and taught the other's pen
All of the days of dragon-herds
Sweep through my soul in happy words.
Dearest of Greeks, of woman best
All of my fancies sought your breast.
Like artist-friends we planned to make
Each song endure for that hour's sake.
This book, despite that hope, will die—
Have its kind Queen, then buried lie
Even like some frail child of ours
Under the tombstone and the flowers.
Nothing endures but God. His breath
Feeds man forever, saves from death.
Our souls diffuse, renew, transform

Rolling like clouds in his wide storm.
God watched us in his forest dim—
Oak sprig and elm, we bent to him.
Then came the blasting lightning flare,
Then rare re-birth, and pathways fair.
Each soul he winnows with his wings
Nobly to save from earthly things.

>   Nicholas Vachel Lindsay
>   October 12, 1917. Springfield
>   Illinois[6]

A section of *Love Songs* called "Songs Out of Sorrow" shared the National Arts Club Prize of the Poetry Society of America with Edwin Markham's "The Toilers" for the year 1917. And in 1918 *Love Songs* was awarded the country's most coveted honor for poetry, a prize of $500 given through Columbia University, being the forerunner of the Pulitzer Prize in this field.

As Jessie Rittenhouse explained in her autobiography, the first Pulitzer Prizes, established in 1917, did not include poetry, and Mr. Edward J. Wheeler, who was at that time President of the Poetry Society of America, mentioned this oversight to the President of Columbia University. However, since no provision was made for such a prize in Mr. Pulitzer's will, there was nothing that Dr. Butler could do about it. Mr. Wheeler, undaunted, then obtained $500 from a patron of poetry, to be given through Columbia University for the best book of poetry published in 1917 in America, with one reservation: the Poetry Society of America insisted upon naming the judges. William Marion Reedy, Bliss Perry, and Jessie Rittenhouse were called upon to judge for the first year, and they selected Sara Teasdale's *Love Songs*.

For the best book of poetry published during 1918, the judges named by the Poetry Society of America were Sara Teasdale, William Lyon Phelps, and Richard Burton. They agreed to divide

---

[6]This book is now in the Wellesley College Library's English Poetry Collection, and the poem is printed here with the kind permission of the Wellesley College Library.

For My Father.
Nov. 13, 1919.

More than eighty autumns
   you've seen in gold and red,
And still erect, with gentle pride,
   You hold your silvery head.

Observing all things kindly,
   Reverent, and yet with joy,
You watch a horse, a child, a bird
   Freshly as when a boy;

Then take, this birthday morning,
   More love than words can hold—
May my heart be as young as yours
   When I have grown as old!

           Sara.

*Sara Teasdale's poem for her father's
eighty-first birthday*

the honor between Margaret Widdemer and Carl Sandburg. In 1922 the money for the prize was arranged through the Pulitzer family, who established a permanent Pulitzer award for poetry.

Love Songs went through five editions in 1918, an extraordinary record for any book of poetry, no matter how deserving. The honor accorded the volume was totally unexpected by Sara, and a great joy as well as a great surprise. Letters from friends and strangers poured in upon her, and all the critics seemed to be in agreement with the Columbia-Poetry Society of America Prize. Only Harriet Monroe sounded a doubtful note in her "Comment on Sara Teasdale's Prize" in *Poetry*, for she felt strongly that the judges should have all been *poets* of distinction themselves to have been worthy of judging the best volume of poetry for the year. She narrowed the list of other serious competitors for this prize down to four, in her opinion: *Lustra* by Ezra Pound, *Sea Garden* by H. D., *The Chinese Nightingale and Other Poems* by Vachel Lindsay, and *Asphalt* by Orrick Johns. But even Miss Monroe, who never let friendship stand in the way of her criticism, concluded that Sara's "whole book reveals with singular clarity and precision a beautiful bright spirit of rare vividness and charm," and felt that it was certainly deserving of a prize.

Vachel Lindsay was very proud of his friend's award. He commented to Miss Monroe on June 27, 1918, evidently as she was getting ready to write her remarks on the prize for publication in *Poetry:*

"The Chinese Nightingale" came out last September, but you will note on the title page "Dedicated to Sara Teasdale, Poet," so you see I nominated Sara first, and was the original Sara man. Also you will find that "Adventures While Preaching the Gospel of Beauty" was dedicated to her when it came out in 1914 so you can put me down as awarding her two prizes, such as they are, and using my influence such as it is, to further her greatness as a poet, even before the present committee was formed. I consider any honor to Sara, then, in a sense an honor to my critical sense, and as it were, I accept the prize on her behalf. . . .

I have just reread "Love Songs," and I find it a collection of Sara's undisputed best from all her books, and deserves to be spotlighted, if any work of hers deserves it. It represents the calm winnowing of all her work, and does not run thin and uneven in spots as some of her earlier collections. Her style is so simple that the second-raters among her poems are apt to run thin and it takes a long and mature judgment to separate the thin from the simple and classic. I did not find a poem in the book I would omit, and I was glad to renew my memory of them all. I think you could discreetly draw attention to the Chinese Nightingale dedication, especially if you laid emphasis on the word *Poet,* which is exactly in the spirit of that dedication.

Ernst's father sent Sara the clippings about the prize from *Reedy's Mirror* and the St. Louis newspapers and congratulated her. In her letter of appreciation she said:

I feel so deeply that Ernst has been a wonderful help, as well as a deep and lasting joy to me, that the lines of mine called "The Lamp," of which you speak, seem to express only a small part of what I long to say of him. Sometime I hope to write a poem that will express all that is in my heart.

When the shadows of the first World War fell over the United States, and the draft age was extended to forty-five, it seemed for a while that Ernst might be called, and this worried Sara greatly, just as it did countless other women whose husbands' lives were at the command of their government. However, Ernst was not called. Sara was particularly concerned for Stafford Hatfield, who was in Germany when the war started, and placed in a civilian detention camp there. Several times she sent him food packages, but she heard from him very infrequently. In 1918, the English composer, Treharne, was in America, and Sara and Ernst invited him to dinner. He had been confined in the Ruhleben Prison for English civilians in Germany for some months and had been released because of illness. There he had met Dr. Hatfield who had started the Arts and Science Union for the prisoners and kept the camp alive intellectually. Treharne, who knew of Sara's work through Hatfield, had only praise for his friend; and Sara was delighted to get this unexpected word of him.

Though Sara was not in any sense a "war poet," she could not escape the mood and apprehension that war engendered. In *Flame and Shadow,* Section VIII is a little group of poems written during these days; however, Sara was far removed from the grim suffering and horror of the battlefield, and her poems reflect more her own philosophic thoughts at this time than any actual concern with fighting.

She had to write of war in her own way, and she saw it and its fearful consequences as part of the passing pageant of mankind that in no way could affect the eternal elements of nature, the sea, the sun, the stars:

> Years go, dreams go, and youth goes, too,
> The world's heart breaks beneath its wars,
> All things are changed, save in the east
> The faithful beauty of the stars.

In early January of 1919 Ernst had to go to Cuba on business, and Sara went with him, thinking that the two of them might have a little vacation along with his business responsibilities. But Cuba, unfortunately, was in the throes of a general strike, and because of trying conditions there, the trip afforded them very little pleasure. Both came back to New York worn out. One poem, however, remains to mark this journey; called "In a Cuban Garden," it was printed in *Flame and Shadow.*

Before they left for Cuba, Ernst had been told by his company that he might be selected to go abroad on an important and extended business trip; such a selection was, of course, an honor, and when they returned from Cuba they found that this plan had been confirmed. Immediately, they were plunged into a whirlwind of activity to get Ernst ready in time. Ernst had been working hard on his second book, and he finished the final version only the night before he sailed. His secretary typed the last part of it in the apartment, while Sara helped him pack his trunk.

Knowing the penetrating cold of certain foreign countries and the unreliability of the comforts of sleeping-cars while traveling abroad, Sara had given Ernst for Christmas a very soft, warm steamer blanket, and she urged him to carry it everywhere he went in Europe. As he was swamped with a multitude of business details to straighten out before he sailed, she insisted on taking charge of buying his wardrobe, and he was only too glad to turn this task over to her. She provided him well with warm clothes— pajamas, sweaters, underwear, shoes, scarves, gloves, and even a knitted wool cap to go over his ears; she also bought what he needed for the warmer climates, and, with her characteristic sense of order, put his summer weight clothes all together in one of his sample trunks. All of his wearing apparel was gone over with the most painstaking care for loose buttons and flaws, and each article was marked with a name-tape. To Ernst's mother Sara sent a detailed list of the things she had bought for her husband; and she even sent a sample name-tape for his family to see.

Because of the war, every piece of paper that left the United States had to be examined by the censors. This proved to be very much of a burden to Ernst, who had about a hundred letters of introduction, not to mention his great variety of material concerning price lists and samples. However, at last all the details were attended to, and early in February he sailed with everything in order. This was Ernst's first trip abroad, and it was to take him to Germany, Slovakia, Poland, Switzerland, and South America.

He wanted Sara to join him, but she simply did not feel equal to the strain of traveling, and she was afraid that she would be more of a burden than a pleasure to him. Though Marguerite Wilkinson told Sara she was to call on her at once if she became ill or needed her while Ernst was gone, and though Ernst's parents invited her to stay with them, Sara decided to go to California instead.

In Santa Barbara the warm weather, the enchanting view of the mountains and the sea, and the brilliant stars spoke eloquently to her poetic nature. Astronomy had always fascinated Sara, and now she began to study it in earnest. A poem called "Full Moon (Santa Barbara)" recalls the beauty of this California scenery.

Here, too, in December of 1919, she wrote the poem that commemorated her fifth wedding anniversary:

> It will not change now
>   After so many years;
> Life has not broken it
>   With parting or tears;
> Death will not alter it,
>   It will live on
> In all my songs for you
>   When I am gone.

Both she and Ernst were disappointed when they learned that he was not to come home, after all, from South America, but was scheduled to go on to Europe for a business appointment in January of 1920. He was the first American businessman to enter Germany after the first World War. She thought for a time that she would attempt to join him in England, but she finally decided against it, as she did not feel strong enough. Ernst did not arrive home until the end of the summer in 1920. While he was in England, Sara had him call on her friend, Dr. Hatfield, whom he liked at once.

Ernst's sister, Irma, was with Sara in New York to meet his ship when he finally returned after his long absence, and she still recalls the display of affection shown by the couple when their joyous reunion took place: "I shall never forget the ecstatic kissing; her hatpins flew out, and my brother was too demonstrative, but she didn't seem to mind it."

During these early years of marriage, when Ernst had to be

away from her for such long intervals of time, Sara missed her husband intensely. It was one of her greatest disappointments that she had no children of her own. Lacking children and a home that would ordinarily occupy her time, she worked constantly on her poetry, and poetic recognition continued to come her way. In 1920 she was awarded the Brookes More Prize of $200 for the best work published in *Contemporary Verse* during the year. Her prize-winning group of five poems, which appeared in the September issue of the magazine, was called "The Dark Cup," and later was included in *Flame and Shadow*.

Baylor University at Waco, Texas, wanted to confer an honorary Doctorate of Letters upon her in 1920, but knowing that this entailed a personal appearance at the ceremony, and feeling unable to undergo this trip and all the attending drain on her strength, she declined this honor. In 1922 her name was placed on the ballot of the Poetry Society of America as a nominee for a member of the Executive Board, but this honor, too, Sara had to turn down, as she rarely went out in the day time and almost never at night.

Among Sara's most characteristic qualities were her neatness, her orderliness, her tying up of all loose ends. She knew exactly where everything in her desk, her bureau, and her room lay; she knew exactly when a letter that she mailed from one of her lovely places of rest would reach Ernst. A graphologist reading her handwriting might first be struck with the fact that she always put a period after signing her name—an unmistakable indication of a person who likes tidiness and order. In the writing of her poems, this same quality carried through. Where other poets might write on random scraps of paper, carelessly leaving them in odd and forgotten places, Sara meticulously copied her poems in order in little red notebooks. She put down the date each poem was written as carefully as the poem itself. In all, she filled nine of these little red notebooks during her lifetime, three of which she destroyed.

At Santa Barbara Sara gave much of her attention to the poems that were to become her fourth book. She had intended calling this volume *The Wind in the Hemlock,* after one of the longer poems in it, but one day she came across this passage by Victor Hugo:

> Recois la flamme ou l'ombre
> De tous mes jours!

The phrase, *flame and shadow,* seemed to be a perfect title for her book, as her poems spoke of the joys and sorrows of love, and they also contrasted the flame of beauty and the shadows of death. The only drawback was that John Hall Wheelock was about to publish his new book of poetry, *Dust and Light,* and Sara did not want to select a title that would in any way conflict with his. However, he did not object at all to her choice, and *Flame and Shadow,* dedicated to Ernst, was published in the fall of 1920.

Marguerite Wilkinson reviewed the book in the *New York Times,* and comparing it with her other books, called it "the finest of them all." Babette Deutsch wrote: "The beauty that Sara Teasdale is in quest of may be discovered on every page of her poems," and the reviewer for the *Chicago Tribune* prophesied that "Miss Teasdale's glowing reputation will gain an added beauty by this volume." Everywhere it was hailed as another poetic triumph for the author.

As usual, Sara wrote an endearing inscription in the copy that she gave her husband:

> For Ernst, best of critics, and dearest of souls,
> with all the love of Sara. October 5, 1920.

Among the letters from her personal friends that Sara received about this book was one from Edwin Markham, which said:

I always think of you with affection for the friend and with gratitude for the poet....

...I am lighted by your flame and soothed by your shadow. There is no diminution in the fire of your inspirations. You still know how to touch the soul with beautiful words, how to give us the most delicate of all delights—the delight of love and sorrow.

I need not tell you, sweet poet, my heart attends you all the way.

Sara, who was blessed with a keen and discriminating critical sense, had admired Carl Sandburg's work from her first acquaintance with it. It was she who strongly insisted that Mr. Sandburg should share the Columbia-Poetry Society of America Prize with Margaret Widdemer for the best book of poetry published in 1918, when she served as a judge on this award committee. Through the years, whenever possible, she used her influence in Mr. Sandburg's behalf, for she recognized and had the deepest faith in the enduring quality of his work.

Mr. Sandburg's new book reached her hands just as *Flame and Shadow* was being published, and she sent him this message:

Dear Carl Sandburg: I like to think it was you yourself who sent me "Smoke and Steel." You know how much I have loved your work all these years—how it seems to me more real in its tenderness and sympathy than any other poetry being written in our language today. I'm not going to say a formal "Thank you."

My new book "Flame and Shadow" will reach you in a few days. It goes to you with more than my thanks.

Vachel Lindsay also had a book published in 1920, but unlike Sara's, his was a total failure. Through the years Vachel had remained close to Sara and Ernst. They did many kind deeds for him that could not help but strengthen the ties of devotion that he felt for both of them. When Ernst went abroad, he sent back to Lindsay the pictures of foreign places, especially of Egypt, that the poet wanted; now and then, the Filsingers saw that Vachel's new poems were sent to the meetings of the Poetry Society of America to be read and discussed. When a program of Lindsay's work was given in New York, Ernst made an effort to go and to send back a report about it to the poet. The Filsingers entertained a number of Vachel's friends and relatives when they came to New York, such as his brother-in-law, Dr. Paul Wakefield. Sara frequently criticized his poetry, as he requested, and she was the means of his being introduced to Robert Frost, who appealed tremendously to Vachel.

In those days Lindsay was at the height of his popularity, promise, and fame. His ringing recitations held his audiences spellbound, and his vigorous praise of his native land in original and strong, rhythmical verse was like nothing that America had ever witnessed before. The throbbing pulse of his poems awakened an exciting response on the part of his listeners, and the novelty of the man's performance was part of his charm. As the years went by, however, the novelty wore off, and by 1920 Lindsay himself had tired of playing the part of an entertainer. He wanted to cast off the role of the chanting troubadour and write a new and completely different second chapter of his creative life. But a trip to England had already been arranged and, accompanied by his mother, he went through with it. Before they sailed, the two of them had dinner with Sara in New York. The English visit was a great success; John Masefield saw to it that Vachel spoke at Oxford University; he also spoke at Cambridge; and he made new friends, among them Robert Graves and Stephen Graham. But after he came back, the new mood that had been crystallizing for some time and perhaps marks a turning point in his life, certainly in his thought, seems to have settled permanently upon him. To Harriet Monroe he wrote on December 15, 1920:

. . . in Chicago, as in London, a certain public self is forced upon me by my friends, the Vachel I was to them four years ago, and I would as soon wear a plaster cast all over or medieval armor. I suppose there is no living human being who more hates the formula of his yesterday, even if it is forced upon him with the finest affection by his dearest friends. . . .

. . . I would give almost anything to escape forever the reciting and chanting Vachel. Except when immediately under the intense excitement that comes with facing an *extraordinarily* concentrated group, of listeners, I dislike the very name of every poem I have recited very much except The Chinese Nightingale, which, after all I now recite very seldom. My whole heart is *set* on escaping my old self (completely as I may, to be human and frail as we all are).

The only thing that made the English trip possible for me, was to consider it the rounding up and *last* phase of my reciting life. I set Jan. 1, 1921 as quitting time. Of course it would be silly to announce such a thing aloud, as that other very firm resolve that unless I changed my view of life, I would not go to England again for ten or twenty years. Everybody was very good to me, too good to me, in England but I went there aping or recording, as it were, *shouting* the Vachel of ten years ago, for one gets into rhyme only a self that is long dead. I do not like that Vachel very well. What then am I? Certainly when you and I first met, I had made my last water-color design, and last decorative fantasies in gold and silver and silk. You do not even know about them. They are stuffed in great packages there behind the book-case. *If* I had been obliged to exhibit and explain them old and dusty as they are, once a week till now, I would feel about them as I do about reciting. I do not want to be the slave of past performances or habits, I cannot endure to be such a slave, *I care not what the apparent praise or reward.* I am a dead man in my own eyes, and the only resurrection is in the new vista.

Part of the new vista that he had planned for himself was to be the publication of his prose book, *The Golden Book of Springfield*. But Lindsay returned home to face a crushing spiritual defeat. The book, published in late 1920, was a total failure. The tragedy of this to the author was that he had poured more of his dreams, more of his time, ideas, and energy into the writing of this book than into any of the others. He had thought of the volume as the culminating achievement of his writing career; he had expected its publication to change Springfield, as if by magic, into a spiritual universe of goodness, beauty, and flawless democracy. His tremendous imagination, for once, had cast off all restraining bonds, and the visions, revelations, and strange and miraculous happenings that were to take place in his native city in the Mystic Year of 2018, were difficult and confusing for

Sara Teasdale
1920

the reader to follow. About one hundred books were sold in Springfield at this time, and except for those, the volume was largely disregarded by the city. William Rose Benét wrote a highly complimentary and interesting review of the book in which he compared the power of Lindsay's imagination with that of Edgar Allan Poe; but few other reviews appeared. The book was not damned; it was simply ignored.

The depressing reception of *The Golden Book of Springfield* seriously upset Vachel's nerves; and in his bewilderment and disappointment he turned to Sara. On New Year's Day of 1921, after telling her of some of his troubles, he added:

But meanwhile here is your friend Vachel, almost sick in bed, or dead to the world in his ordinary moments—and as I say, only well in the face of a real challenge. That is routine seems to make me physically sick; that is:—my writing-temperament is now also my citizen temperament. If I cannot use my body and blood to write with, as it were on the walls of a town, I do not want to be a citizen and do not seem even to be living. . . .

* * *

If I am the slave of nothing else, I am the slave of my own middle-aged-ness, of my own weariness and boredom, and I am weary too often simply because I burn to the ground every time I *do* catch fire. So I hold off—and keep cool a-purpose. I get so excited when I am excited at all. And I do not want to get excited over trifles, or mere details.

I want to be sure it *is* a real emancipation that excites me. I seem utterly incapable of moderation in anything, these days—and never to my dying day do I want to do a single thing I have done in the past. . . .

Ten days later, he wrote again:

I am in quite a state, Sara. I was never there before, or never for a long time. I seem to get up the highest steam of my life for two hours of a morning, or for a recital, and then I am absolutely a dead one and wish I was dead, from sheer inertia rather than despair. I really should be at a new book, if for no other reason to set my life in order, and quit fretting over details, and give myself so hard to a new project my silly excitement and silly inertia will have some justification. As it is I blow in a terrible amount of steam for two hours over routine, and then nearly die, and get nothing done, at that. And for the rest of the day I am *dead*.

* * *

... If I live I will appear at the Woman's Club, Elizabeth, New Jersey, April 21. I do not care much whether I live or not, I am so bored at myself. Either I am all flame, or silly little ashes. So I should at least reconsecrate the flame. My note books are crammed with projects. And my English letters are not yet sorted, and I have hardly written one thank-you letter to England. It may sound perfectly imbecile, but I spent one month trying to pick out the American letters asking for dates from the English letters, and I haven't picked them out yet. They are all heaped in one corner. I am just stewed, that's all. I am no good except for the race course, so I might as well get on the track.

Sara did what she could to help Vachel through this difficult period. But she was soon involved in her own sadness. For in the summer of 1921 her father died at Charlevoix at the age of eighty-two. At this time, Vachel was on a tramping trip through the Northwest with Stephen Graham, and in his note of sympathy sent from Glacier National Park, he said:

Your father was all courtesy and kindness to me. I remember him for myself with affection and admiration. You owe so much of what you are, that charms us all—to him—as I well know and remember, and I quite realize you are very much his child.

With all my heart
Vachel.

To take her mind off this loss, for Sara had loved her father deeply, she started to work on an anthology of poetry for children from ten to fourteen years of age. She planned to use poems selected from a wide range of English and American verse, and this task entailed much reading and pruning. When the

John Hall Wheelock
1924

book was published in 1922, it contained an excellent selection of eighty poems for children, including Sara's own favorite, Christina Rossetti's "A Christmas Carol." Dugald Walker illustrated the book with sketches filled with the enchantment of a wonder-world of fairy legends and heroic ballads.

Called *Rainbow Gold*, it won a responsive audience from adults and children alike. Elinor Wylie wrote of it: "I should not ask a better fate than to be a child to whom these most adorable toys, these pictures and trumpets and magic rings were given for the first time. . . ." But the review that most pleased Sara was the one written by Eunice Tietjens's daughter for *Poetry*. Janet Tietjens first admitted that the sight of "O Captain! My Captain!" in the book discouraged her before she had read anything in it at all, because she had heard it recited so much in school that the poem was ruined for her. So she put the book aside. Then, she explained:

But I remember "Miss Sara" Teasdale and like her. When I was very small and mother took me to see her, she produced a most extraordinary mechanical tiger, which went through a lot of internal grindings, squatted back on his haunches, and then leaped suddenly forward. Together we sat on the floor and played with it. I have forgotten many people whom I knew then, but never Miss Sara. Even now I think of her as the lady with the tiger.

So after a while I began to think, "That was foolish of me. Probably she thinks, like my teacher, that children are fond of this poem; or maybe she happened to like it when she was young I can see that it might be possible if you had never studied it in school."

So I got out *Rainbow Gold* and began to read. . . . I didn't put it down till I had read every printed word between the covers. Even now that I know it so well, I try not to look up anything in it unless I have plenty of time, because I know that I shall sit down and begin it all over again!

Miss Sara says in her preface that she agrees with Andrew Lang when he says that poems about children, or those written for children, are not those we like the best. So there are none of these in the book. All the poems in *Rainbow Gold* were written for grown-ups, and if I am to be considered a specimen "child" Miss Sara is quite right, and they really do please us.[7]

The dedication of *Rainbow Gold* reads:

To the Beautiful Memory of My Father, John Warren Teasdale

In her prefatory note, the poet mentioned that a number of her friends had helped her by giving her the names of the poems of childhood that they liked best, and she listed these friends to whom she was indebted: John Gould Fletcher, Vachel Lindsay, Amy Lowell, Jessie B. Rittenhouse, Louis Untermeyer, Jean Untermeyer, John Hall Wheelock, and Marguerite Wilkinson.

Meanwhile, Sara thought that Ernst was working much too hard. She wrote to his father warning him that his son was laying the groundwork for an early death and a body broken in health by a life that was filled too full of writing, speaking, holding offices in important business societies, studying languages in the evening, and trying to keep up with all the cultural movements besides. But there seemed to be no time for him to rest. The summer of 1923 found Ernst on business in England, and Sara went with him, although because of her mother's increasing illness, they hesitated for some time before sailing.

Together they went to Shropshire, where Sara's mind was filled with thoughts of *A Shropshire Lad*. On this trip Sara met Charlotte Mew, visited Canterbury Cathedral, and renewed her friendship with Dr. Hatfield, who was living at that time in an interesting eighteenth-century house, which was once described by Thackeray as Clive Newcome's studio. Ernst had planned to return home with Sara in the late summer, but another business trip carried him to Moscow, and she sailed without him in September of 1923.

One person whom Sara did not have a chance to meet on this trip, which was a disappointment to both of them, was Thomas Moult, distinguished English author and editor, today the Presi-

---

[7]*Poetry: A Magazine of Verse*, Volume 22 (1923), pp. 279-281.

dent of The Poetry Society of Great Britain and Chairman of the Editorial Board of *The Poetry Review*. At that time Mr. Moult had already brought out the first of his annual poetry anthologies that were to continue through 1945, *Best Poems of the Year* (1922), in which Sara was represented, and he was then preparing the second edition. But his wife's illness during that summer prevented his seeing Sara, and when he wrote to her soon after her return to America requesting some poems for the 1923 anthology, she sent him a number to choose from and invited him to call on her when he came to New York. Well aware of the arduous labor involved in assembling such a volume, she wrote:

I know how much time and effort this must cost you, and I only hope that it won't interfere with your own poetry. One does not like to feel that it might prevent such rarely quiet and beautiful work as yours from being given to us in full measure.

The year 1924 brought two losses to the Teasdale family. Mrs. Teasdale, the poet's mother, died on February 20, and the sad task of dismantling and selling the family home on Kingsbury Place had to be attended to by Mamie Wheless and Sara. After the depressing effect of her stay in St. Louis, Sara accepted the invitation of John Hall Wheelock's mother to visit her for a while, as Mrs. Wheelock's son and daughter were abroad, and Ernst Filsinger was also away. At this time in her life, especially, Sara appreciated and enjoyed the quiet charm of this lovely East Hampton, Long Island, home.

In July of this year, John Hall Wheelock's long poem, "Noon: Amagansett Beach," appeared in *The Outlook*. This poem, so characteristic of the author, celebrates the glory made manifest by the light of the sun upon the earth and the waters; in it the poet speaks of the "infinite loneliness—pale sand and paler grass," the sea-birds, the sea-wind, the glittering ocean hallowed by the sun, the god of light and of all life on earth. He addresses him as "father," and says:

>   . . . and the whole
> Clear hollow of heaven is full of the wine of thy glory,
>   even as I . . .

and goes on to say of the lonely background of the poem:

> This is my heart's country: these lonely lands
> Are one with my own lonely heart; these winds and
>   waves that roam
> Old, desolate ways forever, they are one with me—
>   these sterile sands
> And bitter waters. Here is my heart's home.[8]

On the margin of the page on which this poem was printed, Sara wrote her own poem to Mr. Wheelock, which begins:

> This is yourself made greater than yourself,
> Set out of reach of time and beyond death;
> The secret spirit is made visible,
> As on cold air the living human breath.

On October 16 of 1924, the poet's older brother, George Willard, died. Sara was in Europe at that time, for as she had not been at all well herself since her mother's death, and as she felt that she needed the renewal of mind and spirit that leisurely travel seemed to give her, she went abroad in September with a cousin by marriage, who was fourteen years older than herself, Mrs. Alice Teasdale. Mrs. Teasdale had stayed with Sara's mother for about a year around the time that Sara married, and the poet had gotten to know her very well then. Ernst was too involved in business matters in the United States to be able to leave the country.

The two travelers went to Paris, to the French Riviera, journeyed on down to Naples, and came home in November. From this trip came the inspiration for "Pictures of Autumn," a section

---

[8]John Hall Wheelock, *Poems Old and New* (New York: Charles Scribner's Sons, 1956), pp. 89-91. Copyright 1956 by Charles Scribner's Sons. Reprinted by permission of the publishers.

of the poet's next book, *Dark of the Moon*. Probably because of the recent losses in her life, a sombre mood seemed to have taken possession of Sara. She saw Fontainebleau in an October setting and wrote:

> The aisles of the garden lead into the forest,
>   The aisles lead into autumn, a damp wind grieves,
> Ghostly kings are hunting, the boar breaks cover,
>   But the sounds of horse and horn are hushed in falling
>   leaves,
>   Four centuries of autumns, four centuries of leaves.

For the first time she was arrested by the sad promise of autumn:

> If I had gone before, I could have remembered
>   Lilacs and green after-noons of May;
> I chose to wait, I chose to hear from autumn
>   Whatever she has to say.

In the fall of 1924, the English edition of *Flame and Shadow* was published, and Sara sent a copy of the book to Vachel Lindsay soon after she returned from France. It reached him at a moment of spiritual crisis. Lindsay had lost his father in 1918; when his mother, on whom he was dependent in many ways although they had intense disagreements at times, died in 1922, his whole world collapsed, and he suffered a nervous breakdown. Soon after this, he was seriously ill with a long siege of influenza that left his vitality dangerously lowered. His time was spent in arduous speaking tours across the country, with moments of rest in various hotels. His papers, books, and possessions were stored in one room of the old Springfield house, which was eventually rented, and he did not return to Springfield for several years except to spend Christmas of 1923 in the old home, when his sister, Olive, and her family came back from China for a few months. Although he did not want to stay in the Springfield home alone after his mother's death, this poet, to whom his roots and his place in the world, in America, and in Sangamon County, meant everything, now felt at times that he was displaced—a man dispossessed of the things he had most treasured. In January of 1923 he had written to Sara of his intense unhappiness in the present pattern of his life:

... I wish I could come as near to composing *music,* in the musical conservatory sense, as I did the year I wrote the Nightingale. I have woefully receded from that strain. The world only loves the orator in me and hates the rest of me and the orator is to my notion nobody much. But every soul in my world is determined to cheer along the orator, even to *pay* him reasonably well, if I will only speak by clockwork—and to punish *all* the rest of me, if it dares to interrupt.... The orator grows monstrously. The musician is destroyed.... They hate the Vachel *you* knew for whom the Nightingale sang, for there is not a cent of income in him or popular acclaim for him....

One thing I am finding out, dear girl. I am just near enough to a Main Street alleged "success" now to find that even my most loyal friends want to *drive me like a slave to do my little act.* The idea of cultivating that very isolated, very lonely creative moment when Booth and the Congo were born—that the better poem of 1923 may be born is utterly beyond them. I am to be spatted on the wrist or tricked like a baby to make me *stop* every time I show symptoms of wanting to write a *new* poem or draw a *new* picture. My manager writes on ahead to the committees, and suggests to the committees that they storm Booth and the Congo out of me—almost suggests that they compel me to recite them. The idea of attempting the creative mood or working out the new stuff in public or private is utterly beyond them—and not till I have taken a vow to seal my lips for three years in spite of every friend in Christendom will I be able to step back to the days when we copied deep books and carved in jade and wove blue silks in the mulberry shade. You *know* I did not recite well when I wrote well and drew well. The orator has destroyed the writer and artist and not till we have destroyed the orator will the writer and artist again appear. And it is utterly incredible to people that I am the kind of person you knew when we first met. . . . Everything is completely perverted or destroyed to fulfill their jazz or oratorical hypothesis.

Of course this is an ungrateful way to write—dear, and it is only my vow of renunciation. Please help me back to living on a penny a day and writing Chinese Nightingales, and drawing pictures of Saraphims. There is a way forward or back. Oratory has made me many friends—but I must tell them a long long good-by. They are sweet—and it has all been worth while—but I *must* go back to some blue day of 1913, when they treated me like the village idiot and the town drunk.

In the intervening months since this letter of early 1923, Vachel had traveled across America, appearing before numerous college, university, poetry, and literary groups; he had taught a class in poetry for a year and a half at Gulf Park Junior College in Mississippi, and there had suffered an unhappy love affair. He had undergone a sinus operation and had never fully recovered from the lingering effects of his illnesses. In the summer of 1924, Lindsay's brother-in-law, Dr. Paul Wakefield, soon to leave the United States for China, alarmed about the state of the poet's health and nerves, went with him to the Mayo Foundation for a complete check-up. There they learned to their stunned amazement that Vachel Lindsay was a victim of epilepsy. This information was never revealed to anyone but the family, and Sara, of course, never knew it. Vachel himself did not recognize his illness and never referred to it by its medical name, though Eleanor Ruggles has noted in her biography of Lindsay, *The West-Going Heart,* that Lindsay later told his wife that he had been subject to nocturnal seizures since childhood.

Epilepsy, as the medical world recognizes, is a disorder of the nervous system characterized by disturbances in the rhythm of electrical discharges from the brain, which may bring on unconsciousness or convulsions. Contrary to popular belief, epilepsy in itself does not necessarily lead to mental deterioration such as Vachel Lindsay experienced in the last harrowing months of his life. Very probably, the killing nervous strain to which he subjected himself through his strenuous tours and recitations, plus the accumulative effect over the years of luminal sodium on his mind, contributed in great part to his ultimate mental breakdown.

When Sara's new edition of *Flame and Shadow* reached Vachel, he was established in the Davenport Hotel in Spokane, Washington. His whole outlook on life had been affected by the depressing events of the past several years, and her book opened the floodgates of all that had been welling up in his heart during these months. On January 4, 1925, he wrote her:

Dear Sara:—You are a queen who sends out eagles, and doves and nightingales to the uttermost parts of the earth, sends out wild swans and strange dragons. And they all die on their adventures except the eagles that come back with broken wings and bloody beak, years and years afterward. Tonight your eagles come home. I surrender. I wish I had sentences to tell of how we differ—for our agreement is always plain and clear. Our first difference is that I am just exactly where I want to be in Spokane and if I went further it would be to Alaska, not New York. I cannot write or think or breathe in the exotic world which is your essence and to which your book pays tribute. Yet I pay them the same tribute from this distance, and I know you and yours are my final audience. Way, way in my soul I know I am writing to please your sense of beauty and nothing else on earth.

* * *

... I know till the day I die I should write and draw only for you. Your hand should always be on my wrist, or at least your letters in my pocket....

When I write to please you I write better, clearer, more beautiful things than all else I have done. The Rachel Jane is you. I wrote that song under your hand, and the Chinese Princess is my Sara.

* * *

I do not want to do anything wild or wicked. I want you and Ernst to help me to be very noble in this matter. And I want you both to be very noble. For my heart is coming home to you Sara— there is no other way out—if I am to write and draw nobly, from the uttermost depths of my heart and my love and my sense of beauty. . . .

* * *

You can say nothing but the most unutterable loneliness has driven me back—but surely I have come home.

I am here with many noble people. They are very loyal. I might marry a girl in the Northwest or Alaska. They are as brilliant, as cultured, as vigorous and as resolute a set as I have ever known in my life—in a city glittering like an inland Venice. But it is not home, dear. I must give you my heart, my pen, my sense of beauty. Only my desperate need has shown me how deeply you were written on my heart. . . .

* * *

The loss of my mother and father lamed me terribly, for all my hard battles with them. Now they are gone—and all the others gone. You are surely home Sara. There is no other home. Take care of me dear—all you can, by letter—be as good to me as you and Ernst think you have a right to be. . . .

* * *

If we do not write for the splendor of life, and our writing does not maintain the splendor of life, establish it, extend it, we have no business to write at all. If you will be good to me, and help me again toward beauty—it will be worth while to take them by storm again. Otherwise I am weary and lonely, and do not care to ape myself. I surrender to you, my dear. Why is Sara like the good God? In her is no variableness, neither shadow of turning. I sleep in peace, tonight.

With love—Vachel

On the next day he sent another long letter, in which he said:

. . . Henceforth all my books are to be inscribed to you. I guess that is what I am trying to say. That puts it the simplest way and leaves us both free. A paper gift for my dear paper doll.

This book is inscribed to Sara Teasdale, Poet.

The torrent of words continued to pour from his pen. On January 6 he mentioned how tired he was of crowds of people and acknowledged:

...I want to live such a life as you do, seeing only a *very* few people, and those *very essential ones,* who can speak for me to the rest. I am nearer to your state of the skin and nerves and blood, where mere casual contacts wear me *out.* I am now like you, far more sensitive to positive and final relations with a few.

And two days later he wrote:

What must I do to be saved Sara? What is my future? What must I do that will please you and Ernst most? I want you to put your hand on my future as a writer all you dare. . . .

Am I simply struggling with a shadow of the past when I try to bring back your first letter to me asking for a Village Magazine, and my first letter to you when you were at Charlevoix?

You passed through Chicago the week after I had been entertained there by Harriet Monroe.

I am wondering what it all meant.

Or are we to go it blind to the end?

* * *

Well child, I am lonely. What an appalling difference it is when both parents are dead and the old house shut up forever. My sister and brother-in-law in China never write and my sister in Cleveland only writes to scold me. So here I am and the ties of blood are cut off and it is about the same as if hands and legs were cut off. You are surely the next of kin—and the hollow of your hand is the nearest to home. . . .

* * *

...Well I have read often enough we are all isolated at last. I have never quite believed it. . . .

* * *

All this series of letters to you began with the arrival with the English edition of Flame and Shadow. I suppose I am the Shadow.

February 17, 1925

Dear Sara: —

I
Will not forget
That golden queen,
For whom I wrote
The best song
Of my days.
Her hand
Was on my hand,
And on my heart,
And we were no more
Than one breath apart, —
The day we wrote
The best song
Of my days.

Rachel —

The storm of emotion that shook Vachel's heart finally passed, and in a few weeks he had recovered his perspective. By February 14, he was able to confess to Sara:

I am so serene now it is hard to believe I turned to you so desperately so short a while ago. But be sure that henceforth on very short notice the dam may break again. I will hold you in reserve before I take Rough-on-Rats! Or drink wood-alcohol! Some days seem so clear and life looks well, and then almost instantly we are incredibly capsized. We have to put on the life-boat mighty quick.

A few days later he sent Sara a newspaper clipping saying that James Stephens, the Irish author of *The Crock of Gold,* had declared that "Lindsay's 'The Chinese Nightingale' is the greatest poem written in America since the Pilgrims came over." With the clipping Vachel sent his own message:

> Dear Sara:—
> I
> Will not forget
> That golden queen,
> For whom I wrote
> The best song
> Of my days.
> Her hand
> Was on my hand,
> And on my heart,
> And we were no more
> Than one breath apart,—
> The day we wrote
> The best song
> Of my days.
>   Vachel—

Vachel sent these same words to Sara on Christmas Day, 1927; he also wrote them in her personal copy of his *Collected Poems* (1925) and his *Selected Poems* (1931).

On the front flyleaf of the 1923 edition of his *Collected Poems,* he had written on May 27 of that year, in her gift copy:

My dear Sara: When it came to assembling this book last summer— I decided instantly that the Chinese Nightingale should be the first poem, as it has always been my favorite among my pieces, and in like manner, synonymously and instantly I decided that the dedication should apply to the entire collected works.

With love,

Vachel.[9]

The printed dedication in these editions reads:

This book is dedicated to Sara Teasdale, Poet

By the end of March, Vachel could write to Sara:

Happiness has come to me tonight, without warrant, and that is the main thing I am writing you. I have had *such* a troubled heart, dear, but for a little while there is peace. I simply marvel that it has come, when I have been so *full* of heartache. . . .

*   *   *

With all my heart I remember you, and Ernst, and you have been real treasures of all treasures to me this month and last. May your light never grow dim.

And a few days later he was even more sure of himself:

There is no doubt I am in possession of my soul tonight, Sara, and I have written you so many feverish letters you have a right to know the patient is coming through.

Several weeks later, on May 19, 1925, Vachel Lindsay married, quite suddenly, Elizabeth Conner, the daughter of a Spokane minister, who was teaching in Lewis and Clark High School of

---

[9]Vachel Lindsay's gift volumes of his *Collected Poems* (1923 and 1925) and *Selected Poems* (1931) are in the Wellesley College Library's English Poetry Collection, and this quotation is printed with the kind permission of the Wellesley College Library.

that city. Elizabeth Conner was an unusually capable girl, with a flair for writing herself, who had finished her four-year college course in three years, majoring in Latin. She had intended to study for a higher degree and ultimately to follow a career in archeology, but, instead, she decided to devote her life to this poet. And certainly she made him as fine a wife as anyone could have; after the first two years, however, during which a family inheritance helped them, their marriage was burdened with overpowering financial troubles.

A note that Elizabeth Lindsay sent to Harriet Monroe soon after her marriage established the tone of friendship that was to endure between herself and Miss Monroe:

Your letter made us both very happy, and then, when the beautiful mystical lotus-flower came to me last week, I was almost *too* happy. The symbolism of the lotus has always been very dear to me, and it was a magical thing for you to do.

Vachel's friends are all, I think, most kind. On the very day of the lotus, there came also a cream white Chinese shawl from Sara Teasdale, and I wondered if it were not a conspiracy of good will on your part, to make me believe that I *am* the queen of China, after all. . . .

As to the Lindsay love songs, I am afraid to make rash promises. It is difficult to live poetry and write it at the same time, but perhaps there will be a fruitful sabbatical hour ere long—who knows? I think, however, that Vachel's most beautiful love songs have been given to the world long since—and I aspire to be, if anything, the background of an epic—or whatever will make him happy.

The symbolism of Sara's gift is most apparent; for Sara well remembered how Vachel had loved her in a white shawl in the days long past and how he had even written a poem to her called "My Lady in Her White Silk Shawl." Now she was surrendering this token of her place in his life and heart to another, as a queen might pass on her crown to her successor.

Thanking Sara for all of her kindness, Elizabeth Lindsay wrote:

... It is sweet and noble of you to draw me into the magic circle of a very long and very dear friendship; and a thing that is most precious to me.

In October of 1925, the newly married Lindsays planned to stay in New York for a month's visit, and Vachel sent a note to Sara and Ernst in advance:

If all goes well I will be with Elizabeth Conner Locust Blossom Lindsay at the Brevoort Oct. 15 to Nov. 15. Our plans are as simple as yours have always been in New York City. We want to see about two friends in our room every afternoon at tea, beginning with the strongest quietest ties, and as for the rest of the day long walks alone around the town, for Elizabeth is a great hiker and as fond of avoiding crowds as yourselves. We do not want to go out to dinner or in the evening any at all. We will talk then and explore.

I know I have written you utterly inconsistent letters this last year, most of them from the deadliest loneliness combined with the most relentless but kindly publicity I ever endured. I was bombinating in a vacuum. But I hope we four can get together for an evening or tea on Sunday and prove to one another this is a good and beautiful world on such occasions.

* * *

We need you two very much our first week in New York. Bring Marguerite Wilkinson if you can find her, or send her to us or us to her. Please share this letter with her and her husband as much as you see fit. I dearly remember *all* their loyalty and devotion.

Sara and Ernst gladly responded to this request and entertained the Lindsays at their hotel; Vachel immediately sent a grateful note:

I very deeply felt the goodness of you and Ernst and Marguerite and Jimmy last night and must hurry to tell you so. I am writing a note to the Wilkinsons also.

It is a great deal for dear Elizabeth to take over and understand instantly—the whole picture of all my old ties and responsibilities, and the willingness of you four to give her the picture of my New

York life is to me most touching and beautiful. I could say much more, but it would only be in her praise and your praise.

* * *

The more you four stand by me the more grateful I will be. I will understand your moral support by wireless, even if you do or say nothing more, and I will be grateful.

Elizabeth is learning poetic New York superbly, and really raising me from the dead.

When the Lindsays' first child was born, Sara sent the little girl her own baby silver and napkin ring; this touched Elizabeth deeply, and she told Sara:

... as I know you better, I realize more and more how it is that you have long been Vachel's dream of a pearl among women, and more and more I love and honor him for it, as well as you.

Another important new friend was soon to enter Sara's life. For in the summer of 1926 Sara received a letter from a young admirer of her poetry, Margaret Conklin, of Rochester, New York —a student at Connecticut College for Women in New London— which was to be the beginning of a warm relationship.

Writing later to her friend, Aline Kilmer, Sara said:

When you come to New York next I want a new young friend of mine to meet you—Margaret Conklin. I was in Washington (Connecticut) when Margaret's first letter came. Ernst usually handles such letters for me when I am away. But this was so unusual that he sent it on to me, and I, mirabile dictu, answered it immediately. To begin with, you know how most "unknown correspondents" ask for advice about writing, or an autograph, or an "original" poem, or a photograph. Well, Margaret asked for a photograph, to be sure—but not for herself, for a former teacher who had fostered her love of poetry. But there was something more than that in the letter—an inherent quality of delicacy, an indefinable something that touched me and made me feel I should like to know the person who wrote it. . . .

After that first letter and Sara's reply, and a box of wild flowers packed in moist cotton from Margaret to Sara, there were other letters. And when autumn came and Margaret returned to college, Sara asked her to stop and see her in New York. That first meeting seemed a miracle to them both. Sara arranged for Margaret to stay at the Martha Washington, where she had so often stayed before her marriage, and to come to the apartment in the early evening. From the moment they met, the sense of accord that had grown with their letters was intensified, and these two —both by instinct shy—found that words would scarcely come fast enough to share their thoughts and experiences.

During Margaret's last two years at college, Sara saw her often, either in New York, where Ernst took them to the theater or the opera; at inns near the college, where Sara momentarily escaped the New York winter that she hated; or on the campus itself, where she met Margaret's closest friends.

For Margaret, the affection of the poet whose work she loved— whose spirit seemed to her all that was finest and most perceptive, whose humor sent her into gales of delighted laughter—opened the door to a new world of happiness. In some strange way, for Sara the friendship meant a re-discovered youth.

In an unpublished poem written to Margaret in January, 1927, she said (in part):

> You had only
>   To open the door
> To bring me the self
>   I was before.
>
>   .   .   .
>
> The years ran downward
>   Still and sloping.
>
> And then—that Autumn night
>   I knew
> The self I was
>   Came in with you.

Margaret Conklin
1931

Together they did foolish, delightful things that Sara had not done in years: they rowed on Central Park lake, went to a flea circus on Broadway, laughed through the vaudeville shows at the Palace, took the Staten Island Ferry back and forth on spring evenings, picked wild flowers in the Connecticut countryside. And together they read aloud, hour upon hour, poetry, essays, biography—even *Winnie the Pooh* by A. A. Milne—each overcoming her shyness in the understanding response of the other.

Margaret had a sympathetic comprehension of Sara's physical frailness and a nature deeply responsive to beauty; and Sara grew to love her as if she were her own daughter.

In an early poem Sara had written:

> The years went by and never knew
> That each one brought me nearer you;
> Their path was narrow and apart
> And yet it led me to your heart. . . .

No one knows now for whom these lines were intended, but they could apply to almost any of the poet's most valued friendships. For the path of her life *was* narrow in the sense that she could not and did not indulge in many of the activities of the average person. Her poetry, her reading, and her literary interests made up a great portion of her life; and much of her life, the most exciting and meaningful part of it, was lived within her own spirit, as it had been since she was a child.

Yet her talent provided many priceless dividends. For her writing brought her not only the rewards of creative work, but also the contacts with and affection of most of the people whose friendships enriched her life. Even in the earlier years, it was because of her literary interests that she was first introduced to Williamina Parrish and became an integral part of the Potter group, forming friendships with some of the members that were to last throughout her life. John Myers O'Hara, John Hall Wheelock, Vachel Lindsay, and Ernst Filsinger, all of whom were important to her in different ways, were first led to her through her poetry. The friendships of Marion Cummings, Eunice Tietjens, Marguerite Wilkinson, Jessie Rittenhouse, William Stanley Braithwaite, Orrick Johns, Harriet Monroe, Amy Lowell, Louis and Jean Starr Untermeyer, Witter Bynner, Aline and Joyce Kilmer, and Margaret Conklin were all brought, also, to Sara initially through her own creative work.

And there were other awards. Because her poetry is essentially lyrical, fluid, and eminently suited for singing, many of her songs have been set to music by such composers as Amy M. Beach, Katherine Glen, Wintter Watts, Mabel Wood Hill, and Rudolf Ganz. Probably the best known of the musical settings is the song cycle by Wintter Watts called "Vignettes of Italy," published in 1920 by the Oliver Ditson Company of Boston. Among the notable performers who have sung Sara's lyrics are Sophie Braslau, Madame Ernestine Schumann-Heink, Eva Gauthier, John McCormack, and Gadski.

Her poetry also began to find an audience in foreign countries. Individual poems were translated into French, Spanish, Danish, Norwegian, and Chinese. Besides the German translation of her work by Rudolf Rieder, a volume of her poems in Japanese was brought out in 1926, translated by Mijutani, a poet of distinction. Other Japanese versions were made by Yaso Saijiyou, considered by many as the foremost poet of Japan at that time, and by Rikuso Watanabe. Mr. Watanabe, a young man who started writing to Sara after being intensely drawn to her work, told her once that a recent "book of beautiful souls" by M. Nakayama had appeared in Japan, in which she was called the "shadow of a green sapphire."

In the literary world Sara had come a long, long way since *Sonnets to Duse* had been published; and if her outward life moved at a rather quiet pace, her poetic and spiritual life was indeed rich, rewarding, and stimulating.

Chapter 10

DEEPENING SHADOWS

•

SEEKING better health, Sara went to Florida in the early winter of 1926 and stayed for a while at Winter Park, where she saw quite a bit of Jessie Rittenhouse and attended a meeting of the Poetry Society of Florida. February found her in Charleston, which she immediately took to her heart. At this time she was engaged in putting together her sixth book, *Dark of the Moon*. She sent Ernst a manuscript of the poems, and the letter that he wrote in reply shows not only his continuing appreciation of her poetic gift, but the hectic pace of his life as well as his genuine concern for her well-being, and his willingness to do many small errands connected with her literary life.

My dear Sara:

Am writing this letter this morning in order to get it into the mail so that you will be sure to have it on Saturday morning. I am so happy that you are enjoying Charleston, which is evidenced not only by your telegram but also from your letter of the 22nd, which reached me this morning before I left the house.

I wired you last night that I would telegraph today about my movements. The whole thing is up in the air and I do not know what to say. Here are the facts: I was asked to appear before a committee of Congress, or at least to be a member of a delegation that was to appear before a committee of Congress on a law involving the parcels post to Cuba. ... This is to be held next Tuesday, March 2nd. Previously I had agreed to speak on the subject of raw materials before the Export Managers Club noon meeting on that same day. There is to be a meeting of the Executive Committee of the Export

Managers Club tonight and the question will then be considered whether to postpone this meeting until March 9th or to go ahead with it. If it must be gone ahead with I shall have to keep my promise and remain here, as I agreed to speak on this subject and it is one that is very interesting in addition to being highly important.

On the evening of Friday, March 5th, I am to speak at the Boston Round Table. I shall have to leave here the morning of the 5th or the night before.

Of course I might arrange to meet you in Washington on Monday night (March 1st), leaving here in the afternoon on the 3 o'clock train, which would put me into Washington in the evening about eight, or a little later, getting there about ten. This [way] we would have Tuesday, Wednesday, and Thursday together.

An alternative proposition is that you would remain in Washington and meet me there on Sunday morning, the 7th, when we could have a few days together. I should like very much indeed to spend a little time with you in Washington, as it is such a beautiful place. Under the circumstances, however, I shall hardly know until after the meeting tonight, when I shall promptly telegraph. Having thought this all over last night, I suggested in my telegram to you to plan to remain and I hope that you will do so. I am suggesting this especially because you are having such a good time in Charleston and it is just the sort of place that appeals to you, and evidently much more so than Florida.

I was immensely interested in your description of the Pringle mansion. I saw it from the outside but did not get in. It was very touching about the lady who is at present in possession of this place. I do hope that you will see the Magnolia Gardens and also the Middleton place. Both of these are most delightful and charming and I know that they will appeal greatly to you.

Now for the book. I cannot tell you how much I love it. It is really a wonderful thing and one that is sure to enhance your reputation. I am immensely impressed with the arrangement and have read over and over again many of the poems. I hope that my telegram which I sent yesterday evening after I got home reached you promptly so that it would not have a disturbing effect after you had retired. I also hope that the letter that I mailed last night will show you still further how deeply I was impressed. All of this we shall talk [about] at greater length when I again see you.

It is fine to know that your trunk arrived in good shape. It is too bad that they have such sketchy arrangements, and to judge from your far more enthusiastic letter about Charleston I am sure that you will not soon again visit Florida or at least you will select a town like Charleston rather than a more southerly one. I wonder how the temperature is in Charleston and whether the weather is nice. It must have been very charming to hear the mocking birds on the Battery.

I am really and truly sorry that you seem not to have received some of my letters. I wrote in one of them about my having taken tea at Margaret Widdemer's. I had told you in one of my letters that she had asked me to come to tea in case I was not going away. I have already told you of my delightful experience at the Tas concert and also at the theatre with Jean.[1] If I have been having a sort of butterfly experience it has been very interesting and certainly no strain, at least it relieves the strain under which I am always working.

You will find from the enclosed letter that one of the poems has been accepted by *The New Republic*. The others I will immediately send out again to *Vanity Fair*. All this is very nice. I do hope that you received Mr. Canby's letter which I enclosed in one of mine; also the one from *The American Mercury*.

In another letter I did speak of meeting Jack[2] on the street when I was up at the Harvard Club for luncheon with Mr. Graham B. Taylor. I should qualify this by saying that I met Jack on the street after I had left the Club. I am going to try to get there to tea in the next few days. My Foreign Commerce Club engagement should really have read Foreign Exchange Club. This is the organization for which I spoke and about which young Bigelow, Marguerite's brother, had made the arrangements. I am to visit their bank tomorrow to meet one of their Vice Presidents and the representatives of the Anglo-Egyptian bank here.

Our business is excellent and things are certainly moving lively

[1]Jean Starr Untermeyer.
[2]John Hall Wheelock.

in that direction. It is a relief, therefore, to get about doing some of these other things.

As I told you earlier in this letter I shall be sending you a telegram probably this evening and hope that you will have it before going to bed. I am certainly glad that you like the Francis Marion Hotel. I too thought it was splendid and not too expensive. I cannot help but believe that inasmuch as you love this place so much it will do you good to remain another week and I hope that you will do so. You can let it serve for what the Germans call an "after cure."

Once more let me send you my congratulations on the beautiful *Dark of the Moon*. I don't know when I have been so enthusiastic about a book of poems and I would be so even if the volume had been written by someone I did not know. That, I think, is the surest test.

Dark of the Moon was published in 1926; and again, with few exceptions, Sara's public and the critics had nothing but admiration for her work, although they detected a new note and a new mood in this volume. As the title implied, the ecstatic rapture of love was not celebrated so much now as the deeper and darker side of life; a new seriousness was evident; the terrible and irresistible magnetism of solitude had begun beckoning to the poet again. In "The Solitary" she wrote:

> Let them think I love them more than I do,
>   Let them think I care, though I go alone;
> If it lifts their pride, what is it to me
>   Who am self-complete as a flower or a stone.

And in "The Crystal Gazer":

> I shall gather myself into myself again,
>   I shall take my scattered selves and make them one,
> Fusing them into a polished crystal ball
>   Where I can see the moon and the flashing sun.

Her heart, which had walked eagerly and joyfully through the rich and colorful spring and summer landscapes of love, seemed now to have moved into the more solemn and austere fields of fall and winter. A sense of loss and the inevitability of the passing of time and the coming of death stain these poems with a sad but compelling beauty.

John Farrar, writing in *The Bookman,* said in his review of this volume what the majority of readers thought: "Sara Teasdale's authentic gift has been accented with the years. Her new collection of poems, *Dark of the Moon,* captures the senses and the heart. These lyrics are deeper with meaning than many of her earlier songs. . . . Now her poems have a clearness, an always crystal beauty. They have lost none of their appeal, they have only gained in that austerity which seems to me to mark the really great in poetry."

Katharine Lee Bates summed up the poet's achievement in her review in the *New York Evening Post:* "Sara Teasdale's most formidable rival is herself. From the appearance of her *Sonnets to Duse* in 1907, hers was a triumphal progress through *Helen of Troy . . .* and *Rivers to the Sea* till that first decade culminated in *Love Songs* with the public recognition of the Columbia University prize. But the volume of 1920, *Flame and Shadow,* so far excels them all that, after these six waiting years, we hardly dare ask if the new volume registers a still higher attainment.

"The earlier qualities are here in undiminished charm—the artistry, the magic, the directness of utterance bearing out her own testimony: 'I try to say what moves me. I never care to surprise my reader.' Our surprise comes in finding our own feeling so exquisitely spoken."

Letters of commendation on the appearance of this book flooded Sara's mail. Witter Bynner wrote her:

It is good to be reminded of our alliance across distances by the receipt of your book. I spent a happy evening with it and found an open fire exactly the right reflection of these curious flames of sadness that have crept into your work. The earlier sadness was a young sadness, to be taken with a smile. This is different. It is more like the sadness in the Chinese poems, a true-seeing sadness, the sadness at the core of even the happiest of us.

From Carl Sandburg came this message:

I have always thought the best poetry something close to the line of silence; it almost crosses over; you get this in *Dark of the Moon;* I put it along with Emily Dickinson; isolate, golden moths. . . .

And Edgar Lee Masters sent the following letter:

Dear Sara: This morning I read your book. My feeling about it is that it contains the most beautiful poems you have ever written. You have captured the music of flowers, of waters and waves, of hills, of autumns, and of stars, and of Villa d'Estes. I am particularly drawn to Fontainebleau, Effigy of a Nun, Those Who Love, So This Was All, Full Moon, Not By the Sea, The Solitary, and Midsummer Night. This is a book to have with one when one is alone and in the composure of quiet nerves, and so to drink in— sitting in a sunny garden, let us say, when the whispers fall this way and that, and Life seems to peer from the changing lights, in wise friendliness. I shall be surprised if the crows (the book reviewers) do not try to sing its praises—the thrushes will.
Sinveerely your friend,

E.L.M.

The poem, "Effigy of a Nun," mentioned by Mr. Masters, was written after Sara and Jean Starr Untermeyer saw such an effigy during one of their visits to the Cloisters together. This experience inspired both poets to write on the same theme, Mrs. Untermeyer's poem being called "A Dead Nun Smiles at Two Poets."

Eunice Tietjens was in North Africa when she received Sara's book, and she sent this message to the author from Tunisia:

Sara dear;—
"Dark of the Moon" is lovely! I have at last had time to sit lingeringly with it, and breathe it in, as your work should always

be breathed in. And I find it quite as good as any book you have ever done. There is, to be sure, no poem that stabs me in the same way that your "Dune Song" does—which I have read twenty times and never without weeping for its sheer beauty—but these are almost all perfect in their own way. And with what a poignant grace you have sung the approach of age! I should think for some people these lyrics would be almost unreadable, they would hurt so. It is strange what time does for us, isn't it, Sara dear?

The book has set me thinking. We are just the same age, and yet fate has dealt with us very differently. You seem, in your heart, to have skipped middle age—at least I find no suggestion of its values. Very likely this is because you are so sure a craftsman, and middle age is not lyric. But it is fine human stuff all the same. I am splashing in it, and enjoying myself. Youth is all hope and passion and cob-webs. Age is all memory and resignation and wistful pale-gold sunshine, clear and cold. But middle age is strong and vital—and silent. It is middle age that gets the work of the world done. It builds the bridges and the cities, and it carries the weak years, before and behind. They feed on middle age. But it has not much time to sing. . . .

I am sending a little poem to add to the sheaf of "Poems that have been written to me" which you were once collecting! It is a purely personal reaction to the book, but you won't mind that, knowing that personal reactions are the deepest.

The lines that Eunice sent with this letter follow:

OLD FRIENDSHIP
(For Sara)

Beautiful and rich is an old friendship,
Grateful to the touch as ancient ivory,
Smooth as agèd wine, or sheen of tapestry
Where light has lingered, intimate and long.

Full of tears and warm is an old friendship,
That asks no longer deed of gallantry,
Or any deed at all—save that the friend shall be
Alive and breathing somewhere, like a song.[3]

[3]Eunice Tietjens, *Leaves in Windy Weather* (New York: Alfred A. Knopf, 1929), p. 10.

As her physical strength was limited, Sara rarely granted interviews; the Macmillan Company gave out all the publicity and information about the poet, and in answer to many requests had prepared a little grey booklet about her, which was revised in later years. The public in general did not have access either to her address or to her telephone number, which was unlisted. To simplify answering the numerous appeals that came to her, Sara had Tiffany's print a formal white card which read:

Sara Teasdale wishes to express her appreciation of your inquiry, but as she never makes public or semi-public appearances, she is unable to comply with your request

However, because of the persistent pleas of Victoria Unrub Harvey, a journalist from St. Louis who was doing a series of articles for the *St. Louis Star* on Missouri authors, the poet finally granted one of the two interviews that she gave within a period of almost twenty years of writing and publishing. Sara tried to discourage the interviewer from her task by first writing to her from Old Lyme, Connecticut:

I am in this village resting but if I feel well enough upon my return in a week or so I shall be glad to see you though I am a complete failure from the standpoint of a reporter. The only news about me is that my new book, *Dark of the Moon,* a collection of my lyrics written during the last six years, was published by the Macmillan Company last month and the initial edition of five thousand copies was exhausted on publication, and the book went immediately into a second edition, which means an unusual interest, and gives me a great satisfaction. I live so simply and quietly and find it so hard to talk to new acquaintances that I don't believe I'd be worth your taking time for an interview.[4]

This message only made the reporter more interested than ever in meeting Sara, who, reluctantly, but astutely, granted the interview at twelve o'clock, noon. No doubt the reason for this rather

[4]*The Missouri Club Woman* (St. Louis, Missouri), March, 1933, p. 11.

strange hour was that the interviewer would, in all decency, have to leave shortly, in order that lunch might be served.

Sara greeted her guest in a gray satin dress and gray shoes. She wore one ornament, a necklace of jade beads. She surprised her visitor by descending from the realms of Parnassus to discuss the difficulties of keeping coal dust out of her New York hotel apartment. She also mentioned that she loved the seclusion of New York—where she could go on long walks alone and never meet a soul she knew—and where she was not obligated to people as she was to her many friends and acquaintances in St. Louis.

Mrs. Harvey described Sara's apartment as "a most restful one—for she has used shades of pale blues and greens and lavenders and pale orange and tan and amber in her furnishings and in her decorations. Her pictures are restful—many of them water scenes with long shadows of trees with their reflections in the water."

The poet pointed out the shelves filled to overflowing with books of poetry, many of them first editions with inscriptions by their authors. She also showed Mrs. Harvey the volume containing her own poems translated into Japanese, and remarked: "When I look at those vertical lines, they remind me of wisteria blooms." The time passed all too quickly for the reporter; she came away deeply impressed with the genuine simplicity of spirit of this writer, who was apparently untouched by the torrent of sophisticated life swirling around her in the great city.[5]

In the spring of 1927, Sara decided that she and Margaret Conklin must see her beloved England together. Such a trip, with someone she had known a comparatively short time, was a departure from her usual carefully planned way of life. But her detailed arrangements for it were typical. She introduced Margaret to Dr. Dana C. Atchley, her physician and friend, to Mrs. Wheelock, mother of John Hall Wheelock, to the representative of her bank, to Harriet Monroe, in New York from Chicago—and to others whose opinion she valued. Margaret believes that all

[5]*St. Louis Star,* February 1, 1927.

this was a test of her inexperienced and unsophisticated self, but certainly Sara gave no direct indication of that. In June, 1927, they sailed to England to spend a summer that remained in both their hearts a shared adventure, every moment of which was a joy.

Ernst, who stayed behind because of his business duties, was, as always, concerned about Sara's health and happiness, and lonely for his wife, and he wrote her on June 25, 1927:

I have been thinking a great deal about you, as I always do when things are so beautiful and happy, and wish very much that you were with me. . . .

By this time you must be getting pretty close to England and will doubtless be landing shortly. I hope that you will arrive at a good hour and that you will not have to be up so early in the morning as we had to be when we reached Plymouth. I also pray that you may find the weather delightful and the accommodations all that you had dreamed of. I do hope that you are already feeling rested and that you are going to be helped greatly by the English climate.

In the copy of Muirhead's *Guide to London,* which Sara had given Margaret the previous Easter, she had written:

> Margaret, may London be
> As dear to you as it is to me:
> Its reticent, proud way of keeping
> Loveliness hidden for our seeking . . .

and expressed her love of London in these lines:

> Hyde Park, so meadowy and clean,
> Kensington Gardens, fluttering gay
> With decorous children, all the day

and

> The lucent, unexpected green
> Of leafy squares in crowded places.

London was sheer delight to them both, and the whole trip an almost unbearably moving experience to Margaret—a born Anglophile who had never before traveled. But it was the Lake District and Devon that perhaps meant most to them: Dove Cottage where both Wordsworth and De Quincey had lived—and the cliffs at Lynton with fox-gloves and sea pinks growing in wild profusion. It was at Lee Abbey Hotel in Lynton that Sara wrote:

> How can these wild cliffs ever forget you
> Or so good a day be done?

It was also on this trip that Sara wrote to Margaret her lyric called "To a Child Watching the Gulls," which came from their experience at Queenstown Harbor:

> The painted light was on their underwings,
>   And on their firm curved breasts the painted light,
> Sailing they swerved in the red air of sunset
>   With petulant cries unworthy of their flight;
> But on their underwings that fleeting splendor,
>   Those chilly breasts an instant burning red—
> You who are young, O you who will outlive me,
>   Remember them for the indifferent dead.

When the travelers returned home in September after a rather hectic voyage of storms and intense heat, Ernst and Sara decided to move from the Beresford where they had lived for ten years. Sara, not too well after the strenuous trip back, was sent off to Boxwood Manor in Old Lyme, Connecticut, to recuperate; and Margaret and Ernst took the responsibility of moving the Filsinger possessions to the Hotel San Remo at Central Park and 74th Street. Excerpts from a letter written by Ernst to Sara at this time will show again how Ernst had Sara's welfare at heart, how he wanted to spare her any strain, and how much he, too, thought of Margaret:

Dear Sara,

This morning I received a letter written on Sunday evening. I am glad to know that everything is green and lovely and hope that you are well taken care of at Boxwood.

As I explained to you over the phone yesterday afternoon, all is going well. I was at the San Remo this morning and found the painters hard at work. All the little details will be completed by this afternoon, including the floors. They are going to lay paper over the floors so that, in moving in, they will be kept nice and fresh.

We shall definitely move to-morrow morning and Morgans promised to have the van there at 7:30 a.m. This was confirmed in writing. I had a talk with Mr. Kramer this morning and both of us were as sweet as peaches and cream. He promised to let me move all our furniture out of the 81st Street side, only heavy cases are to go out through the Central Park West door. I shall, of course, be on the job and see to it that there is someone on the elevator.

Margaret came to the apartment this morning before I left and we discussed such details as were in doubt. She will keep an eye on the work at the San Remo during the day and will report to me later. . . . The bookcases arrived this morning—they match our others quite perfectly.

The view from the new apartment this morning, in a sort of hazy atmosphere, was very lovely. The boss painter was also commenting on the beauty of the scene to his workmen. I am sure that you will like it. The new color is perfect and the improvement as a result of the light shade of cream on the woodwork, mantelpiece and so on, is very pleasing. It was certainly a happy idea of yours to persuade these people to do that job for us.

* * *

There was some mail this morning, including two envelopes from the Guarantee Trust Company which I am sending you herewith. There was also a magazine from Japan with a translation of one of your lyrics and an article by Mr. Watanabe on your autographed poem or poems.

Margaret is, to me, a wonderfully fine girl and I can see why you like her so much. I am trying to take all the load that I can from her shoulders but she is really very efficient and is managing things with neatness and dispatch. . . .

As I told you over the 'phone yesterday, I am delighted that you did escape that bad cold. I felt that it was coming on and that was the thing that upset me so much. I did not want you to get sick over this whole thing and the realization also that you had taken it terribly hard and would likely have a siege in bed, gave me a great deal of worry. I am certainly glad that you have been out of the mess because the condition of the apartment, with the packing cases and so on, would certainly have got very much on your nerves.

Margaret and Mrs. Curlin took down a lot of stuff yesterday and it is all locked up in the closet. There is, of course, no chance for anyone to break in there as it is carefully locked with a yale lock. I made a careful note of the various items that you discussed with me and shall have the thumb lock removed. I am looking after the change in the mail and telephone.

* * *

The view at sunset yesterday evening was superb; the golden spire of the Hotel Netherlands seemed especially attractive. On your return I think you will find everything in pretty good order. I do hope that you will not take too seriously the finishing touches and will allow them to come along in due course. I want you to have a pleasant and happy autumn free from serious colds which so easily take hold of you.

In spite of Ernst's solicitude and sincere concern for her well-being, and Margaret Conklin's frequent trips to New York, the next months were not happy ones for Sara. Early in 1928, Marguerite Wilkinson was drowned in the waters off Coney Island. She had suffered a nervous breakdown the summer before her death, and to prove to herself that her fear emanated from the spirit rather than from physical causes, she made herself learn to pilot a plane. Every afternoon she flew from Curtis Field, and every morning she took a strenuous swim, engaging in aquatic stunts, as a means of conquering her fear. Jim Wilkinson, her husband, sent Sara a string of Marguerite's beads after her death, which Sara treasured.

When Vachel Lindsay received Sara's and Ernst's wire about Marguerite's death, he wrote at once from Spokane on January 14:

Elizabeth and I have just sent our word of affection to James, and that is all we can do, except hold in noble memory, the good and beautiful Marguerite Wilkinson.

It is all like the breaking up of the Round Table to me—and if we are to live at all we must gather new circles about us to hearten ourselves. I have not forgotten a single thing in which Marguerite had her hand. She always was a stateswoman for us all, a friend and destiny-maker, just by being naturally a high adventurer for poetry, with such *splendid innocent enthusiasm.*

So many things happen now—that make us say:—"It was not like that in the olden days—in the days beyond recall." I have been so fiercely "discussed" and almost villified, and all my friends—you would suppose we were worth destroying, if mere dust from the wind could destroy.

For a long time we had the privacy of a comfortable circle that understood one another—and we had nothing that any man coveted. Now we all have so little—yet the little we have we must watch.

If we are to be poets at all—it is with a second courage—that rises above all shadows and death—and I confess I am merely struggling—*not* triumphant. . . .

Our circle was the most innocent circle of birds that ever sang. That we can boast of to the end of time. And we truly know it now—when we must face death and infidelity at every step, at this hour.

I pledge my belief in the eternal soul of Marguerite and its eternal goodness. Her prayers were not in vain and not shadows and we know she died at peace with the dear God.

We were all singers together in those old days—innocent singers who loved the sun—and I have not forgotten a day of it. We asked for nothing but to please our own circle, and had not the remotest notion of trying to please the world. "Bluestone" should be on Marguerite's monument in bronze.

With love from Vachel and Elizabeth

Captain Bentley and Ernst Filsinger

Ernst Filsinger

A few months later, on March 25, Sara was injured in a taxicab accident, and the rest of this arduous year was spent in trying to recover from the serious and painful effects of this misfortune.

Early in September of this year, Ernst's father died. Though Sara had not seen him for some time, she had never lost her affection for Mr. Filsinger, and she sent this message to his widow:

I am in such grief over the news. . . . I have thought of you all, you and Wanda and Irma and Auntie and my own Ernst, so far away and having to bear his trouble alone, until my heart is sick. . . . I feel so badly not to be near Ernst to try to comfort him at this time. . . . I have never known a more splendid man than Father Filsinger—he and my own father were equally fine and lovable and full of goodness. . . . I feel sorry now that I never put into words when I spoke with him, my admiration for his wonderful knowledge of life and of books, his broadmindedness and his sympathy for all people. He was a gentleman in the finest sense of the word.

Meanwhile, Ernst was working harder than ever. Business took him on his first trip to Africa, and in order to save time covering the territory, he chartered a moth plane piloted by an Englishman, Captain Bentley, and both flew from Johannesburg, ending the flight in Berlin, after various business stops. At that time Ernst was President of the New York Export Managers Club, and since he was not in the United States when the Club was to meet in Baltimore, he addressed the gathering by telephone from his hotel room in the Adlon Hotel in Berlin, transmitted by radio. This was the first experiment of its kind and was widely publicized.

Because of the pressure of Ernst's business interests, he and Sara were apart almost more than they were together; and the tragedy of their marriage and the root of its dissolution lay in the living conditions of their life. The fact that ill health prevented Sara's traveling with her husband left no alternative to a gradual growing apart. Though Ernst loved people, loved the theater and the opera, enjoyed having friends in to visit and going to parties, and though Sara required a quiet life with little out-side activity, they were very happy when they were together, and Ernst made few demands upon her. Occasionally, when some friend like Margaret Conklin or Nancy Coonsman was visit-ing them, Sara would urge Ernst to take their guest tea-dancing or to the theater, for she knew how much pleasure Ernst derived from these social activities in which she could not participate.

It was the being apart so much that doomed their marriage. The two who had such a radiant future before them gradually found themselves seeing little of each other. Ernst was absorbed in his business life, as indeed he had to be to make a success of it; Sara became more and more of a recluse, as her health made it difficult for her to live otherwise. There was no question of a third person, no open disagreements such as usually bring about separation; slowly, they drifted into two very different ways of life.

Sara intimated to Ernst's family that he was coming to live only for his business. She talked seriously with him about separa-tion and divorce, but he was shocked and unaccepting of any such proposal and did not want even to discuss it, because he could not bear to think of losing her. In 1929, leaving Margaret Conklin in charge of her mail and various affairs in New York and telling almost no one else, Sara went quietly to Reno with a friend of Margaret's, who was a nurse, as her companion. John Hall Wheelock, one of the few with whom she discussed her plan for a divorce, advised her strongly against it. At that time Ernst was in South Africa, and when he received word from her that she was determined to carry out her previously expressed intention, he was broken-hearted. But he knew that Sara, having made up her mind, could not be swayed, and there was nothing that he could do except let a lawyer handle the sad affair for him.

Margaret Conklin, having graduated the previous June, was now working in the Publicity Department of the Macmillan Com-pany, and was able to quiet to some extent the anxious questions as to Sara's whereabouts that came to her from friends.

A letter that Ernst wrote to Jessie Rittenhouse immediately after the divorce shows his continuing devotion for Sara; for in it he said:

...I know that you know, dear Jessie, that I love Sara today, more completely, more desperately, more tenderly than in all the time I've known her. Never for a moment did I cease to love her, to admire her—to respect her wonderful independence of spirit. I find it hard to believe that all that has happened is anything but an ill dream.... If only I had not taken that trip to South America.

When Sara told Vachel Lindsay of her action, she had a swift reply. An ending of another nature, about which he had been thinking more and more ever since Marguerite Wilkinson's death, was very much on his mind, and he mentioned it in his letter of September 24:

My dear Sara:—Your letter came yesterday and left us stunned. The best comment from us is no comment. I send you both my goodwill, and earnest prayer.

An utterly impersonal comment, about the whole New Poetry Movement, and all the great brave days of the past, naming no names and calling no names, and praising the glory of 1910 to 1914 comes out in The Landmark, organ of the English-Speaking Union for October. I am sure all members of the old gang however separated will highly approve for it says in substance we met late, rejoiced exceedingly as poets and companions, and separated soon, first because of death by the war and grief over the war causing death, and secondly because of death by natural causes, such as the death of Marguerite and Jimmy and the death of Amy Lowell. I try to say that those who are living are still singing, though they seldom meet. I want all the old gang still under your hand to approve of this article.

I am tired of the critical dictum that the New Poetry Movement has grown careless, as though it were a matter of the fading away of technique, when it is a plain case of the death of your parents, the death of my parents and all such, and we must put on a far sterner and more solitary harness to go forward.

Certainly all the survivors are still singing though separated, and it is merely the separation of the once bright banquet board that the critics are talking about, though they do not know it.

They merely mean there is no longer a clatter of Poetry Society conversation to enlighten them.

Tell us more, tell us everything, and come to see us, noble lady.

Most fraternally
Vachel.

Elizabeth Conner Lindsay also included her note with Vachel's letter:

Dear Sara,

We were simply stunned when we had your letter this morning. It was the last thing on earth to have happened; and you are being unimaginably brave and self-contained about it. It would make us love you the more—if that were possible!—as it is, you are right: we are still here, and always will be, for you—mind, heart, and soul.

You are so good to want us to come to New York. We should love to. I am sure you will see Vachel this winter—I hope, often—I am more of a fixed star at present, for the usual domestic reasons. We should so love having you here—our guest-room is always ready, and I think you would be comfortable and happy in it. When next you are lonely, don't just *think* of us, come to us. *Please!*

The infants flourish and send Aunt Sara their love, now and always.

Vachel, of course, is writing, too. I think he is too shocked for speech just now.

Our hearts for yours, gallant lady!
Elizabeth

We have the bust here. Come and see it! E.

The Reno experience was a terrible ordeal for Sara, physically and spiritually. Music, which had always been an important part of her life, was her deepest consolation through these trying days. After she was free of her marital bonds, she told her lawyer that she wished to retain the name of Filsinger always.

She came back to New York and took a small apartment in the Hotel Gramercy Park. The shadows of her personal world were deepening. A part of her life that had been very precious to her was now over. One cannot help but recall her own prophetic lines of poetry published in *Dark of the Moon* three years before, and fittingly called "An End":

> I have no heart for any other joy,
>   The drenched September day turns to depart,
> And I have said good-bye to what I love;
>   With my own will I vanquished my own heart.
>
> On the long wind I hear the winter coming,
>   The window panes are cold and blind with rain;
> With my own will I turned the summer from me
>   And summer will not come to me again.

Her family and many of her friends were amazed at Sara's quiet action, as she and Ernst had always seemed so completely in tune, spiritually. One of her sisters-in-law, now deceased, who visited her about a year before the divorce, remarked afterwards that she had rarely seen two such harmonious people as Sara and Ernst.

But there were two conflicting desires within the poet's nature that had been battling for supremacy since childhood. One was the desire to love and to be loved and to be with the person she loved; the other was the old, old wish for the refuge of solitude where her spirit found its greatest delight and its greatest renewal.

She and Ernst remained friends, though they saw little of each other. Towards him she retained an attitude of sympathy and concern, for she knew how deeply his sensitive and loving nature had been hurt by their separation and how hard he was driving himself to achieve success in his business. At her suggestion, once, he came and spent a quiet and pleasant evening with her.

Resolutely, she turned her mind to other things and began to gather together a charming group of children's poems for a little volume called *Stars To-night*, which was published in 1930. The verses, some of which were new and some of which were selected from previous books, were delightfully illustrated by

Dorothy Lathrop, and the book was dedicated to Margaret Conklin.

To an intimate friend Sara once referred to her divorce as "this tragedy behind me." Life moved now at a muted and slower pace for the poet. Her days were filled with reading, letter writing, and resting. Very infrequently did she see people or go out. Many of her old friends who used to make the city a place of radiant enchantment in those far-off days were no longer present. Joyce Kilmer, Marguerite and Jim Wilkinson, and Edward J. Wheeler all had died. Jessie Rittenhouse no longer had an apartment in New York, and a number of her other friends were now scattered. There were times when loneliness, more than solitude, laid its hand upon her heart.

Her friendship with Margaret Conklin was a brightening influence in her life and the source of a great consolation for Sara during these later years. Margaret came directly from her job at the Macmillan Company to Sara's apartment three or four evenings a week, and they read aloud or talked of gayer times in the past, of their childhood, and of the things they had done, or wanted to do.

It was at this time that Sara wrote this tribute to Margaret:

> Till the last sleep, from the blind waking at birth,
>   Bearing the weight of the years between the two,
> I shall find no better thing upon the earth
>   Than the wilful, noble, faulty thing which is you.
>
> You have not failed me; but if you too should fail me,
>   Being human, bound on your own inviolate quest,
> No matter now what the years do to assail me
>   I shall go, in some sort, a victor, down to my rest.

Sara's sense of fun never deserted her, and Margaret remembers with delight a brief trip to Washington where they stayed at the Mayflower Hotel. The dining room was crowded with members of a club-women's convention and Sara, whose rich, lovely voice was penetrating, in a sudden hush was heard to say:

"How many happy husbands and sons there must be at home tonight!" That episode reminded them of their visit to the National Museum in London where they had burst into spontaneous giggles before a huge and very bad portrait of the royal family. A horrified guard, standing near by, said to Sara: "Madam, in England one does not laugh at the Royal Family!"—probably the first and last time that Sara was ever reprimanded for deportment.

John Hall Wheelock was one of that small group of old friends who were still an important part of Sara's life in these days. For time had only enhanced her opinion of him formed long ago as a man who seemed to her high above other men in many ways. The years had strengthened her early affection for and devotion to him into a rich and abiding friendship, and it is well known that many of her later poems were written to him. Perhaps her feeling for him was most perfectly expressed in these lines:

It is enough of honor for one lifetime
To have known you better than the rest have known. . . .

"A November Night" in *Love Songs* was, one must conclude, written to Mr. Wheelock, and the entire Section V of *Flame and Shadow* would seem to refer to him. "I Know the Stars," "Understanding," "Nightfall," "It Is Not a Word," "The Nights Remember," and the exquisitely musical and haunting "Let It Be Forgotten" clearly appear to have been written with Mr. Wheelock in mind.

Sara thought that she recognized in him many of the virtues that she had so loved and respected in her father; yet she was also, one may note, thoroughly aware that he, even as all men, was not perfect, and she translated an actual incident into her poem, "Appraisal":

Never think she loves him wholly,
Never believe her love is blind,
All his faults are locked securely
In a closet of her mind. . . .

Yet, she went on to say, these things were relatively unimportant:

> Let them be, oh let them be,
> There is treasure to outweigh them,

and she spoke of his "proud will," "his gentleness to beast and bird," and:

> Humor flickering hushed and wide
> As the moon on moving water,
> And a tenderness too deep
> To be gathered in a word.

"Appraisal" appeared in *Dark of the Moon* in the section entitled "Portraits." Another poem in this same section called "Those Who Love" might well have been a portrait of Sara herself:

> And a woman I used to know
> Who loved one man from her youth,
> Against the strength of the fates
> Fighting in somber pride,
> Never spoke of this thing,
> But hearing his name by chance,
> A light would pass over her face.

Occasionally, whenever he was in New York, Vachel Lindsay came to see Sara. His life and spirit during this period were at a low ebb, for fortune had not smiled upon him since his marriage. But the glory of their friendship was one thing that time never dimmed.

After their second child was born, the poet and his wife were beset with the financial problems that must be solved by growing families, and since Lindsay was without a regular position of any kind, their problems were acute indeed. Now and then, although he disliked the idea more and more, he continued to give recitations, but the strain of travel and speaking exhausted him completely, and seriously aggravated his nervous disorder. Furthermore, not only the pressure of mounting financial difficulties, but also his belief that his poetic talent had run its course and burned itself out contributed substantially to the shattering of his nervous system. A number of disagreeable experiences had brought about this state of mind.

Unfortunately, after his English trip, a book of his collected poems was published in England with the title, *The Daniel Jazz and Other Poems,* this being taken, evidently, from the poem, "Daniel," in which this line occurs: "He stirred up the jazz in the palace band."[6] Ironically, this particular line has no bearing whatever on the point of the poem. Lindsay himself detested jazz; he used the syncopated rhythms of the music of his day as a means of catching the ear of the public, and only to get his messages across to his audiences. He never intended for these meters to glorify jazz music. When many who had never read *The Daniel Jazz* at all drew their own conclusions from this breezy title, the volume got off to a very poor start. Lindsay had not been consulted about the title, and he was deeply hurt at the book's reception, at the reviews it inspired, and most of all at the reputation it established for him in England as a "jazz poet." What he considered his most representative poem, "The Chinese Nightingale," was not even included in the book.

There were other matters that upset him emotionally. He had never wanted composers to set his work to music, as he said, "Other men's music kills my poems," and when he was now approached on this subject, he became highly excited and irritated with the prospective composer out of all proportion to the matter at hand. He could not understand, even after all these years, why the prose book to which he had devoted his greatest effort, *The Golden Book of Springfield,* had been completely ignored and left unread and unreviewed. Nor could he understand why his later books drew adverse criticism, or why his drawings had never found the acclaim that he thought they deserved. It was hard for him to overlook Amy Lowell's reference to him as a typical middle-westerner of the middle class, when his mother had

---

[6]Lindsay changed this line to: "He stirred up the music in the palace band," in his later edition of *Collected Poems.*

never let him forget for a minute that he was descended from two fine Kentucky families.

> They went west to the new blue grass,
> When it was still Virginia.
> When people say "Kentucky," they mean Virginia ...

Vachel once wrote. He considered himself a Virginian in the finest sense of this word's cultural meaning, and once he even dared to tell proper Bostonian Amy Lowell that he was a Virginian, when she spoke to him of being a middle-westerner.

All of these things began to trouble him deeply; his mind turned back to the days when he had been younger, when his nervous system had not been permanently injured by being subjected to the strains and anxieties of forced readings and recitations—to the days when life stretched out before him in a long golden road, and he was going to answer its challenge by chanting the Gospel of Beauty to all America. He remembered how he, a young poet, had thrilled the distinguished audience at the Chicago dinner in honor of Yeats, when his newly-written "The Congo" drew round after round of applause. The inspired dreamer of those days seemed far, far away from the tired, ill, and distraught man that he had become. It was hard, almost impossible, for him to face the realities that now confronted him. His creative power seemed to have deserted him, and he became convinced that he would never write another poem.

Harriet Monroe, who had kept in close contact with Elizabeth and Vachel, clearly perceived what was happening to the poet in whom she had had such faith. She wrote him a thoroughly typical and straight-forward letter, thinking it would help him to pull himself together. She urged him not to get excited over composers, genealogy, or "your very secondary talent for drawing," and begged him to put his mind on poetry and poetry alone, for she was confident that he was capable of giving the world more great poems.

But the old Vachel, the old ringing exuberance and assurance were never to return. As it has done for others, England recognized the ability of Walter de la Mare while he was a young man and granted him a pension, freeing him to write lest the spirit of song should perish with the battles of age and the fight for survival in the material world. And it seems incredibly tragic that Lindsay, who dedicated his life work to the glorification of his country, could not have been granted a small yearly pension by his city, state, or nation that would have saved him. For all Vachel Lindsay needed, as Edgar Lee Masters pointed out in his biography, was just enough money to have a plain but comfortable home, good nourishing food regularly, and many hours of rest. But such security as this was never to be his after his mother died and he married. His temperament was not suited to teaching or to normal positions in the business world. When the pressure of financial worries crowded in upon his spent nervous system, his creative spirit simply gave up.

In March of 1928, after Harriet Monroe had sent the Lindsays a check of $100 from an unknown admirer to tide them over a particularly bleak time, Elizabeth wrote to her:

...meanwhile, your kindness has pulled us out of our panic-stricken paralysis, and enabled us to start forward with light hearts. Vachel particularly is simply stunned by worry; he just sits and broods and gets absolutely *clammy* and cold with misery, which, of course, does no one any good—especially himself.

* * *

The trouble began when Vachel cancelled his fall dates—increased when some of his fall articles came back (as articles will) and reached a crisis when he became panicky and paralyzed and stayed that way.

It seemed unbelievable and bewildering to this poet that his youth should be slipping away and with it, his creative power. The young Lindsay, standing with his feet firmly placed on the rungs of the magic ladder of literary achievement, was the one he wanted to find and become again.

Harriet Monroe's magazine, which awarded him the only three poetry prizes that he won, now presented him with the last of these, the Award of Honor; this was the first $500 prize ever offered by *Poetry*. And in the spring of 1929, Lindsay made one last attempt to re-establish his life. Using the Award of Honor prize money to pay some of his debts at Spokane, and with further financial help from friends, he moved his family back to his old boyhood home in Springfield, where his heart had always been.

But, even here, financial problems were still pressing, and desperately, he tried to pay the taxes and upkeep on his old home by lectures and readings when he could get them. Elizabeth, too, gallantly helped out by way of writing and teaching, although she was very busy looking after her two small children.

Late in January of 1931, Lindsay was in New York, and he sent this note to Sara with a copy of his *Selected Poems,* in which he had written the tribute beginning, "I will not forget that golden queen, for whom I wrote the best song of my days . . .":

January 23, 1931.

Darling Sara:—

I have called, and phoned, and no reply.

Here is the new book for you—my due return for Stars Tonight which was received with silent devotion.

Fred Melcher of The Publisher's Weekly is my host for over Sunday, out at Plainfield, New Jersey.

Stoddard King is in town, burning up the banquet tables for about three days.

Bless you my dear. I remember everything.

With all my heart
Vachel.

The terrible strain under which he had been living was beginning to make itself felt. On February 22 of 1931, Lindsay wrote a passionate letter to Sara, while on a train, telling her that people were only interested in hearing him recite his old poems, of which he was deathly tired, and that no one cared a bit about his writing new ones, which he longed to do. He begged Sara to influence him to write something new, as she had done in the days of old.

... "Vachel, won't you please do the Congo just for US?" I hear it till I nearly crack. Every town it is the same. "Why don't you like the Congo, Mr. Lindsay?" ...

I want *one soul on earth* to say "Create, create, create, do nothing *but* create!". ...

You would suppose I could ask this of hundreds. It is *not so*. They look *vague* if I talk about it.

I have no *chance* for a group of the inner ones. I have no strength left, after my tours, to form one. When we first met—that was *all* I had. I concentrated on them as I do now on audiences.

Even at Rochester where I have recited seven times and where they are as letter-perfect in my work as any crowd could ever be— they said sententiously, apologetically, etc. and audibly—behind my back after the recital was over:—"Mr. Lindsay is regrettably touchy about the Congo—" etc. Not *one inch* of artistic curiosity about new ms. of which I read three. Twenty people yelled "Congo" to me between every piece. You have in you the power to save me from the exhausion of this running fire. With love   Vachel

A month later, he wrote her an even longer and more desperate letter from Charleston, South Carolina, with this note at the top: "I never *write* letters. Elizabeth writes them *all*, and has since marriage. I am not given to outpourings like this to anyone, and have been *corked* since about 1920. Corked myself for my own good, in fact!"

March 21, 1931

Dearest Sara:—God knows how long this letter may be, maybe a page, maybe a book. But do not be alarmed, Golden Eyes, you are not going to be overwhelmingly corresponded with. But if you care for what is left of the man who dedicated his best song to you, you will forgive his egotism, and bear with him while he tries to clarify his artistic battles in the presence of your own clear brain. Most every one else seems satisfied with a photograph a little out of focus.

I did *not* see any of the Selected Poems book till it came out. I knew Spencer would have a hard enough battle to get it printed at all, so I left him utterly unhampered. It had been vaguely postponed several years. But one of his petitions to me was that I throw out all dedications as personal. I said yes—if you put the nightingale first and leave it dedicated to Sara. ...

So far as I know, to the day of my death I will have to spend my days away from home, earning my living and being only a nuisance the few hours I am at home. Speaking is the only thing the public will pay me for, or *anyone* really wants and I can hold 5000 as easily as one, and often that many have been turned away because the committee knew so little about me they rented a parlor. Yet [in] every big *auditorium* 2 or 3 thousand have been packed. Often for weeks at a time no books are present, and I am vaguely known as the "Author of Booth and the Congo" from previous (?) literary histories circulated in 1916, etc.

So the bigger the crowd the bigger the ignorant persecution for these two songs, and even if I recite two hours, as I did here in Charleston, the chairman or the crowd mob me like Lindbergh. It's *Booth* and *The Congo,* and that's all I came for apparently. *The Building of Springfield* is nothing to them, *The Chinese Nightingale* nothing even though their own reporter says these are well done. Generally they work me politely politely politely politely, but I give you my word if I recite two hours to the point of complete exhaustion till my will power and sense and even power of refusal seem completely gone, the committee will drag me to the private home of somebody, and load themselves up on liquor, (which I generally refuse) and keep me till one A.M., if possible till they have extorted these two poems out of me before I get my check, *due* the instant I leave the platform. Obviously that is all I mean to them, a stunt artist. I tell you with my soul I would be crucified for the ideals in *The Building of Springfield,* and people who do not welcome me as representing such ideas should let me entirely alone. Springfield tea-cup hell-cats likewise, should let me alone.

I have been traveling too fast for my nerves, but must travel *even faster* and speak even harder, if I am *ever to support my two children.* Elizabeth has been wearing other women's clothes ever since I married her, and I travel, till I am ready to fall flat in the aisle of the Pullman, and *no* one comes to the rescue, and hardly a soul in America knows "The Building of Springfield" represents the very soul of my soul, and I have been crucified more than once, because there I pinned my faith and there is more immediately impending. I do not want to have anything to do *ever* with people who do not like the ideals in that poem, with people who utterly ignore The Congo as a memorial to a missionary, or who sneer at foreign missions, or people who think General Booth "lovely," but would not sleep in Salvation Army Quarters as I have done, no, not if their lives depended on it. I want to take to the road so bad I am nearly frantic. I want to meet the real people again, and Elizabeth is still fighting off the bill collectors at home. . . . And I want to take the road leaving Elizabeth provided for and serene. If I stay home and write till I drop I will be in a worse case financially. I get $15 to $50 for poems. I hate dress suits and dress suit crowds and tea-sets as much as any ploughboy straight from the farm and *always will,* and offer no apologies. I stand with the majority on this: with the people who elect Presidents. Yet I have smiled and smiled 19 years while I was tea-partied to death, in and out of Springfield, and at Spokane till I was ready to yell murder.

But all this is merely human—and I want to appeal to the artist in you, for there is where we meet more than ever before.

I *do* want to write, and keep my standard as crystalline as yours and long after we parted, I kept it there. The Chinese Nightingale and The Building of Springfield represent as near as *I* can do, our standards of art and happy aspiration.

I have never had so much creative force in me in all directions, as *right now* yet I am thwarted in *every* direction, since my only way out is to ape my 32nd year in *public,* doing Booth and my 33rd year, *in public* "doing" "The Congo."

You know how much the Nightingale was keyed to the *hour* it was written and if anyone in the world applied such a literary standard to my fresh work, in writing I could go on as never before. But where is the leisure to find or argue with the people or form a circle? I loafed all last summer, dead in heart and mind through furious recital tours charging like a bull in the ring in the winter all to pay the summer's bills and poor Elizabeth is hectored to this hour by bill collectors for last summer's bills, and we wear our clothes till they drop off.

So when I *have* the leisure, even on tour I haven't sense left to seek out the most intelligent person on the committee and take a museum tour, or draw the picture that begins every poem. Do you know we have five very big dragons in Springfield in color, and somewhere an old poem around them about an old laundryman, done in 1909—as the beginning of the Nightingale?

Museum tours and years of art study and pen and ink drawings *are the very substance of literary concentration* with me. I have said in every way I know how (to yet be polite) that nearly every drawing in the Collected Poems was done one to five years before the poems it illustrates and nearly every one illustrates in *some fashion* three or four poems written afterward. Look at the censer drawings for the beginning of The Golden Book of Springfield. I drew for years in all fashions, however crudely, "The Boats of the Prophets" and finally it came out in the Congo climax:

"There where the wild ghost gods had wailed
A million boats of the angels sailed."

Booth goes all the way back to a 1902 Chicago drawing I made which was a variation of Jacob's Ladder—long lost by whoever I gave it to. It was then called "very obscure," a picture with crowned and robed saints climbing a ladder to the sky. Booth at least is not "obscure" till it is very carefully read, and Booth began in an "obscure" drawing!

Why do I insist on this point? Because yours is the most pointed and concentrated brain I have ever known and it is by art study and museum study that I have kept pointed and concentrated, being otherwise the log-cabin brand of a human being. Museums, and drawings in pen and ink—(and I was still *packed* with them when we met)—are *my* civilized substitute for tea-cups, dress suits, reception lines, Yale, Harvard, Princeton and Columbia. . . .

* * *

To the point: my literary concentration has always come inversely by long lonely art-study, and *all* I *need* is a chance for leisure, concentration and art study to *write* something that represents the 51st year of my age and will make people forget to try to hector my far distant past out of me. You *know* I teem with new ideas. I wake up with as many every morning as I ever did in my life. Yet I have to kill them with a fly-swatter and have quit all notebooks in despair. . . . If I try to write them I have not time and strength left after holding people 3000 at a time to put them down with the old force.

Over and over, in nearly every recital new ideas and images and tunes for new poems and drawings float through my mind and eyes so vividly as to confuse me—till I have to literally howl them down, and find my place again on the page, for that audience is demanding stale poems I *forget*. So *all* the new creative force in me that has been on me of late in a tremendous tide is not completely exhausted by my audiences, but only thwarted and dammed up to the torture point by their howling for old things. I think of at least one new poem or drawing every day, yet do not even put it down, knowing that when I get to Springfield I will not have force enough left to concentrate as I did in the old days, and have to use all my energy *not* being angry about my situation away from home.

Vachel Lindsay with Elizabeth Conner Lindsay and their children
1929

Vachel Lindsay
from the bust by Adrian Voisin
Spokane, Washington
1929

In the old days I saw only three things (1) Beggary when possible, and log cabins (2) Museums and art study (3) Small groups of artists and later poets. Now I see none of these three things. I begged, loving with all my heart the shanty-living American people. I talked with artists and poets, begging them as you well know for the most critical scrutiny, and *accepting it,* and putting down all their amendments to my poems as you well know, and now I have to howl for gangs who want "that wonderful poem about the Indians called The Congo" or that other one about Edwin Booth, no—it was Bramwell Booth? No—Evangeline Booth, wasn't it?

Beggary was the freest and most emancipating thing I ever did. Now it would cost me wife, children and home, yet I consider its possibility with more and more conviction. I am only waiting a gentleman's chance.

They are civil to me in Springfield but I am not specially wanted. I *don't* like the drunk country club, or the *addled* woman's club. It will take twenty years for them to rebuild the city. If I recite, I want to recite my Springfield poems everywhere till Springfield in spite of itself builds Lincoln's city and it will *not* be the tea cup set that rebuild it! I *believe* in the apotheosis of *Lincoln* the Railsplitter. The people who hate it love tea-cups and hate log cabins. I *believe* with all my heart and soul that Christ is King of the Universe and Lincoln is the nearest to the Christ type the world has seen since. . . .

* * *

I believe in faithfulness and clean love and high aspirations all the way to the cross.

* * *

I *love* everyone who was ever *good* to me, and only the utter exhaustion of platform work gives me that dead eye and stopped heart and quenched laughter that makes them think I do not want to see them any more. I was born talkative, telling *everything* but I am so full of the things in this letter I would unload and be bad company so I sit in my hotel room alone swearing not to say any of these things to anyone and in Pullman cars alone too frustrated to read or think when every creative force in me is at its height, and completely thwarted by the only way I am allowed to earn my living, or even function. Sara I have to *keep still* to *every intimate* about the things in this letter till gag rule ruins me. Lest I tell all this to *everyone* with an indecent explosion I tell it to you, and to you only. I will never write any of it again. Do not be afraid of an avalanche of words, from me, again.

I wish you would read this letter through ten times when you have the kindness. I doubt if I will ever write you anything more than notes henceforth. Let this letter be as 100 letters. But it ought to be something worth doing for you to raise Chang from the dead. You *are* a great clean diplomat. The Nightingale might sing again, and in a brand new tune.

* * *

My *very life routine* and increasing audiences, (the bigger the more ignorant) cut me off from the thinking I want to do clearly.

And poor dear Elizabeth pays a *bigger* price—hectored by bill collectors every day who are the meaner because I am so much advertised. They do not know that even when travelling as fast as I do now—the fastest for years, I have to put 51 per cent into car-fare and hotels and 25 into lecture fees. She has put up a brave brave fight and though young and strong needs a rescue party—a *real* one, not *one* lecture with a fat fee, but genuine public understanding that we are dead in earnest about things.

With love
Vachel.

In November of 1931, Sara saw Vachel for the last time. During the fall of that year, he had an engagement to speak in Severance Hall in Cleveland as one of the offerings of the Mc-Bride Lecture Series. The hall was filled, and Lindsay was given a great welcoming ovation. But for some reason, after he began to read and chant in his individual style, many in the audience got up and walked out; though he made a humorous reference to the "thinning ranks," and continued his program, valiantly, this experience and a similar disheartening one in Washington cut him deeply and convinced him as nothing else had done that his star was setting and his power was waning. At this time Lindsay was, in fact, weary and ill, spiritually and physically, and the stress under which he had been living not only was hastening his mental collapse, but was actually killing him.

It is true that he gave his most successful reading of his work in Springfield at the First Christian Church not long after this and felt, for the first time, that he had won the city to himself and his ideals. But it was too late. His funeral was held in this same church exactly one week after his reading there. The ominous shadows that had been darkening his life had now closed in upon him, and he could not find his way out again. It may well be that two lines from "The Chinese Nightingale" echoed in his mind during those last terrible days:

> While the monster shadows glower and creep,
> What can be better for man than sleep?

But as Edgar Lee Masters said, "Fatigue had entered into him so deeply that no sleep but that of death could rest him."[7]

In the early morning of December 5, 1931, his mind and body wrecked by the agonizing torture that only a nervous system strained to the breaking point can inflict on a human being, Lindsay drank a bottle of Lysol and found at last and for all time the peace that passeth understanding and the spring that comes on forever.

When Sara learned of Vachel Lindsay's death, the news came as a shattering blow and, in her own words, "shook me to my very roots." Stricken with grief, she called John Hall Wheelock immediately to tell him. But she was so upset that she could hardly speak, and though he called her back twice, she was too distressed to discuss the matter with him. Alarmed, he left his office at once, though it was in the morning, and hurried to her hotel. But there was little that he or anyone could do or say to comfort her.

To Sara, Vachel Lindsay was the "last knight errant." Because she did not move in large circles and did not know or have any desire to know great numbers of people intimately, Sara's few chosen friends were all the more precious to her. She liked to take people one at a time and savor to the full her association with that one person. Louis Untermeyer said of her, "Once a friendship was established, nothing could shake it for Sara; she was the most instinctively loyal person I knew."[8] Lindsay's death

---

[7]Edgar Lee Masters, *Vachel Lindsay: A Poet in America* (New York: Charles Scribner's Sons, 1938), p. 355.

[8]Louis Untermeyer, *From Another World* (New York: Harcourt, Brace and Company, 1939), p. 173.

made her realize, acutely, the diminishing number of the people to whom she had once felt very near. The doors of her life were closing, one by one.

Not long before Vachel's death, Sara was a guest at the Untermeyers' farm in the Adirondacks. She wrote her host and hostess later that her brief joy in that visit "seemed to be given as the prelude to what was so soon to be a tragedy—Vachel's death."[9]

Mrs. Untermeyer recalled that visit years later: "She came at Thanksgiving time, and I deplored the lack of foliage. But she insisted that she liked the austerity of the branches against the wintry sky, and the trunks against the rime that covered the fields. She wrote a poem (I have the manuscript) and laid it on my pillow. It is a poem of thanksgiving to be among friends, who have weathered much together." This poem, "Grace Before Sleep," appeared in *Strange Victory*.

Soon after Vachel's death, Sara wrote a memorial poem to him, using in it his own words from his tribute to Governor Altgeld:

> "Deep in the ages," you said, "deep in the ages,"
>   And, "To live in mankind is far more than to live in a
>   name."
> You are deep in the ages, now, deep in the ages,
>   You whom the world could not break, nor the years tame.
>
> Fly out, fly on, eagle that is not forgotten,
>   Fly straight to the innermost light, you who loved sun
>   in your eyes,
> Free of the fret, free of the weight of living,
>   Bravest among the brave, gayest among the wise.

Elizabeth Lindsay, who had experienced an exceptionally difficult life from the very first years of her marriage, seemed hopelessly trapped in a labyrinth of horrors toward the last. And it must be said to her exceedingly great credit that never once, by the slightest intimation, either before or after her husband's death, did she let Sara know how profound was her agony. Elizabeth

[9]*Ibid.*, p. 182.

seemed determined to withhold the bitter truth from the woman above all others whom her husband had worshipped for so long. And knowing the true terror of her life at this time and how much younger she was than Sara, one can only admire her fervently for this course of action.

In March of 1931, in a mood of discouragement, Elizabeth had written to Sara:

As to knowing me, Sara dear, I doubt whether there is anything left to know. Vachel doesn't know me at all; and the few glimpses he has caught have been so utterly disconcerting to him, that it seemed wiser to adopt a kindly anonymity, and I do fear that it has become a permanent gesture. Perhaps not. We shall see. At all events, I shall dream of and plan for the quiet hours with you, here or there, and hope that they may come soon. I am afraid you would find me very dull and plodding, and be horribly disappointed. You might have to be wise and free and starry-hearted for two; and employ all the Greek as well as the Roman virtues, and what a strain that would be! I shall try hard to grow up to you.

Of course, I spend my days tutoring in the morning, a high school pupil, all subjects; and attending to Vachel's routine and business affairs; and managing the house, and looking out for the babies, who by the way are flourishing, and full of delicate surprises; and getting up these eternal talks and book reviews of a mildly cultural nature (I detest the word culture!) and making outlines for the religion study group of the local A.A.U.W., and worrying; and trying very hard to give a tremendous tug to my bootstraps and be a mystic, instead of twenty-nine and happy, and interested in spring clothes. And I see our friends here who are dears, one and all; and try to do everything I think Vachel wants and nothing he doesn't want, which is not Christianity but pragmatism; and of course I don't succeed. And I think I have not had a really healthily rebellious feeling about anything since Susan was born; just sort of cowed and subtle reactions. And does that sound like a person anyone would like to know? I doubt it! Anyhow, you can't say you weren't warned.

And thanks a lot for your letter. I'd love more, when you feel up to it. And can't you come to see me here? It's not so terribly far, you know; and it is quiet, once you are here. Do, please.

My love to you,
Elizabeth

Sara was, of course, very much aware of the disastrous financial struggle that Elizabeth and Vachel were involved in, but the even more distressing circumstances of Lindsay's mental deterioration—the hallucinations of persecution, the (unrealized) fear of harm to Elizabeth and her children, the irrational moods that soared from outbursts of exhilarated passion to searing accusations that marriage had destroyed his manhood—were never mentioned by Elizabeth to Sara.

On December 27 Elizabeth sent Sara a message of gratitude for all that she had done:

How shall I thank you for all your kindness, your wire, the flowers, your letters, the beautiful memorial song? They have all meant so much, helped so much; and the poem I am particularly glad of, because it has been shared with so many who loved him, and who needed such a brave word to let him go free, as he wanted to go.

* * *

Dear Sara, you have been with us all the way. I am sorry this had to come to you, as well as to us, for, first and last, you have had so much. . . .

I am glad he had a visit with you in New York this time. He saw you and he saw so many of his oldest and dearest this last time, and came home to an overwhelmingly successful recital here. It all seemed so happy. And it was. It was the completion of the pattern, but we didn't know it. Some day we can say that it was right and beautiful, but now it is too near, and too hard.

* * *

. . . he was very tired, and never quite belonged in such a world as this; and I know he will rest, and then be happy, and find his full stature and glory, and we must be glad of that. It's just too soon.

* * *

Harriet Monroe was able to come down for Monday and Tuesday, and it was a comfort to have her here. There's a gallant soul. He was one of her fledglings, and she never forgot. Her article in the January *Poetry,* which she wrote here on the Tuesday after the funeral, and flew back to Chicago with, to be in time, is beautiful and conclusive. Full of the memory of golden days, a memory you have, too; and strong in faith to the end.

And as for Springfield itself, that little town, for a season at least, the censers were swinging over the town, everyone knew it; and Springfield, the symbol, and Springfield, the reality, came close to being one.

A little later, in discussing one of the last pictures taken of Vachel, which she liked, Elizabeth wrote to Sara:

...Of course you would feel differently from me about this, or any portrait. The young, eager, undefeated Vachel whom you knew and loved—the boy for whom "life was a rebellion with banners" was scarcely a remote relative of the Vachel of twenty years after. I always believed in that boy, and tried to find him—but it could not be. He had lost himself. The lonely—lost, weary-hearted, self-tortured man for whom I tried, quite in vain, to build up some kind of liveable universe, was beyond himself or any of us, beyond any thing but temporary memories of what he had hoped might be, and such small surface alleviations as could be sought out from time to time. Such a world as this was both too small and too cruel for him. The one comfort in his death is that, tragic as it is, the tragedy now is ours, whereas before, it was his. He has passed beyond that, too, now—and it would be the height of selfishness to wish him back. There is no suffering, I think, worthy the name except that of watching another suffer—and knowing that there is nothing at all to be done about it. I wish I had been better able, stronger, and more fortunately circumstanced, to care for him, protect him, find for him, somehow, peace, happiness, rest, and after that, the way forward. But one cannot begin so late; and even with a perfect world at hand, perhaps it would have been the same, in the end. The unraveling of old causes, unhealed wounds burning more with the years—consequences of events before I was born; even, some of them, before he was. So it is that a picture which shows strength, peace, a steady forward look into light, not darkness—is very precious to me—almost like an act of faith—the image, if not the substance, of things hoped for: the evidence of things not seen. Naturally it could not mean the same to you: one wouldn't want it to. I am glad that, knowing half the truth, I had the courage to attempt the impossible. Had I known all of it, I could not have. But it was not altogether without meaning for him; and in the larger pattern, which, again, we cannot see, but only believe in, may take its appointed place.

Chapter 11

THE LATER DAYS

•

WITH Margaret Conklin on leave from Macmillan, Sara had made a brief trip to France in 1930; and in 1931, with Miss Conklin's friend who had accompanied her to Reno, Sara went to England again. Here she met Virginia Woolf, whose work she admired greatly. In search of her Willard relatives, she looked in the London Telephone Directory, but not a Willard could she find listed. But she did locate some interesting tombs of the Alards in the very old churchyard at Winchelsea, in Sussex, and she longed to know if the effigies on the tombs were those of her distant ancestors.

While in England, Sara began to think seriously of writing a biography of Christina Rossetti, of whom she once said: "She has always been my favorite woman poet. I consider her one of the finest lyric poets of modern times. No poet who has ever written in our language, except Shakespeare in his songs, was the master of a more ecstatically fresh melody than hers. Her mixed blood, three-quarters Italian and the remainder English, may be the reason for her individual vocabulary, in which every word seems newly minted."

With such a biography in mind, Sara made a special effort to visit the various places connected with the English poet's life. Writing later of her London research, she said: "This summer I followed Christina Rossetti from the house where she was born— the house has been torn down to make way for an apartment building which bears the name Rossetti House—off Portland

Place in London, through all the different streets that had associations with her, and finally to the quiet old square in Bloomsbury, Torrington Square, where she died in 1894. She is buried in Highgate Cemetery, overlooking London."

Sara also went to the National Gallery to see Ford Madox Brown's picture, "Christ Washing St. Peter's Feet," as Christina Rossetti was said to have posed for the face of St. John in this painting; and she jotted down in her notes: "The disciples were painted from Brown's friends, C. B. Cayley [whom Christina Rossetti is said to have loved] being a blond seated figure in the central foreground. The bearded face is vague and gives no striking sense of character."

By a fortunate stroke of luck, Sara unearthed and bought a letter that Christina Rossetti wrote to her brother, Dante Gabriel, about a public reading of *Goblin Market*. She was delighted to have this, for she wrote:

It is almost impossible to find an unpublished letter of Christina Rossetti's for sale and I am especially happy that mine is to her beloved brother Gabriel. Many of her letters to him have been published in "The Family Letters of Christina Rossetti," and they always have a whimsical touch which is absent from her usually reserved correspondence with the other members of her family or even with her most intimate friends. . . . But she never in any case dated her letters, and beyond knowing that the one I possess must have been written between 1867 and 1878 because it is headed 56 Euston Square, I cannot assign a date. I have not found a record of the date of the public reading from her book "Goblin Market" to which the letter refers. She writes that it is to take place at the Queen's Concert Rooms, Hanover Square, on the following day, Tuesday, and her wish that Dante Gabriel would go to the reading is the reason for her writing. But one surmises that that colorful gentleman, then at the height of his fame as a painter, a lover and a poet, probably forgot all about the matter before Tuesday night came. He was the only person from whom Christina ever took criticism—indeed he is the only person from whom she ever seemed to take anything. Her gentle stoicism masked an impassioned heart so effectually that even the two men who wished to marry her must have felt afraid of her unvarying self-command. And her sense of humor showed itself only in slightly terrifying, if very rare, shafts of wit. But her tenderness toward all suffering and toward all small and helpless creatures was constant throughout her life. Her nobility was never shaken.

Trying a new medium of creative work lent a heightened interest to her life, and settled in New York again, Sara started reading and doing the necessary research in earnest. She was led into a study of the entire Pre-Raphaelite movement; and she visited the Metropolitan Museum to see Dante Gabriel Rossetti's picture, "Lady Lilith," which she found in an alcove with William Morris's tapestries and wall-papers and a cabinet painted by Burne-Jones, all of which interested her.

In her notes she left some particularly telling passages, one being: "William Rossetti had a gift for not interfering with other people."

Another reads: "C.R.'s sense of music in English verse is infinitely more acute than E.B.B.'s.[1] Note the flat, ugly singsong of even such a nobly conceived poem as 'Cowper's Grave' in comparison with any poem by C.R. Even her least verses have a sense of the necessity of variety in the beat. Her music is to E.B.B. what a song of Schubert is to a street-melody."

And in speaking of Christina Rossetti's poems, she concluded: "The Italian lyrics lack the sure modelling as well as the rainbow coloring of her English poetry. I am reminded of what Eleonora Duse said of Dante Gabriel Rossetti's Italian poems, that they sounded as though they had been written by a blind man."

Of Christina Rossetti's deep religious beliefs, Sara wrote: "Christina R.'s religion may have given her peace at times—never apparently for long—but it never gave her ecstasy. The raptures experienced by St. Theresa would have been considered unseemly by Christina. Her Anglo-Catholicism was almost Calvinistic in its rigour."

---

[1]Elizabeth Barrett Browning.

Another observation of Sara's left among her notes that is certainly provocative reads: "We all know that the poetry of young people concerns matters about which they know nothing from experience—the revelation that is made is a forecast of their lives, not a record, and the forecast is infallibly correct."

Perhaps the most interesting of all of Sara's conclusions in her Rossetti note-book are these remarks upon the English poet and marriage, for the reader cannot help but think how nearly Sara's own spirit paralleled her deductions about the English poet: "With due regard to the fact that everybody who has written about Christina Rossetti says that she refused to marry Cayley on religious grounds alone, I feel that her disinclination to marry him sprang chiefly from her disinclination to marriage in general. She wished to be free to follow her own thoughts, to meditate in her own way. She was a born celibate in spite of her impassioned heart."

There are indeed many likenesses that the perceptive reader can find between the spirits of these two poets, and when Sara wrote of Christina Rossetti: "Her nobility was never shaken," she could have well been writing of herself. When she declared: "Her life, one of the most perfect examples in literature of intensity in reticence, consistent, delicately and consciously moulded as a Tanagra figurine, kept its inner quiet inviolate until the end," she could also have been painting a word picture of herself.

The poet's title of her study was to be: *Christina Rossetti, An Intimate Portrait,* and the dedication page was to read: *To the Memory of Vachel Lindsay Who Loved the Poetry of Christina Rossetti.*

The Prefatory Note that Sara completed is of especial interest, for it illuminates the background of her desire to write this book and contains a number of observations, which, again, could very well apply to Sara's own life and art.

Prefatory Note

For years I have wanted to write a short account of Christina Rossetti's life. Until recently there was only one biography of her, the too reticent book by Mackenzie Bell published long ago, in 1898. Now that the poet's centenary has come and gone, several biographies have appeared, but I hope that there may still be room for what I want to say. My attitude toward Christina Rossetti differs from that of several of her biographers for I consider her life, as lives go, a reasonably happy one. There was no more interesting family in England than the one into which she had the good luck to be born. Her birth, coming as it did in 1830, was in the nick of time—a great change in thought and in manners was about to occur. The boisterous England of the last of the four Georges was transformed in Christina Rossetti's lifetime into the formal country of Queen Victoria. Such changes are a strain on the individual called upon to undergo them. We cannot live through one of the crucial acts of the drama of civilization without paying for the privilege. Christina paid heavily, but that is our good fortune, for without conflicting impulses she would not have written poetry. Her method of getting through the ordeal of life was to withdraw into herself and to make her art serve as her solace. She had two consuming desires, to write poetry and to serve God. She fulfilled the first superbly; the second she fulfilled according to her lights. These lights illumined a rigid doctrine, a somewhat narrow form of Christianity, but her own intensity lifted her into the realm of the great religious mystics. Her poems on love and death are finer, even, than her devotional poems.

On the score of happiness in her youth she had association with the most interesting young men in London, the Pre-Raphaelite Brotherhood. She need not be pitied because of what is called her limited experience and because she chose to remain unmarried. She was an impassioned woman, but not a passionate one. Neither of the two men who wanted her in marriage would have made her happy; and with Dorothea in *Middlemarch*, she "liked giving up."

Christina idolized her brother Dante Gabriel though she was well aware of his faults. To both men and women he was vividly magnetic; her own two wooers were pale beside his flame. The members of the Rossetti family got on well together and Christina had her poetry and her jealous God. Anything more would have taken her from these three.

There is no need to make an analysis or appraisal of her poems because people either like or dislike lyric poetry; they cannot be changed. Those who dislike it find it lacking in decorum to an embarrassing degree, as well as ridiculously egotistical. And for the others there is no occasion for praise or criticism in Christina Rossetti's case. . . .

It is amusing that so seclusive a poet was considered for the laureateship when it was left vacant by the death of Tennyson. Christina Rossetti would have been even less happy as a laureate than as a wife.

She carved her life carefully as she might have carved a gem. A person who knew Christina, but who insists on remaining nameless, told me that the poet loved deeply a man who was married—a facet of her emotion that has never caught the light—but that she would not have his love at the cost of sorrow to his wife. I cannot feel that the incident is of much importance. It would be odd if there had not been such an occurrence at least once in her life. She was singularly self-sufficing; the affair passed and left no trace.

In the loneliness of her arrogant heart she made a shifting and exquisite music. If we want a wider range of thought than hers, we may find it without searching farther than the poets of her own day. Christina Rossetti was fitted by temperament and genius to use certain limited aspects of experience. When she went beyond these she was only a cultivated Victorian lady doing her best.

But her finest poetry was effortless; it was singing, a music of clear colors, fresh and yet exotic, that rang with easy rapture; it will last as long as our language.

The less than one hundred pages that Sara left of her manuscript are enough to convince the reader that the unfinished book was a distinct loss to literature. The opening paragraphs of the biography are sufficient to give the charming and compelling prose style that was as much Sara's own as her poetic voice was her own.

A lyric poet is always a contemporary. He works in the changeless feelings of men and not in their changing thoughts that shift restlessly from decade to decade. Christina Rossetti was a lyric poet.

She would write no differently today, if she happened to belong to our time. Of all the Victorians, she is the least stamped by her period. And it is for this reason that I always feel, whenever I am in London, as though I had only to present myself at the door of her sedate old house at 30 Torrington Square, to hear her voice and see her face to face. I have gone to that house often and stood before it wondering whether the crystal chandelier that Dante Gabriel Rossetti gave to his mother and Christina was still hanging in the drawing-room. The light from the west, shining over the green square, struck the chandelier at sunset and made prism reflections on the walls. The two large windows looked out on the trees that Christina loved. She spent the last twenty years of her life here, as the bronze tablet between the windows tells us. It gives her dates: "Born 1830— Died 1894."

To an American, the stillness in this part of Bloomsbury seems incredible. But it must have been broken in Christina's day as it was for me the last time I stood before the house. A street piano was playing "Connais-tu le pays?" and a meditative English rain began to fall.

I was a child when Christina Rossetti died and I did not visit London until ten years after her death, but since then I have followed her over the city from the place where she was born, through her long pilgrimage that ended at last in this house. Hers was essentially a London life. No other major English poet was so constant a dweller in the city. And to a lover of London this makes her all the more intimate; we encounter her at every turn.

While Sara was in the midst of writing the book, several other biographies of the English poet were published, as she mentioned in her Prefatory Note, and she decided that it would be advisable for her to return to England to speak personally with Miss Rossetti's two nieces and to acquire some fresh material. The Macmillan Company, which was eager to publish the book, gave her an advance on the project and in the summer of 1932 Sara sailed again, making the trip alone for the first time in her life. Everything went well at first. On July 26, she wrote to Margaret Conklin:

I have the same room (at the American Women's Club on Grosvenor Street) that I had last year, that is, the one you had in 1927. . . .
Miss Rossetti wrote most kindly to ask me to tea Thursday. She said that she and her sister Mrs. (Signora) Angeli would be happy, and so on. It is sweet of them to ask me to tea . . . they are living in the same house that they have lived in since about 1888.

. . . Three weeks is a painfully short time to be in this adorable, cold grey cosy darling city,—I doubt if I do much in the way of going out of it except to try to see one or two places (Little Missenden for one) connected with C.R.

. . . I think of you always and always with love. I wish you were here! Oh why don't I live in this city? Yet in winter everybody says it is detestable. . . .

Altogether Sara had a pleasant and successful time, until in August she contracted double pneumonia and became critically ill. Not wanting to remain abroad among strangers in this condition, she made a supreme effort and came home, although the doctor on shipboard said later that he did not see how she survived the trip. When she arrived in New York, weak and ill, her left lung had not cleared, and she was left with unresolved pneumonia.

Nervous exhaustion followed, and she continued to be pitifully weak and ill and deeply depressed. Her heart was also affected. Thinking that a warmer climate might effect a quicker recovery, she went to Florida for about two weeks, where she visited Jessie Rittenhouse. But the doctor whom she consulted there only added to her distress by telling her that she had a heart murmur. Her blood pressure was very high, and she felt that a stroke was imminent. She thought of her brother, Warren, who had lived on for twenty years after a paralytic stroke, and to whom she had written these lines in "The Silent Battle":

> In winter fog, in gathering mist
> The gray grim battle had its end—
> And at the very last we knew
> His enemy had turned his friend.

Seven doctors were consulted about her condition in January of 1933, but none could do anything to alleviate her suffering or to hold out any hope. Shortly before she died, the blood vessels in her hands broke, and paralysis seemed inevitable.

Before Sara had gone to Europe in the summer of 1932, she had rented an apartment at One Fifth Avenue, as her lease at the Bolivar, where she had been living, was to expire on October 1. In the midst of her illness, at the worst possible time, all of her possessions had to be moved from the one apartment into the other. Her sister, Mamie Wheless, and Margaret Conklin accomplished this for her. Sara was established in one of the hotel's furnished apartments until her own newly rented apartment could be painted, extra closets built in, and her furniture arranged as she wished. However, she never did recover enough strength to unpack and decorate the apartment as she had intended doing.

In March of 1932 Vine Colby had sent Sara a framed Morpho Sulkowski butterfly, which came from the jungle of some tropical country. It was large, of opalescent and iridescent colors, and as the light fell upon it, an enchanting blue would appear and disappear. It had fascinated Sara from the moment she saw it and was one of her most beloved possessions.

Writing of it later to Vine Colby, Mamie Wheless said:

We both loved the butterfly very, very much, and I am glad that you wish me to have it for I shall enjoy it more than I can tell you. It was one of the things which gave her pleasure even in her great suffering.

... About two weeks before she died, I told her that I tho't she had better let us put up a few embroideries and the butterfly even if we did not place them just where she would like them to be permanently as the color would help to make her apartment cheerful, and she chose the place for the butterfly herself—right where she could see it all the time from the bed. You may imagine how dear anything is to me which contributed to taking her mind from her troubles. . . .

Near the end of January Sara called her sister and gave her power of attorney over her affairs. Always systematic and orderly, she had already carefully thought through her desires for the future, and on May 30, 1930, she had made a will, in which, among other things, she said: "I give and bequeath to Ernst B. Filsinger my diamond ring in a crown setting as a mark of my esteem." Some afterthought prompted her to add a codicil to the will, over a year later, on November 12, 1931, including her former husband as one of her heirs. This fact alone seems to be conclusive proof that she never lost her concern and affection for him, although their lives drifted apart. Sara's family was also remembered with bequests, as was Margaret Conklin, and to Susan Doniphan Lindsay she left $5000 as a token of what her father's friendship had meant to her.

Miss Conklin was later named as Literary Executor of Sara's estate. After leaving the Macmillan Company, she moved to New Haven, where she is now Administrative Assistant with The Connecticut Association for Mental Health.

According to Sara's will, Wellesley College was to select and receive one hundred books from her library, the balance to go to Margaret Conklin together with her other personal possessions. Today, because of this clause, the books that Vachel Lindsay gave to Sara, personally inscribed and decorated with his drawings, are in the Wellesley College Library.

Eventually, Wellesley will receive the income from Sara's estate. On April 25, 1930, Sara had written a letter to the Trustees of Wellesley College setting forth the conditions under which this money is to be used. This letter, so complete in every detail, shows the precision and foresight that were such characteristic qualities of this poet, and is reprinted here with the kind permission of President Margaret Clapp and the Trustees of Wellesley College.

To the Trustees of Wellesley College:

It is my desire to leave money to Wellesley College for an annual award for notable poetic achievement. Upon receipt of such money it shall be used to establish a permanent separate fund, the gross income of which for each calendar year shall constitute the award to be made during the next calendar year. The fund shall be administered by the Trustees of Wellesley College and the award shall be made under the following conditions:

1. As soon as reasonably may be in each calendar year after the establishment of the fund, the Trustees of Wellesley College shall appoint an English scholar who shall be an American citizen. He or she shall be a member of the faculty of some American college or university and a person definitely interested in and in touch with contemporary American poetry. In making this appointment, due regard shall be paid to varied and impartial representation of colleges and universities. As soon as may be after accepting such appointment, the person so selected shall appoint two poets of recognized standing who shall be American citizens, and upon their acceptance of such appointment their names shall be communicated to the Trustees of Wellesley College. The same person shall not be appointed under this paragraph in successive years.

2. The three persons so appointed shall constitute a jury which shall select a poet as the recipient of the award. The poet so selected shall be an American citizen and the author of at least one printed volume. The award shall not be divided. Every reasonable effort shall be made by the members of the jury to make their selection unanimous, but a majority vote shall be sufficient to select the recipient of the award. No person shall receive the award more than twice or without an interval of at least five years between the first and second awards.

3. The jury shall, at least thirty days before the commencement of Wellesley College next succeeding its appointment, communicate the name of the recipient of the award to the President of Wellesley College who shall announce it at commencement, and the recipient shall thereupon become entitled to receive the award forthwith. Before such announcement the decision of the jury shall be held in confidence.

4. Members of the juries and recipients of the award shall be selected without discrimination of sex.

· 318 ·

5. It is the earnest desire of the donor that the principles govern-ing the selection of juries and recipients of the award shall be cath-olic, open-minded and progressive.

6. All expenses in connection with the award or the administra-tion of the fund shall be paid by Wellesley College from other funds.

7. This letter of instructions shall be published annually in some official publication of Wellesley College, and with it an estimate of the amount of the award for the current year.

(Signed) SARA TEASDALE FILSINGER

On the night of January 29, Margaret Conklin read to Sara and played an English recording of Beethoven's *Fifth Symphony.* The evening passed quietly and uneventfully. Early in the morn-ing the nurse discovered that Sara was not in her room, and upon investigating, found that she had died while taking a bath. The bath water was still warm. Her death was first thought to have been due to drowning, but later it was established that she had taken an overdose of a sedative. One remembers the poet's own words:

> I have loved much and been loved deeply—
> Oh when my spirit's fire burns low,
> Leave me the darkness and the stillness,
> I shall be tired and glad to go.

For her, "the last complete reunion with the earth" had been made. The solitude that she had sought ever since she was a child had taken her back into its infinite peace.

In writing of those last dark hours to Williamina Parrish, Mrs. Wheless said:

She realized that a stroke was impending and thought constantly of our brother, Warrie. . . . She knew that it meant, finally, helpless-ness and that the brain would be involved. You may imagine her deep depression. It was all so sad and pitiful, I cannot get rid of the terribleness of it night and day.

I am thankful that Sara is over her suffering. I could not wish her back as she was. Her doctors said it was best that she died, but it is so lonely without her.

And a little later, Margaret Conklin wrote to Miss Parrish:

... I want the people who loved her and knew her well to know her tremendous courage. Through all the long illness that followed pneumonia, she was afraid of a stroke.... Her doctor has told me since that it is probable that she would have been completely helpless, and neither she nor anyone who loved her could have wanted that. The night before she died, I was with her all evening.... Never by a word or a look did she show me what was in her mind, though I knew she was terribly depressed. Late in the evening she sent me home because she thought I looked tired. I had sprained my ankle the day before and her concern for that slight pain of mine was very beautiful. I went because I thought it would worry her if I stayed any longer, and she had a nurse....

One can trace through Sara's poems in her last book, published after her death, the shadow of the inevitable ending of her life; for the thought of what she intended to do had evidently been very close to her for some time before she died. And, unquestionably, Vachel Lindsay's death influenced her to some extent.

Long ago, as a girl thrillingly in love with life and beauty, she had told John Myers O'Hara that only the thought of death could drive her to sheer madness, but she added that it would be terrible to think of life without this final release. And this dual weighing of the final darkness was apparent even in *Helen of Troy*, where a sonnet about death contains these lines:

I am afraid, oh I am so afraid!

. . .

How can they leave me in that dark alone,
Who loved the joy of light and warmth so much,
And thrilled so with the sense of sound and touch,—
How can they shut me underneath a stone?

E. O. Hoppé, London

Sara Teasdale
1932

Yet, even in this volume, she had written in "Youth and the Pilgrim" these lines, spoken by the pilgrim:

"There is a place where Love is not,
But never a ship leaves land
Can carry you so quickly there
As the sharp sword in your hand."

As the years passed, her fear changed to a rebellion that death should deprive her of earth's beauty, and, finally, as the loneliness and illness of the last months descended upon her, her thoughts turned to death with the kind of relief that she had long ago prophesied it might hold for her. Her later poems are almost all concerned with what is so soon to come; they are clear and revealing testimony of the spiritual climate of her last days and lead the reader almost to the very act of suicide. In "Wisdom" she wrote:

Oh to relinquish, with no more of sound
Than the bent bough's when the bright apples fall;
Oh to let go, without a cry or call
That can be heard by any above ground;
Let the dead know, but not the living see—
The dead who loved me will not suffer, knowing
It is all one, the coming or the going,
If I have kept the last, essential me.

There is no mistaking what she meant in "Since Death Brushed Past Me":

Since Death brushed past me once more to-day,
Let me say quickly what I must say:
Take without shame the love I give you,
Take it before I am hurried away.

Because the poet requested in her will that her body be cremated, her wishes were carried out, and her ashes were placed in the family plot in St. Louis. Not long before she died, Sara had written:

All that was mortal shall be burned away,
   All that was mind shall have been put to sleep.
Only the spirit shall awake to say
   What the deep says to the deep;

and:

Laid in a quiet corner of the world
There will be left no more of me some night
Than the lone bat could carry in his flight
Over the meadows when the moon is furled;
I shall be then so little, and so lost,
Only the many-fingered rain will find me,
And I have taken thought to leave behind me
Nothing to feel the long on-coming frost.

Funeral services were held in Grace Episcopal Church in New York City, conducted by the rector, Dr. Walter Russell Bowie, according to her wishes. Not long before Sara died, she had sent a little note to Dr. Bowie, requesting him to come to see her. He responded at once, and they began what he hoped might be the first of many conversations about life and the faith needed for living. Dr. Bowie was greatly drawn to Sara, and she gave him a copy of *Dark of the Moon*. It is very probable that Sara, with her essential orderliness, and with the thought of death so close to her in those last trying days, purposely asked Dr. Bowie to call because she already had in mind the service that would be requested of him.

Another private service was held in Bellefontaine Cemetery in St. Louis, attended only by her nephews, her sister-in-law, Mrs. Willard Teasdale, and Ernst Filsinger's two sisters. The stone that marks the resting place of her ashes has on it the name *Sara Teasdale Filsinger*, as she requested in her will.

John Hall Wheelock, after looking upon her face in death, was moved to write his "Resolute Silence":

In your stern mien I read it, in the high, inflexible air
And resolute silence that the dead,

Even for those they have loved, are used to wear—
The secret fallen between us, the strange new thing unsaid.

It is evening: the first, tremulous stars come into view,
Which you praised so well; while I, who watch here, caught
In the web you have broken, probe the old secrets we two
Warred on once with the spears of thought.

And it is as if you had deserted, gone over to these
That are leagued in their silence against us. You, too, in
    the end,
Sealed your lips, and are one now with the unforgiving
    mysteries—
Who were my friend.[2]

With the same meticulous care that characterized all of her actions, Sara left twenty-two poems in her notebook marked for future publication, and had even included the title for the final volume, *Strange Victory*. Her two close friends, John Hall Wheelock and Margaret Conklin, arranged the poems for posthumous publication, and in October, 1933, the world received its final lyric treasure from one of its best-known and best-loved poets. A facsimile of a poem in manuscript, "Truce," was included in the little book, as well as a drawing of her by the French artist, Marcel Maurel. The title, *Strange Victory*, signified, perhaps, that though she lost her mortal life, her spirit would live on through her poetry.

Jessie Rittenhouse had a slightly different interpretation of this title. Eight years after Sara's death, she wrote to John Hall Wheelock:

... Her tragic ending came very close to me as she had been with me in Florida until two weeks before her death. I have always wanted to tell you of those weeks she spent with me in which I tried to rouse her from the melancholy (melancholia) into which she had

2John Hall Wheelock, *Poems Old and New* (New York: Charles Scribner's Sons, 1956), p. 139. Copyright 1956 by Charles Scribner's Sons. Reprinted by permission of the publishers.

fallen, though I myself was in deep sorrow over Clinton's[3] death which had just occurred.

... you were the great love of her life as she often told me, and this love persisted to the end. It all went to the making of her beautiful lyrics, the price of song. This was her "Strange Victory.". . .

These words take the reader's mind back to a poem written when Sara was happily married, which was published in *Flame and Shadow:*

It is not a word spoken,
    Few words are said;
Not even a look of the eyes
    Nor a bend of the head,
But only a hush of the heart
    That has too much to keep,
Only memories waking
    That sleep so light a sleep.

Ernst Filsinger was abroad when the news of her death reached him. Shortly before 1929, Ernst had left Lawrence and Company and had become associated with Standard Brands, where he became one of the Vice Presidents. When the financial crash of 1929 struck with devastating force, he left Standard Brands, and, with another partner, established his own New York firm of foreign trade agents, which necessitated his traveling much of the time, from 1932 on, through the Orient. His work took him to Africa, India, Siam, China, the East Indies, Japan, and the Philippines. Always a hard worker, and a man determined to do his best, he pushed himself unmercifully; the hot climates, the endless travel, the constant pressures under which he worked, all took their toll of the man, though he was born with a splendid physical vitality. On his first trip to Africa, he had learned of his wife's divorce; on his second trip to that continent, he learned of her death.

---

[3]Clinton Scollard was Jessie Rittenhouse's husband.

In November of 1933, Margaret Conklin received a letter from Ernst written in China:

By this mail I received your letter of October 20. I am distressed beyond words that you are ill and that you have been compelled to take a six months' leave of absence. . . . I know that you have been under a terrible strain and I can realize how it pulled you down. Do take good care of yourself and get well quickly.

A friend sent me a copy of Sara's last book: "Strange Victory." Is not it perfectly superb? In my opinion it contains some of the most exquisitely beautiful and moving poems she ever wrote. As you can imagine, I was deeply stirred and touched by several of the poems in particular. What a glorious poet and what a magnificent person she was!

I was also touched by the review written by Charles Hanson Town(e)? which appeared in the Hearst papers, and by the one in the *Tribune* written by Miss Deutsch. I shall memorize most of the poems as I have with so many of the others that appeared in her previous volumes.

The drawing which serves as a frontispiece is lovely and an excellent likeness. It was a happy thought to include a facsimile of one of her poems. What memories her handwriting brought back to me! I shall treasure this volume perhaps more than any of the others which I always carry with me.

That Ernst never ceased caring for Sara was apparent to his friends and family. Eunice Tietjens has related how "two years after the divorce, he sat with me, more distinguished-looking than ever, in a glittering New York restaurant, and spoke of her in the same awed adoring voice he had always used, while the tears dropped unheeded on his waistcoat. And he recited to me again her poetry, only now it was the beautiful later lyrics she had written to him. And I wept with him, for something lovely lost beyond recall."[4]

---

[4]Eunice Tietjens, *The World At My Shoulder* (New York: The Macmillan Company, 1938), p. 56.

To Mamie Wheless, shortly before his own death, he wrote: "I not only loved Sara to the end, but she lives in my life, soul, and spirit today. What a wonderful person she was!—Memories—only exquisite memories forever."

The years after her death passed, for him, in days spent abroad in ceaseless travel. In January of 1937, he wrote to his sister of the endless strain that his work entailed and of an attack of recent illness. The breakdown in health that Sara had always predicted would come because of continual overwork and travel seemed imminent. In May of 1937, his family received word that he had died in Shanghai, China. A postmortem revealed that the immediate cause of death was stomach trouble, but his family attributed it to an overworked heart that had already given a warning of what was to come if he did not change his mode of life.

By a strange coincidence, long before the Teasdale and the Filsinger families had had any connection whatever, Ernst Filsinger's father had bought a family lot not more than seventy-five or one hundred feet from the Teasdale lot in Bellefontaine Cemetery in St. Louis. Early in July of 1937, Ernst's ashes were sent to the home of his sister, Mrs. Wetteroth, and they were immediately placed in the family lot on that side of the Filsinger monument that lies closest to the remains of Sara. Among the personal possessions of Mr. Filsinger at the time of his death was the manuscript of the first version of Vachel Lindsay's *Collected Poems,* which Lindsay had instructed Mr. Harold S. Latham of the Macmillan Company to give to Ernst in 1923.

In a letter to Williamina Parrish after Sara's death, Vine Colby said: "In thinking constantly about her since her death, it has seemed to me that no one we knew lived a more consistent life than Sara, from start to finish. Not that she did not grow and develop, for she did. But she changed little, and her growth was harmonious, not jerky and obscure, like that of most of us. In her every act and word as a girl, you can see the woman she became. Her elements were never at war with each other."

Memorial poems and tributes to the poet and articles about her flooded the press after her death. Though her physical presence was gone, her spirit and poetry were very much in evidence in the world. In 1937 a volume of the poet's *Collected Poems* appeared, carefully selected and arranged by John Hall Wheelock and Margaret Conklin. In the first month after publication, over four thousand copies were sold. Very few poets can claim such a record.

Various critics have mistakenly maintained that Sara Teasdale's popularity as a poet waned in the later days of her life and that she lost her public after the schools of cerebral and experimental poetry came into full force; but the actual facts are irrefutable evidence to the contrary. Evidently, these critics were momentarily distracted by the noise made by some of the new poets, as they were trying to shock the world into listening to them; perhaps it was impossible for the critics to keep their fingers on the pulse of the reading public at the same time. It is true that *Love Songs,* which won the forerunner of the Pulitzer Prize for poetry in 1918, was the most popular of her books. It is also true that her more serious, later poems were not sung, recited, and quoted extensively, as her earlier songs had been, and consequently, perhaps they were not known to as large an audience as her lighter lyrics. But the tremendous sales of *Dark of the Moon, Strange Victory,* and *Collected Poems* prove conclusively that this poet never lost the devotion of her public, and even more convincing is the fact that many of her poems live on in the hearts of people who loved them when they were first written and love them still today. The record shows that the period of the greatest sales from her books (not counting the posthumous volumes) was the fiscal year of 1931-32, at the very close of her life.

John Hall Wheelock, who knows her work as perhaps no one else in the world knows it, said of the poet on a radio program honoring her, after her death:

"Sara Teasdale was a lyric poet, and lyric poetry is intimately personal, even confessional in character, is wrung from the spirit capable of it by genuine experience only. Its greatness is in direct ratio to its simplicity, and its art, in the highest form, is the art of simplicity. Of all the lyric poets who have written in the English tongue none illustrates these truths better than Sara Teasdale. To know her was to realize the integrity, the almost painful honesty, of one of the most sensitive beings that has ever lived. She could not be brought to read these poems of hers in public at any time; she could hardly bear to say them aloud, even to her closest friends. What she wrote was forced from her—as a cry, or an exclamation—by the sheer torment or ecstasy that life laid upon a spirit excruciatingly vibrant and responsive.

"But this high degree of sensitivity is but one aspect of a nature equipped and disciplined for great tasks. There is, in this poet, a vein of iron, a proud inflexible strength, that many readers, familiar chiefly with the earlier, softer poems, have missed. Sara Teasdale's later books, *Flame and Shadow, Dark of the Moon,* and *Strange Victory,* are her best. These later poems increasingly reveal her courageous outlook upon the mysteries of life and death; in them she asserts her faith in the inviolateness, the aloofness, of the human soul amid perishable things and fugitive emotions."

Nine years after her death, the Yale University Library received the six remaining notebooks in which Sara wrote her poems, the diary that she kept when she was abroad in 1905, and other irreplaceable material concerning the poet. The special bookplate used by the Yale University Library for these articles notes that they were

Given in memory of
SARA TEASDALE
by her friend and literary executrix
Margaret Conklin
1942

Ted Malone, in January of 1940, gave a radio broadcast on her poetry that elicited national praise and an overwhelming amount of mail. And in 1943, on October 30, at Richmond, California,

John Hall Wheelock
1951

the United States Navy christened one of its Liberty ships the *Sara Teasdale,* which seemed particularly fitting when one recalls the intense love that this poet had for the sea.

The singing voice was stilled, but the music that it left the world—the rich heritage of pure, lyrical song—could not be forgotten.

> The rest may die—but is there not
> Some shining strange escape for me
> Who sought in Beauty the bright wine
> Of immortality?

For her, the "shining strange escape" was an escape of the spirit, not the body; for the spirit will endure, forever singing to the heart of man—of love and joy and sorrow—in delicately beautiful words that even death cannot destroy.

Chapter 12

THE WORK OF SARA TEASDALE

·

THE name of Sara Teasdale is imprinted on eleven books as either author or editor. Besides her two anthologies, *The Answering Voice* and *Rainbow Gold,* her book of children's poetry, *Stars To-night,* and her *Collected Poems,* she left seven volumes filled with songs that are eloquent testimony to the growth of her creative stature from the first book through the last. For there was no lessening of her poetic genius or her craftsmanship as the years went by. She grew in artistry and spirit until the very end.

Marguerite Wilkinson once said that Sara Teasdale's books may be compared to "ascending terraces on the side of that mountain, whose summit, the absolute beauty, no mortal can ever reach." And if the higher terraces of later years have the shadows of evening lingering about them, they are no less compelling, no less memorable. For the depth of night only served to emphasize how the spirit grew as it moved out of the April sunlight into the winter darkness.

Her haunting and poignant poems, written in a pure, lyrical music, illuminated the moods of love in all their rainbow splendor as few singers before had illuminated them. She laid bare the soul of one woman when rapture, anguish, solitude, longing, or loveliness had burdened the heart to overflowing. And because her lyric testimony communicates emotion that is the same for all men, all hearts everywhere, her poetry possesses a timeless quality.

Her work is almost totally without figurative or ornamental imagery, without a large and pretentious vocabulary; it is not scholarly or cerebral. It is completely free of the influences that sifted through the poetic world during her lifetime: the awakening of a social conscience, the experimentation with new verse forms, new idioms of expression, poetry devoid of capitalization and clarity, and poetry depicting the emptiness and shallowness of the twentieth century. Essentially an individual in her life as in her art, she was affected by none of these.

For she did not see the world either through a social conscience or as an empty Waste Land; she wrote from the world within, a many-colored land whose shifting lights fell over the horizons of solitude, love, and beauty. The objective world was never as real or important to her as the castle of her own heart and mind.

It is true that her poetic latitude was limited: she was not closely concerned with the everyday struggle of the common man and his problems, or with the great philosophical probings of the world, or with the contemporary scene. But her range was wide enough to include the infinite spaces in the human heart—the eternal emotions of joy, sorrow, longing, and love that are of grave importance to every human being.

Speaking of the simplicity of her singing style, Sara Teasdale once wrote: "I try to say what moves me—I never care to surprise my reader; I avoid, not from malice aforethought, but simply because I dislike them, all words that are not met with in common speech and all inversions of words and phrases. My poems aren't written in the literal sense of the word. They sometimes never meet pen and paper until they have been complete for days in my mind. Perhaps that habit of composition is partly responsible for the fact that I never use intricate stanzas—it would be too hard to compose them in my usual way. For me one of the greatest joys of poetry is to know it by heart—perhaps that is why the simple song-like poems appeal to me most—they are the easiest to learn."

Reading through her poems, one is struck with the number of times that the word "gray" (or "grey") appears. From the very first book where grey ashes of Japanese incense are mentioned, through all the others, this word is used over and over. We read of "grey quiet," "gray pilgrim," "my spirit's gray defeat," "gray fog," "grey sea-weed," "gray bells," "a world as hard and gray as stone," "gray cities," and "gray, high-flung bridges." Perhaps this softly indefinite color was symbolic of the silver-gray solitude and peace that the poet's heart was seeking all her life.

Besides Sappho, Christina Rossetti was her first, last, and most enduring poetic influence, and many times the two poets have been compared. Both had the gift of pure and unaffected melodic grace and of distilling deep emotion into delicately written lines. But much of Christina Rossetti's ecstasy of spirit was channeled into a religious and moral dedication of life, while Sara Teasdale's consuming passion was for spiritual beauty—and this included love.

Many of Christina Rossetti's lines reflect that her life was an unswerving devotion to her religious faith, a deliberate choice as binding as a marriage vow; and most of Sara Teasdale's poems reflect her lifelong worship of beauty. For all of her intense enthusiasms grew out of her eager adoration of loveliness; her identification with Sappho and her flight back to the Greeks, the high priests of beauty, were only early manifestations of this. For her, the sea, the stars, the moon, and all outward aspects of nature held strange and sublime wonder that her heart responded to with joy, and this gift of rapturous response was hers until the end.

The element of renunciation entered into the life and work of each of these poets, but it was with a great difference. Christina Rossetti, though unwell in her later years, resisted the world and purposely closed her heart to its pleasures for reasons of religious scruples; Sara Teasdale, on the other hand, in withdrawing into her own spirit as the years went by, followed the natural course that ill health and her love of solitude brought about. Her cycle of spiritual development was a completely unaffected one, and because of this it is fairly easy, when one is reading a poem by Sara Teasdale, to know to what period of her life it belongs. The same thing cannot be said of Christina Rossetti. Since her life was directed, from early days, to a religious devoutness, her spiritual outlook on the world never varied. Many of her poems were written to please her God, while Sara Teasdale's were written to please herself.

Yet when Christina Rossetti cast off her studied moral absorption and let her own heart sing through the lines, one finds that rare blending of vision, music, and emotion that is found in Sara Teasdale's best work; and in this respect the poetry of the two is strikingly similar.

The early poems of Sara Teasdale have much in common with the songs of A. Mary F. Robinson, an English poet of the nineteenth century, whose books Sara Teasdale treasured and whose work influenced her greatly. For in this poet's work, as in Sara Teasdale's, are found a simplicity of expression, a delicate and lyrical music, and a passionate concern with love.

A number of critics have linked the names of Sara Teasdale and Elizabeth Barrett Browning, because of their ill health and a similarity of theme; but there is no likeness whatsoever between these two in poetic expression. Although Sara Teasdale was moved by the overwhelming passion of the Browning sonnets and intrigued by the romantic story of the English poet's life, her work itself was entirely untouched by the actual style of Mrs. Browning. Louis Untermeyer once referred to the *Sonnets from the Portuguese* as "those overcolored and heavily drooping waxflowers." This criticism could never be applied to Sara Teasdale's work. For she was born with a gift of flowing lyricism that Elizabeth Barrett Browning did not possess. There was never anything the least contrived, strained, or awkward in the poetry of Sara Teasdale; her work was like natural speech in a setting of song.

Perhaps William Stanley Braithwaite best described the relationships of these poets when he wrote:

A. Mary F. Robinson's poems are full of Sara Teasdale's wizardry, but flavored more sharply with a mellow anguish of love and memory. Passion burnt her as it burnt Emily Brontë—but the dust of them is alive today in that invisible light never on land or sea. She and Sara Teasdale have the same flute-like quality of music.

And as in Sara Teasdale's work it tightens with a poignancy that stirs the senses into a common echo with nature.

There can be no kinship established between the art and spirit of Elizabeth Barrett Browning and Sara Teasdale. The former's passion was intellectual, but once something—the warm mystery of Robert's love perhaps—melted the guardian gates of her mind, and the ecstasy of possession flowed down into her heart and launched the *Sonnets from the Portuguese.* All this beauty and magic, springtime and stars, sunlight and shadow, the human dream and urgency— were in Sara Teasdale's heart from the beginning, which her mind, like a sun, drew up and there shaped into those images vibrant with music, and then showered forth as a balm for human aches and joys.

Sonnets to Duse (1907) is important today as the first step on the path that led to poetic fulfillment. Divided into two sections, it contains a group of poems to Eleonora Duse and a group of miscellaneous songs, lyrics, and sonnets. Reproductions of three of the pictures of the actress that Sara Teasdale received in 1905 and that were examined so enthusiastically by the Potters are included in this little book. Most of the poems in it had appeared in *The Potter's Wheel.* None of them had ever appeared in any public periodical.

Though it was the song quality that especially appealed to Arthur Symons when he reviewed the book for *The Saturday Review* of London, one cannot help but feel that the sonnets to the actress, Duse, are the most arresting and finished part of the small volume. For though they were written over fifty years ago, they still move with a stately and classic grace.

Only eight poems were selected from this little book for inclusion in her *Collected Poems,* and four of these were sonnets to Eleonora Duse. One was the sonnet, "To Joy"; and among the three lyrics was the much-quoted "Faults," written to Bessie Brey:

> They came to tell your faults to me,
> They named them over one by one;
> I laughed aloud when they were done,

I knew them all so well before,—
Oh, they were blind, too blind to see
Your faults had made me love you more.

One poem in two parts, "To Sappho," reveals the young
poet's deep interest in the Greek lyricist and is a worthy predecessor of the later Sappho poems.

Sonnets to Duse was youthful testimony to the poet's overwhelming attraction to beauty, and in it are to be seen the three
chief influences of her early period: the musical quality that she
had absorbed from Heine's poetry, her admiration for Eleonora
Duse, and her identification with Sappho and deep love for ancient
Greece.

Helen of Troy (1911) represents a great step forward. A
much thicker volume than *Sonnets to Duse,* it consists of 109
pages, and contains a variety of poetic forms, including blank
verse, lyrics, sonnets, and the little verse drama called "On the
Tower."

The first six poems are monologues in blank verse, concerning
some phase of love and spoken by various women: Helen of Troy;
Beatrice; Sappho; Marianna Alcoforando, the Portuguese nun;
Guenevere; and Erinna, a student of Sappho's. Not wanting to
write of such deep emotion in a personal voice, the poet created
lines of intense feeling, speaking as she felt these women would
have spoken. Although there is no rhyme to enhance the lyric
mood, and though the monologues are rather long, they are
remarkable for their sustained moods and flowing quality; and
they contain some memorably fine lines. Marianna Alcoforando
says that she knows what it is

To feel the weight of love upon my heart
So heavy that the blood can scarcely flow.

And Sappho says:

There is a quiet at the heart of love,
And I have pierced the pain and come to peace . . .

and:

> Ah, Love, there is no fleeing from thy might,
> No lonely place where thou hast never trod,
> No desert thou hast left uncarpeted
> With flowers that spring beneath thy perfect feet . . .

and:

> Close, close against my heart I hold my world.

This book contains a number of poems that any talented young girl might have written; yet there are some that rise far above the average because of their simplicity, impulsive beauty, and emotional appeal. Typical of these are "Song" ("You bound strong sandals on my feet"), "The Faëry Forest," and "Wild Asters."

For the first time the poet weaves definite places into the thoughts of her lyrics. In this book appear, for instance, poems that refer to her beloved New York, among them "The Metropolitan Tower," "Gramercy Park," "In the Metropolitan Museum," "Central Park at Dusk," "Union Square," and "Coney Island." Here, too, are the poems that allude to some of the places that Sara had seen on her first trip abroad with her mother in 1905: "The Wanderer," which recalls the land of Egypt, "Paris in the Spring," and "Madeira from the Sea."

Duse's influence, which was waning, and Sappho's, which was growing, are both apparent. Only one sonnet to Duse is found in this collection; called "Silence," it celebrates the

> Deep stillness pure of any speech or sound,

with which the great actress crowned her art, and speaks of

> The silent music of infinity

and is notable for the high value that the poet herself put on solitude and quiet even this early in her life.

Three poems recall Sappho: "To Erinna," the "pale Erinna of the perfect lyre," who was a student of the Greek poet's, "To Cleïs," the daughter of Sappho, and a "Triolet" originally written in a book of Sappho's poems. A sonnet, "To an Aeolian Harp," reminds the reader of the harp that the poet had once owned, loved, and dreamed over.

Helen of Troy was revised in 1920, and the little verse drama, "On the Tower," was omitted, as well as a number of the merely competent poems; because of this winnowing, the revised version is an improvement, but the first edition is immensely interesting to the person who wishes to make a close study of the growth of this poet.

Rivers to the Sea (1915) shows a still greater arc of achievement. The poet no longer speaks through characters of ancient times; the emotion is her own, and she writes of it in the pure music that was her native language. The very first poem in this candid volume marks the poet's awareness of the struggle that was to be apparent all through her life: the desire for beauty and the ability to enjoy it in solitude, and the conflicting desire for love and the presence of the lover. In "Spring Night" we read:

> Why am I unsatisfied,—
> I for whom the pensive night
> Binds her cloudy hair with light,—
> I, for whom all beauty burns
> Like incense in a million urns?
> O, beauty, are you not enough?
> Why am I crying after love?

These poems possess an eagerness and a spontaneity that reflect the fresh and passionate rapture of youth. The poet declares:

> Joy was a flame in me
> Too steady to destroy. . . .

Love has now become an intensely personal experience, and its miracle sings through many of these lines. Here are found the very popular "The Look" and "I Shall Not Care." Though these songs are a personal revelation of one young heart feeling the first stirring of romantic ecstasy and agony, they owe their great appeal to their universality; almost any reader can apply them to some point in his life. And even when the poet was writing of the sadder side of love, she did it with a light and delicately appealing touch, as in "Doorway Roses":

I have come the selfsame path
    To the selfsame door,
Years have left the roses there
    Burning as before.

While I watch them in the wind
    Quick the hot tears start—
Strange so frail a flame outlasts
    Fire in the heart.

There are a number of poems in free verse included that provide a note of variation, and many of these reflect the New York scene: "New Year's Dawn," "Broadway," "Summer Night," "Riverside," "The India Wharf," and "From the Woolworth Tower." Typical of the poet's achievement in this field are the following lines from "A Winter Bluejay":

For suddenly, with lifted eyes you said,
"Oh look!"
There, on the black bough of a snow flecked maple,
Fearless and gay as our love,
A bluejay cocked his crest!
Oh who can tell the range of joy
Or set the bounds of beauty?

Sara Teasdale also experimented with the Sapphic stanza form, and though she did not adhere rigidly to the ancient prescribed form of long and short accents, her work followed the given pattern in its general outline. One of the most successful of her poems in this form is "Indian Summer" with its memorable first line:

> Lyric night of the lingering Indian summer....

Included in this volume, also, are the "Vignettes Overseas," lyrics written while the poet was abroad with Jessie Rittenhouse, and "From the Sea," a long poem in blank verse, full of the mystery of the ocean and of love, and filled with sensitive and compelling lines, such as:

> Listen, I love you. Do not turn your face
> Nor touch me. Only stand and watch awhile
> The blue unbroken circle of the sea.

The book reaches its climax in the final section called "Sappho," and the entire group of three poems in this series sustains the same high level of expression and emotion. Almost any lines from this section contain a fluid and unforgettable loveliness, such as these:

> There shall be swallows bringing back the spring
> Over the long blue meadows of the sea,
> And south-wind playing on the reeds of rain,

and there are many single lines that linger in the mind, like:

> The precious pain of arms that held me fast.

Love Songs (1917), a volume in which love is further illuminated, contains a selection of some of the poet's most successful lyrics from earlier books, as well as a number of new poems. Again, looking into her own spirit, Sara Teasdale brought forth from her personal universe poems of memory, delight, sorrow, and wisdom, set to her clear-voiced and graceful music. And again the poet proved her ability to handle with what William Stanley Braithwaite called "exquisite sensibility" the prismatic moods of love—its burning joy and sadness, enchantment and disillusion, longing and fulfillment, ecstasy and suffering. Because of the lyrical spell of their musical appeal and their simple directness, these poems of love sing themselves into the heart.

Among the new poems there is found emerging even more strongly the poet's deep belief in the supremacy of beauty as one of life's greatest gifts. She says in "Barter":

> Spend all you have for loveliness,
> Buy it and never count the cost. . . .

And in "Wood Song," a poem inspired by the song of a bird in Cromwell, Connecticut, she realizes that the loveliness of a thrush's song makes the bitterness of life bearable:

> Three shining notes were all he had,
> And yet they made a starry call—
> I caught life back against my breast
> And kissed it, scars and all.

There are a spiritual enrichment, a new understanding and awareness of suffering, and a deepening sense of wisdom in the section of the book called "Songs Out of Sorrow." The lyric heart, momentarily turning from the rapture of love, observes now how something durable and triumphant may be salvaged from the anguish of the spirit.

> From naked stones of agony
> I will build a house for me;
> As a mason all alone
> I will raise it, stone by stone,
> And every stone where I have bled
> Will show a sign of dusky red.

In this group of poems is first foretold the new and more serious mood that was to absorb her so completely later.

In *Flame and Shadow* (1920), a book of still greater maturity of thought and spirit, both a radiance and a wisdom are evident. Now the eager and ecstatic tone of early youth has been tempered, though the music is still as liquid and melodious as it was before. This is a book of transition; the key is slowly and almost imperceptibly changing to a soft minor. Against the leaping flame of beauty, the poet now balances the gathering shadows of death. The very first poem, "Blue Squills," states this conflict:

> Oh burn me with your beauty, then,
>   Oh hurt me, tree and flower,
> Lest in the end death try to take
>   Even this glistening hour.

Over and over the gift of loveliness to man is celebrated. The poet says:

> O Beauty, out of many a cup
> You have made me drunk and wild
> Ever since I was a child,

and:

> "Forever
> Seek for Beauty, she only
> Fights with man against Death!"

She cries with passion:

> What has man done that only he
> Is slave to death. . . .

This theme is dominant from the first poem through the last, "The Wind in the Hemlock," where the poet reaches a solution by realizing that man, through his power of consciousness and the enriching effects of loveliness, may make his life on earth, no matter how fleeting, a triumph instead of a defeat:

> *If I am peaceful, I shall see*
> *Beauty's face continually;*
> *Feeding on her wine and bread*
> *I shall be wholly comforted,*
> *For she can make one day for me*
> *Rich as my lost eternity.*

Yet now and then the poet weighs the eventual solitude, the eventual release that death is sure to bring:

> Even love that I built my spirit's house for,
> Comes like a brooding and a baffled guest,
> And music and men's praise and even laughter
> Are not so good as rest.

Over some of these poems fall the first shadows cast by thoughts of death, of loss, of grief, of inevitable endings, and the merciless passing of time—shadows that foretold the promise later fulfilled in the restrained and sombre music of *Dark of the Moon* and *Strange Victory.* And with the far-off promise of eventual winter, the faint stirring of an autumn wind prophesying a coming chill seems to blow gently across some of these lines:

> My heart is a garden tired with autumn,

she says, and:

> The heart asks more than life can give,
> When that is learned, then all is learned. . . .

"The Long Hill," which begins:

> I must have passed the crest a while ago
> And now I am going down—

is almost symbolic of the crest of emotional joy in youthful love that was reached in her previous books. Yet, in *Flame and Shadow,* she sings of love, though it is now in a slightly more subdued form. Occasionally, the tone of ecstatic emotion is still in evidence, for the autumn mood is only suggested, not wholly consummated yet. One of the most memorable songs of love that she ever wrote is found in these pages and closes with these lines:

> In many another soul I broke the bread,
> And drank the wine and played the happy guest,

But I was lonely, I remembered you;
The heart belongs to him who knew it best.

Solitude's cool haven beckons to her in these poems, and she says:

When I am all alone
Envy me most,

and alluding to that greater and more final solitude:

I am alone, as though I stood
On the highest peak of the tired gray world,
About me only swirling snow,
Above me endless space unfurled;

With earth hidden and heaven hidden,
And only my own spirit's pride
To keep me from the peace of those
Who are not lonely, having died.

Though there are many delicate and appealing songs in this book that linger on in the reader's heart, such as "Compensation," "It Is Not a Word," "What Do I Care?" and "It Will Not Change," the jewel of them all, flawless, pure, and beautiful as a pearl, is the incomparable "Let It Be Forgotten." Few poems in the English language are as musically perfect as these lines:

Let it be forgotten, as a flower is forgotten,
Forgotten as a fire that once was singing gold,
Let it be forgotten for ever and ever,
Time is a kind friend, he will make us old.

If anyone asks, say it was forgotten
Long and long ago,
As a flower, as a fire, as a hushed footfall
In a long forgotten snow.

In *Dark of the Moon* (1926), the book that brought her spiritual maturity to its fullest blossoming, the minor key that was

suggested in *Flame and Shadow* has now become fully established; the music in these poems is as melodious and graceful as
ever, but the pulse of the music has slowed to an autumnal measure. These poems are enriched with an austerity, a nobleness,
a resignation with no self-pity and no bitterness; they are stripped
down to the very essence of wisdom born out of suffering. Having
drunk deeply from the cup of beauty and love in rapturous delight, the poet now turns her thoughts irrevocably to death; where
autumn was once a whisper of coming loss, now the promise is
fulfilled; now the winter landscape is a certain and inescapable
thing. And the snow, the winter sadness, the sinking of Arcturus
absorb her completely now. Though the book opens on a gay note:

> It was not you, though you were near,
>   Though you were good to hear and see,
> It was not earth, it was not heaven
>   It was myself that sang in me . . .

the mood that is to prevail is soon established:

> You have taken a drink from a wild fountain
>   Early in the year;
> There is nowhere to go from the top of a mountain
>   But down, my dear. . . .

Her old passionate concern that the elements of nature—the
sea, the stars, and the moon—will endure long after man has had
his brief hour of joy on earth, is again mentioned, but now there
is no struggle against this fact and no distress in the acceptance
of it. For in her maturity of spirit, her attitude toward death
has undergone a change. No longer is she afraid of it; no
longer does she rebel against it. The spirit is disciplined now to
accept the inevitable:

> There will be stars over the place forever,
>   There will be stars forever, while we sleep.

No longer is the poet absorbed with the dream, the promise,
and the realization of love; for from her later wisdom she has

evolved a philosophy that recognizes the poverty that makes the spirit rich. In "The Wise Woman" we read:

> How much more safe it is to lack
> A thing that time so often steals,

and in "Wisdom":

> It was a spring that never came,
>   But we have lived enough to know
> What we have never had, remains;
>   It is the things we have that go.

The old conflict within her own spirit, the old unresolved desire between solitude and love, are shown clearly within these pages. One section of poems called "The Crystal Gazer" reveals the essential and unchanging solitary quality of her spirit. She, who was "self-complete as a flower or a stone," says:

> There are no highroads to my heart;
> The gates are locked, they will not stir
> For any ardent traveller.

But she also has left evidence of the equally powerful place that love has taken in her life; the last section of the book contains the few love poems in this volume. One says:

> When I am not with you
> I am alone,
> For there is no one else
> And there is nothing
> That comforts me but you.

Here, too, is found the beautiful tribute called "The Beloved."

Prophetic in a sense is the final poem, "The Flight," which concludes:

> We are like eagles,
> But when Death harries us,
> Human and humbled

When one of us goes,
Let the other follow,
Let the flight be ended,
Let the fire blacken,
Let the book close.

For except for her children's book of verse, the poet never opened another new book of her own poetry.

Strange Victory (1933), a small volume of only twenty-two poems, is an extension of the mood first felt so deeply in *Dark of the Moon*. Born, as its predecessor, of the winter of the spirit, this is a book that reflects deep emotional suffering and anguish, but it shows, too, a spirit that resolves its grief by the promise of the infinite peace and release that death is sure to bring. As in *Dark of the Moon*, the poet no longer wonders about death; she is preoccupied with it, and seems now, in these later days, to desire it and prepare for it.

The title, *Strange Victory*, apparently has more than one meaning. For the book as a whole, it indicates that though mortal life is lost, the poet may attain immortality through her poems; and the title poem itself refers to a person much beloved by her, who is still aware of her, still found in the living circle of those who remember her and move with her "across the stricken plain" of life:

To this, to this, after my hope was lost,
    To this strange victory;
To find you with the living, not the dead,
    To find you glad of me;
To find you wounded even less than I,
    Moving as I across the stricken plain;
After the battle to have found your voice
    Lifted above the slain.

A prelude for the mood of her final poems is sounded in the opening quatrain, "Moon's Ending":

Moon, worn thin to the width of a quill,
   In the dawn clouds flying,
How good to go, light into light, and still
   Giving light, dying.

Her touch that had always turned everything to song had not lost any of its artistry. Now the songs, however, are all set in an elegiac mood; a classic restraint and sombre grace enter into the very syllables. This poet had always sung from her heart, and when her heart was filled to overflowing with thoughts of imminent darkness, she sang as movingly of death as she had sung of love. The sea, which had always been so much a part of her life, is spoken of again, but now she sees it in relation to the final silence:

Bitter and beautiful, sing no more;
Scarf of spindrift strewn on the shore,
Burn no more in the noon-day light,
Let there be night for me, let there be night.

Three of the poems in this book are addressed to Margaret Conklin. Here, also, are the elegy for Vachel Lindsay and the poems so intimately concerned with the poet's own death: "All That Was Mortal," "Since Death Brushed Past Me," "Ashes," and "Wisdom."

Though dark shadows possessed her spirit, the stars still held out their ancient promise of peace, and to the very end she was concerned with their burning and changeless radiance. The final poem in this small volume, "There Will Be Rest," brings the book to a perfect close:

There will be rest and sure stars shining
   Over the roof-tops crowned with snow,
A reign of rest, serene forgetting,
   The music of stillness holy and low.

I will make this world of my devising
Out of a dream in my lonely mind,
I shall find the crystal of peace,—above me
Stars I shall find.

The *Collected Poems* (1937) are arranged by the order of the individual books in chronological sequence, so that the reader might trace for himself the line of development so apparent in the work of this poet. *Dark of the Moon* and *Strange Victory,* which were part of the same period of her growth, are the culminating volumes in which her genius was brought to the highest level of its artistry. She died at forty-eight at the height of her poetic achievement; though there was a turning toward the valley of the shadow from the high pinnacle of ecstatic romantic love, there was never any lessening of her lyric genius.

If one word could be used to describe the poetic artistry of Sara Teasdale, it would be the word *pure.* From a purity of spirit, she gave the world poems of pure music, pure emotion, and pure beauty. Even the suffering and resignation of later years could not mar this quality of purity; for as the darkness grew deeper, the true essence of the spirit shone even more luminously.

The best of her work will live, like that of other lyric singers of permanence—Sappho, Christina Rossetti, Housman. The haunting melodies and the golden words will not be lost or forgotten; they will endure as long as man is conscious of his own heart and spirit.

SELECTED BIBLIOGRAPHY

Selected Bibliography

•

Bulletin of the Willard Family Association, 1937-1938.

CUMMINGS, MARION. *Poems.* Privately printed, 1957.

DUNBAR, OLIVIA HOWARD. *A House in Chicago.* Chicago: University of Chicago, 1947.

EARLE, FERDINAND. *The Lyric Year.* New York: Mitchell Kennerley, 1912.

A FRIEND. *Elder John Teasdale.* Nashville: Southern Baptist Sabbath-School Union, 1860.

GRAHAM, STEPHEN. *Tramping with a Poet in the Rockies.* New York: D. Appleton and Company, 1922.

HARRIS, MARK. *City of Discontent.* Indianapolis: Bobbs-Merrill, 1952.

JOHNS, ORRICK. *Time of Our Lives.* New York: Stackpole Sons, 1937.

JOHNSON, ANNE ANDRE. *Notable Women of St. Louis.* St. Louis: privately printed, 1914.

LINDSAY, VACHEL. *Adventures While Preaching the Gospel of Beauty.* New York: Mitchell Kennerley, 1914.

———. *The Chinese Nightingale and Other Poems.* New York: The Macmillan Company, 1917.

———. *Collected Poems.* New York: The Macmillan Company, 1937.

———. *The Golden Book of Springfield.* New York: The Macmillan Company, 1920.

———. *Letters of Nicholas Vachel Lindsay to A. Joseph Armstrong.* Waco, Texas: Baylor University Press, 1940.

———. *The Village Magazine.* Springfield, Illinois: Privately printed, 1910.

MASTERS, EDGAR LEE. *Vachel Lindsay: A Poet in America.* New York: Charles Scribner's Sons, 1935.

MONROE, HARRIET. *A Poet's Life.* New York: The Macmillan Company, 1938.

POPE, CHARLES HENRY (ed.). *Willard Genealogy.* Boston: printed for the Willard Family Association, 1915.

RITTENHOUSE, JESSIE. *My House of Life.* Boston: Houghton Mifflin Company, 1934.

RUBINCAM, MILTON. *Historical Outline of the Teasdale-Teesdale Families.* Washington, D. C.: Reprinted from the National Genealogical Society Quarterly, 1939.

RUGGLES, ELEANOR. *The West-Going Heart.* New York: W. W. Norton and Company, 1959.

TEASDALE, THOMAS COX, D.D. *Reminiscenses and Incidents of a Long Life.* St. Louis: National Baptist Publishing Company, 1887.

TIETJENS, EUNICE. *The World at My Shoulder.* New York: The Macmillan Company, 1938.

UNTERMEYER, LOUIS. *From Another World.* New York: Harcourt, Brace and Company, 1939.

WILKINSON, MARGUERITE. *New Voices.* New York: The Macmillan Company, 1924.

INDEX

Index

·

Rossetti, Dante Gabriel, 64, 116, 309, 310, 312, 314
Rossetti family, 312
Rossetti House, 308
Rossetti nieces, 314, 315
Rossetti notes for biography (Sara Teasdale), 310-311
Rossetti, William, 310
Rossettis, 47, 108
"Rubaiyat of Friendship," 37
Rubens, 58
Ruggles, Eleanor, 259
Ruhleben Prison (Germany), 242
Ruskin, John, 179
Ruth, 54

S

S. S. *Arabic*, 48, 49, 50, 53, 56
"Sadie" (Sara Teasdale's nickname), 3, 19, 22, 107, 108-109, 211
Saijiyou, Yaso, 270
St. Anthony, 50
St. Aspinquid Hotel, 236
St. Augustine (Florida), 134
Ste Chapelle, 58
St. Francis of Assisi, 92, 96, 132, 180, 216
St. George, 147
St. John, 309
St. John's Hospital, 226
St. Louis (Louis IX of France), 58
St. Louis (Missouri), 6, 7, 9, 10, 11, 12, 13, 19, 21, 28, 29, 59, 72, 74, 76, 77, 82, 84, 97, 103, 104, 105, 113, 118, 125, 131, 132, 137, 141, 142, 145, 146, 156, 163, 170, 174, 178, 185, 188, 189, 190, 191, 195, 196, 197, 198, 221, 223, 224, 226, 230, 233, 235, 242, 255, 278, 321, 326
  beginning of 6-7
  cultural aspects of in early twentieth century, 23-28
  personalities of late nineteenth and early twentieth centuries, 23
St. Louis Artists' Guild, 16, 25, 42
St. Louis Bird Club, 77
St. Louis Children's Hospital, 74
St. Louis Globe-Democrat, 27, 43, 88, 223

St. Louis Mirror, 27
St. Louis Post-Dispatch, 19, 42, 43
St. Louis Public Library, 26, 104
St. Louis Republic, 21
St. Louis School of Fine Arts, 24, 33, 34, 97, 103
St. Louis Star, 278, 279 ff.
St. Louis University, 3, 23
St. Margaret's Church (Durham), 8
St. Margaret's Church (Horsmonden), 4
St. Peter's Church, 56, 57
St. Theresa, 310
Salerno, 148
Salome, 131
Salon Carré, 58
Salon Club of America, 30
San Antonio (Texas), 111
San José (California), 119
Sandburg, Carl, 27, 167, 241, 276
Sandwich Islands, 24
Sandys, T., 89
Sangamon County, 182, 203, 258
Santa Barbara (California), 236, 245, 246
Santa Catalina Mountains, 116
"Santa Fé Trail, The," 182, 189, 190
Sapphic stanza, 338-339
"Sappho," 164, 171, 228
Sappho, 32, 34, 40-41, 123, 168-169, 237, 332, 335, 336, 337, 348
Sappho (John Myers O'Hara), 113, 115
Sara Teasdale (Liberty Ship), 329
Sarafimm; see Saraphim
Saraphim, 177, 182, 185, 187, 191, 213, 259
Saturday Review, The (London), 99, 334
Saxton, Mr., 82
Saxton, Mrs., 82
Saxton's Farm, 81, 82-83, 95, 97, 134, 142, 197
Saxton's Hill, 83
Schooley's Mountain Church (New Jersey), 9
Schubert, Franz, 310
Schulenburg, Adele, 24, 79, 80, 97-98
Schumann-Heink, Madame Ernestine, 270
Schuyler, William, 25, 74

PAPER: Warren's "66"

TYPE: Baskerville

ILLUSTRATIONS: Lithography

TEXT: Letterpress

PRODUCTION: By Whittet & Shepperson

Richmond, Virginia